TELENOVELAS

**Recent Titles in
The Ilan Stavans Library of Latino Civilization**

Baseball

Border Culture

Cesar Chavez

Health Care

Immigration

Latina Writers

Latino Identity

Mexican-American Cuisine

Quinceañera

Soccer

Spanglish

Telenovelas

The Ilan Stavans Library of Latino Civilization

TELENOVELAS

Edited by Ilan Stavans

AN IMPRINT OF ABC-CLIO, LLC
Santa Barbara, California • Denver, Colorado • Oxford, England

Copyright © 2010 by Ilan Stavans

All rights reserved. No part of this publication may be reproduced, stored in a retrieval system, or transmitted, in any form or by any means, electronic, mechanical, photocopying, recording, or otherwise, except for the inclusion of brief quotations in a review, without prior permission in writing from the publisher.

Library of Congress Cataloging-in-Publication Data

Telenovelas / edited by Ilan Stavans.
 p. cm.
 Includes bibliographical references and index.
 ISBN 978-0-313-36492-1 (hard copy : alk. paper) — ISBN 978-0-313-36493-8 (ebook)
 1. Television soap operas—Latin America—History and criticism.
 2. Television soap operas—Social aspects—Latin America. I. Stavans, Ilan.
 PN1992.8.S4T4435 2010
 791.45′6—dc22
                                                                       2009042546

13 12 11 10 9   1 2 3 4 5

This book is also available on the World Wide Web as an eBook.
Visit www.abc-clio.com for details.

ABC-CLIO, LLC
130 Cremona Drive, P.O. Box 1911
Santa Barbara, California 93116-1911

This book is printed on acid-free paper ∞
Manufactured in the United States of America

Contents

	Series Foreword *by Ilan Stavans*	vii
	Preface	ix
I	**PANORAMAS**	1
	What Is This Thing Called Soap Opera? *Laura Stempel Mumford*	3
	The International Telenovela Debate and the Contra-Flow Argument: A Reappraisal *Daniël Biltereyst and Philippe Meers*	33
	Telenovelas and Soap Operas: Negotiating Reality from the Periphery *Christina Slade*	51
	Romancing the Globe *Ibsen Martínez*	61
	Understanding Telenovelas as a Cultural Front: A Complex Analysis of a Complex Reality *Jorge González*	68
	Opening America? The Telenovela-ization of U.S. Soap Operas *Denise D. Bielby and C. Lee Harrington*	79
	Engaging the Audience: The Social Imagery of the Novela *Reginald Clifford*	93
II	**CASE STUDIES**	101
	Cultural Identity: Between Reality and Fiction: A Transformation of Genre and Roles in Mexican Telenovelas *María de la Luz Casas Pérez*	103

Fact or Fiction? Narrative and Reality in the Mexican Telenovela 110
Rosalind C. Pearson

Whose Life in the Mirror?
Examining Three Mexican Telenovelas as Cultural
and Commercial Products 116
Laura J. Beard

Selected Bibliography 133
Index 135
About the Editor and Contributors 143

Series Foreword

The book series *The Ilan Stavans Library of Latino Civilization*, the first of its kind, is devoted to exploring all the facets of Hispanic civilization in the United States, with its ramifications in the Americas, the Caribbean Basin, and the Iberian Peninsula. The objective is to showcase its richness and complexity from a myriad perspective. According to the U.S. Census Bureau, the Latino minority is the largest in the nation. It is also the fifth largest concentration of Hispanics in the globe.

One out of every seven Americans traces his or her roots to the Spanish-speaking world. Mexicans make up about 65% of the minority. Other major national groups are Puerto Ricans, Cubans, Dominicans, Ecuadorians, Guatemalans, Nicaraguans, Salvadorans, and Colombians. They are either immigrants, descendants of immigrants, or dwellers in a territory (Puerto Rico, the Southwest) having a conflicted relationship with the mainland U.S. As such, they are the perfect example of *encuentro*: an encounter with different social and political modes, an encounter with a new language, and encounter with a different way of dreaming.

The series is a response to the limited resources available and the abundance of stereotypes, which are a sign of lazy thinking. The 20th century Spanish philosopher José Ortega y Gasset, author of *The Revolt of the Masses*, once said: "By speaking, by thinking, we undertake to clarify things, and that forces us to exacerbate them, dislocate them, schematize them. Every concept is in itself an exaggeration." The purpose of the series is not to clarify but to complicate our understanding of Latinos. Do so many individuals from different national, geographic, economic, religious, and ethnic backgrounds coalesce as an integrated whole? Is there an *unum* in the *pluribus*?

Baruch Spinoza believed that every thing in the universe wants to be preserved in its present form: a tree wants to be a tree, and a dog a dog. Latinos in the United States want to be Latinos in the United States—no easy task, and therefore an intriguing one to explore. Each volume of the series contains an assortment of approximately a dozen articles, essays and interviews by journalists and specialists in their respective fields, followed by a bibliography of important resources on the topic. Their compilation is designed to generate debate and foster research: to complicate our knowledge. Every attempt is made to balance the ideological viewpoint of the authors. The target audience is students, specialists, and the lay reader. Themes will range from politics to sports, from music to cuisine. Historical periods and benchmarks like the Mexican War, the Spanish American War, the Zoot Suit Riots, the Bracero Program, and the Cuban Revolution, as well as controversial topics like Immigration, Bilingual Education, and Spanglish will be tackled.

Democracy is able to thrive only when it engages in an open, honest exchange of information. By offering diverse, insightful volumes about Hispanic life in the United States and inviting people to engage in critical thinking, *The Ilan Stavans Library of Latino Civilization* seeks to open new vistas to appreciate the fastest growing, increasingly heterogeneous minority in the nation—to be part of the *encuentro*.

Ilan Stavans

Preface

My father is a *telenovela* actor in Mexico. I came of age in the seventies visiting Televisa, the largest manufacturer of soap operas in the Spanish-speaking world. It was a world of make-believe: actors' physiques reshaped by surgery and cosmetics and hiding behind the panoply of the day, spotless artificial sets where it was always spring, and an overabundance of emotions spilling out in every direction. (I wrote about it, tangentially, in my memoir *On Borrowed Words* [2001].) The academic exploration of *telenovelas* is a much-needed field of study that has grown exponentially in the last couple of decades with probing explorations of the transnational projects manufactured in Mexico, Brazil, Venezuela, and Miami. Spanish- and Portuguese-language soap-operas are spiritual sustenance in places as remote as Russia, Israel, and the Philippines, their casts a constellation of celebrities competing against Hollywood power.

In this volume I've collected essays on a variety of topics. U.S. scholar Laura Stempel Mumford and Venezuelan playwright Ibsen Martínez look at the phenomenon through a wide lens. There are studies of particular cases like *Xica*, *Betty la fea*, and *Laberintos de Pasión*. The connection between stereotypes and gender roles, particularly among young women, is analyzed. Another area of exploration is the relationship between fact and fiction. The impact of television in the Hispanic world, from Buenos Aires to Los Angeles, is enormous. The closing episode of a prime-time *telenovela* is capable of bringing a country to full stop. Indeed, I remember when Mexico's president apologized for cancelling a meeting with congressmen because he didn't want to miss the finale of his favorite soap-opera. I forget which one it was but I do remember that it wasn't his favorite. Proof of its impact was that the following day, almost every major Mexican daily reported the news of who the father of the *telenovela's* illegitimate child was.

My hope is that these reflections open lines of research. A single episode of a popular *telenovela* in the United States is watched by more viewers in Univisión than the sum of readers of Gabriel García Márquez's masterpiece *One Hundred Years of Solitude* since its publication in 1967.

PART I
PANORAMAS

WHAT IS THIS THING CALLED SOAP OPERA?

Laura Stempel Mumford

> The name given to the new genre is as interesting as it is unusual. Isn't it unprecedented for a cultural product to indicate so crudely its material origin . . . and its conscription in the battle between different commercial brands? At the same time, a whole *household* definition of a broadcast literature reveals itself plainly, making unambiguously clear a twofold function: to promote the sale of household products, and to subsume the housewife in her role by offering her romantic gratification.
> —Michele Mattelart, "From Soap to Serial"

Despite the close critical and theoretical attention that has been paid to soap operas over the last decade, few writers have offered a very clear definition of the genre. Many have identified general characteristics, compiling lists that may include everything from major features of the programs' narrative structure to the work habits of their female characters.[1] Others have remarked on viewers' understanding of "the poetic and generic rules that govern soap opera programs."[2] Still others have joined Charlotte Brunsdon in calling soap opera "in some ways the paradigmatic television genre (domestic, continuous, contemporary, episodic, repetitive, fragmented, and aural)."[3] Yet for the most part, theorists have been content to employ a commonsense definition of the form, such as Robert Allen's simple equation of soap operas with "daytime dramatic serials."[4]

Among the things that have allowed work on soap opera to proceed without a more detailed basic definition is the fact that, as with many other television forms, industry parameters for the original and still-dominant version, U.S. daytime soap operas, have so closely tallied with viewers' understanding of the genre that the category has appeared already to be defined. Because

---

Laura Stempel Mumford: Excerpt from "What Is This Called Soap Opera? Public Exposure and How Things End," first published in *Love and Ideology in the Afternoon: Soap Operas, Women, and Television Genre*, Bloomington and London: Indiana University Press, 1995: 14–46.

there is little argument over whether or not, for example, *General Hospital* qualifies as a soap, the need for a more precise definition has not seemed especially urgent.

Yet this apparent clarity disappears the moment we move beyond such an obvious example, and the category of soap opera is no longer as transparent as it may once have seemed. The days when all the U.S. programs that could potentially be identified as soap operas shared a clear set of characteristics—notably, daily daytime broadcast—ended with the 1978 debut of *Dallas*, the first major "prime-time soap." Since then, we have watched a seemingly endless set of variations on the soap opera form. Today, the very same commonsense definition that is on one level so self-evident that even relatively inexperienced viewers can immediately recognize, not only that *General Hospital* is a soap opera, but that SCTV Network's *Days of the Week* is a parody of one, dissolves into incoherence when we ask only slightly more complex questions: Are weekly prime-time serials like *Dallas* and *Dynasty* really soaps? What about the murder-centered *Twin Peaks* or the law drama *L.A. Law*? How is it that programs as diverse as the police series *Hill Street Blues* and the family drama *thirtysomething* can both be called soaps?[5] And where do parodies like *Soap* and *Mary Hartman, Mary Hartman*, or productions from Europe and Latin America, fit in?

Efforts have, of course, been made to differentiate among programs like these. Some critics have drawn a line between television serials and other forms of television melodrama (a category that is, as I will argue below, also far less transparent than its usage often suggests), while others have explicitly separated daytime soap operas from so-called "prime-time soaps." Muriel Cantor and Suzanne Pingree, for instance, discriminate between soap operas and prime-time serials such as *Dallas* in terms of production values and costs, number of episodes produced, and content, and Ien Ang makes a similar case when she insists that "an important formal difference between *Dallas* and the daytime soap opera is the much greater attention to visualization in *Dallas*."[6] Because daytime and prime-time serials share so many features and are so often equated,[7] the distinction between them is perhaps the most crucial one, and Gabriele Kreutzner and Ellen Seiter identify two possible stances: regarding prime-time serials as simply "a modification of the US daytime soap opera," or considering series like *Dynasty* and *Dallas* "as an expression of significant changes within the category of texts geared toward an adult audience."[8] Still, the more basic problem of marking soap operas off from programs that exhibit similar characteristics has not been adequately addressed.

A closer look at one attempt to distinguish among closely related program forms suggests just how difficult this task can be. Christine Geraghty's work on soap opera dates back at least to her contributions to the British Film Institute's important 1981 publication *Coronation Street*. Her 1991 book *Women and Soap Opera* can thus be seen as the culmination of over a decade's analysis of both the British and U.S. versions of the television serial. It also represents an attempt to move beyond a text-based understanding of the genre in favor of one that defines soap opera in terms of how viewers make use of it, and thus reflects a major trend in television studies. In *Women and Soap Opera*, Geraghty, a British scholar, equates U.S. daytime, U.S. prime-time, and British serials, calling all of them "soaps." In explaining the principle that unites this group of programs, she writes that "soap operas ... can now be defined not purely by daytime scheduling or even by a clear appeal to a female audience but by the presence of stories which engage an audience in such a way that they become the subject for public interest and interrogation."[9] As a defining characteristic, however, this produces a category called "soaps" that potentially encompasses nearly all of television. Although Geraghty has in mind the public fascination with the identity of J.R.'s would-be murderer on *Dallas* and speculation about the fates of characters on British serials like *Coronation Street* and *EastEnders*, it is easy to recall other instances of "public interrogation" inspired by programs that can in no way be defined as soap operas, especially in the United States. Think, for instance, of the 1992 debate about Murphy Brown's sitcom pregnancy or the controversy over PBS's 1991 airing of Marlon Riggs's controversial film *Tongues Untied*, to name just two recent U.S. examples.

The problem here is that Geraghty is, quite understandably, trying to define the genre in mainly functional terms, emphasizing what she calls "the capacity of soaps to engage their audiences in the narrative and their ability to open up for public discussion emotional and domestic issues which are normally deemed to be private."[10] Yet we could argue that this capacity is not actually special to soap operas at all, but is instead a characteristic of television as a simultaneously public and domestic medium. As it has done from its beginnings, television introduces public concerns into the private viewing space of the home through news and public affairs programming, fictional uses of current events (sitcoms or crime dramas that incorporate issues from recent headlines), and the presentation of public performances, sports, and political events for consumption in a domestic setting.[11] At the same time, TV's position as the dominant medium of entertainment and information makes it an obvious and constant topic of both private conversation and public discussion. Geraghty implies that, outside of the programs she refers to as "soaps," such talk about television has traditionally focused on subjects that are neither "emotional" nor "domestic," and that it is only through prime-time serials aimed at women that these topics enter the sphere of public talk about TV. Yet cultural-studies-oriented audience research makes it clear that viewers are capable of raising personal issues in connection with programs that encompass a variety of genres.[12] And even if this were not true, the phenomenon of the daytime talk show—*Donahue*, *The Oprah Winfrey Show*, and the like—has institutionalized the public discussion of intensely "private" issues, such as sexuality, domestic violence, parent-child relationships, and so on.[13]

As Geraghty acknowledges, the important thing "is not so much to give [particular programs] the correct label but to recognise why there is a problem about definition."[14] One of the complicating issues is the tendency for television as a whole to incorporate aspects of the melodramatic mode of address into previously established genres, particularly through the increasing personalization of all television expressions, from comedy to the news, a subject to which I will return later in this chapter. Although this has intensified since prime-time serials such as *Dallas* and *Dynasty* became popular, it is a medium-wide trend—at least in the United States, Canada, Australia, and the United Kingdom—and one that renders essentially pointless any strict identification of the personal with soap opera.

To avoid the kind of confusion that arises from a definition that emphasizes function in this way, we need to develop one that focuses instead on the specific characteristics of the genre itself, a definition that allows us not merely to describe and categorize a wide range of programs, but to imagine other possible permutations. Otherwise, theoretical developments will be limited by the fact that those of us who work in the field can never be sure that we are all talking about the same thing. What, for example, does it mean to speak of closure's function in soap opera (to cite only one major theoretical issue) if the "genre" includes daytime and prime-time serials, episodic series that follow a single plot trajectory, episodic series with multiple storylines, and limited-run prime-time series?

Although several important theoretical questions need to be considered before we can examine the following definition in detail, let me begin by specifying as precisely as I can what I mean by the term "soap opera":

> A soap opera is a continuing fictional dramatic television program, presented in multiple serial installments each week, through a narrative composed of interlocking storylines that focus on the relationships within a specific community of characters.

These are the elements I see as "necessary and sufficient to constitute and delimit [the] genre,"[15] and define the term as I will use it throughout this chapter. Although the traditional U.S. soap opera serves as my primary model, I have deliberately tried to define the form in such a way as to allow for the possibility of a wide range of permutations beyond those that have actually been produced (such as future soaps from nonbroadcast and noncommercial sources and from other than U.S. producers), without sacrificing the specificity that makes a definition useful. Although these parameters are to a great extent derived from commercially produced U.S. daytime serials, there is no reason to imagine that such programs represent the limits of the genre. (At least one national cable service has already produced a serial that meets my criteria, the Christian Broadcasting Network's *Another Life*, which ran from 1981 to 1984.) In particular, we need not expect future examples to be limited to daytime, and the fact that other programs, especially British and Australian serials, already meet most of my criteria suggests that we have by no means seen all the possible variants on the form.

Before I look at the individual elements of my definition in more detail, however, I want to consider why the issue of definition itself has been problematic and to suggest what the effort to define soap opera as a unique genre implies for work on other television forms. The project of genre definition has at least one obvious function for TV theorists: Because it allows us to distinguish among programs that might otherwise seem quite similar, it permits us to separate the operations of specific *forms* (genres) of programming from the operations both of individual televisual *practices*—which may occur in a variety of genres—and of television as a *medium*. (An example of this would be my attempt, above, to separate the formal operations of soap opera from television's capacity as a medium to introduce domestic issues into the public arena.) In the case of soap operas, the need for this kind of separation becomes more and more urgent as conventions traditionally associated with daytime serials bleed into prime time. At least since the U.S. debut of *Dallas*, and certainly since the 1981 premiere of *Hill Street Blues*, televisual practices such as serial-style episodic nonclosure and complexly overlapping storylines have become more and more common on programs that bear few other obvious affinities with daytime soap operas. (Some people might argue that the 1965 debut of *Peyton Place* actually marked the beginning of soap opera's invasion of prime time, but while popular, that series never had *Dallas*'s impact on television conventions.) Jane Feuer has argued that U.S. television exhibits a "general movement . . . towards the continuing serial form."[16] In fact, it is impossible to isolate a single major generic characteristic of soaps—with the possible exception of multiple weekly installments—that is not now also employed by other types of fictional television programs. If we expand the landscape to include nonfiction forms, such as news programs, talk, or game shows, we cannot even except daily presentation.

Nevertheless, certain problems face those who attempt to define specific television genres, and these are not unique to the field of soap opera. A profound theoretical uncertainty underlies most discussions of television form: the lack of an adequate theory of television genre as a whole. While genre has long been a site of debate within film theory, it has only recently begun to be dealt with seriously in television studies. And not surprisingly, questions about the validity of genre itself have accompanied theorists' first serious efforts to move beyond broad generalizations like "television melodrama."

A major objection to the project of genre definition is that television is resistant *as a medium* to the rigidity that such categorization is thought to require. Television is seen, for example, as both the ultimate representative and the primary purveyor of a postmodern sensibility, the site of a self-reflexive mix of ahistorical pastiche and apolitical parody, filled with programs that refer mainly to other programs, and emblematized by MTV. Its fluid formats, argue postmodern theorists, have borders far too permeable to fix into anything that resembles the genres of the past.[17] Others object on the grounds that television categories are too changeable to anchor anything as stable as genre definition, arguing instead that the medium is characterized by constant movement within which, as John Fiske claims, "Each new show shifts genre boundaries and develops definitions."[18]

Yet claims like these seem to ignore a basic characteristic of television, especially in its commercial broadcast incarnation. Indeed, in John Caughie's words, "Questions of genre . . . seem fundamental to television,"[19] particularly in the United States, where television is uniquely genre-driven—not least because the industry obsession with ratings has led producers, broadcasters, and, more recently, cablecasters on a perpetual quest for the programming formula that will guarantee a large and dependable audience. However malleable TV formats may seem, industry self-promotion and trade publications make it clear that programmers rely heavily on viewers' realization that specific programs belong to specific genres. This has several important consequences: While literary and film theorists can, for instance, usefully distinguish between "genre" fiction or movies and other forms, such a distinction is not very useful for television.[20] Even industry discussions of programming innovations demonstrate the importance of a basic genre stability, and most new shows are designed to be immediately recognizable in terms of familiar existing genres, whether as traditional members or as new variations on them. This process is a self-perpetuating one: Programs that viewers find impossible to understand in familiar genre terms tend to be interpreted as mocking audience expectations—as indeed they are, since audiences have been led to expect that new programs will conform to old patterns.

The most prominent recent example of this phenomenon, and one of the most complex demonstrations of the dominance of genre, is *Twin Peaks*. Its initial popularity can probably be attributed to the combined effects of co-creator David Lynch's cult status and the fact that the program's challenges to television conventions—its overt expressions of sexuality and violence, black comedy, allusions to film culture, and so on—seemed at first to take place within a format that mixed the already popular genres of the prime-time serial and the crime/mystery series. Ultimately, however, *Peaks'* loss of audience and both critics' and viewers' intense alienation from the series can, I think, be traced directly to the fact that the audience found it nearly impossible to continue to understand the show in terms of recognizable genres.[21] (It is interesting to note that the few programs that do resist this kind of categorization—including *Twin Peaks*—tend at some point to be identified as soap operas, as if this serves as a default genre.)

An important factor here is the way in which the basic programming structure of U.S. commercial broadcast television (and its noncommercial and cable imitators) interacts with audience expectations to reinforce familiar genre categories. As Caughie has pointed out, "the schedules of the majority viewing channels ... [concentrate] particular genres and subgenres within the same time-slot: the competition is directed quite blatantly at the same demographic group or taste constituency, and, characteristically, for the network viewer, the choice is *within* genres and subgenres rather than between them."[22] Nowhere is this more evident than in the case of low-caste genres such as soap operas, children's programs, game shows, and talk shows, which tend to be clustered together in fringe time periods. That is not to say that the individual programs within these clusters are identical. Patricia Mellencamp contends that "While there is still a programming block of time and general set of conventions which define 'soap opera,' each serial is also marked by differentiation," yet such "differentiation" does not necessarily mean, as Mellencamp concludes, that "genre analyses of TV no longer cohere."[23] For both programmers and viewers, genres are to a great extent defined by their placement on the schedule: To place a series in a particular spot on the schedule grid is implicitly to locate it within a particular genre.

The centrality of genre to the operations of the TV industry, then, makes it ironic that, while specific individual forms such as soap operas and sitcoms have received an enormous amount of analytic attention, television genre theory itself is still at a relatively early stage of development. What Caughie calls "assumptions of genre" pervade TV studies, but major books on television form have only recently begun automatically to include detailed discussions of genre theory, and that theory has only begun to deal with the impact of television's unique combination of repetition and difference on notions of genre.[24]

One reason for this late start is the relatively recent separation of television studies from the study of film and literature. Although the issue of television's difference from film was raised early on, it has taken a long time for critics and theorists to recognize just how limited an application there may be in TV for concepts originally developed for the study of film.[25] Much work continues to draw on film theory, but it is crucial to remember that, in Jane Feuer's words, "television as an apparatus differs in almost every significant respect from cinema."[26] The role of the major U.S. broadcast networks in shaping the television programming agenda, the effect of commercials on the narrative structure of individual programs, the simultaneous availability of anywhere from 4 to 150 viewing options, the networks' changing relationships both to their affiliates and to cable services, and the domestic setting in which television is consumed are only a few of the things that set the medium apart from film.

This insight is particularly important in the case of soap opera, which has almost universally been understood as a form of melodrama, and therefore has frequently been discussed using the analyses developed for the stage and film versions of it. Melodrama may be invoked as a meta-genre, a mode of address, a form of imagination, or a performance style. Or it may be used as a blanket term that means roughly the same thing as "television drama," as David Thorburn seems to do when he includes in the category of TV melodrama "most made-for-television movies, the soap operas, and all the lawyers, cowboys, cops and docs, the fugitives and adventurers, the fraternal and filial comrades who have filled the prime hours of so many American nights for the last thirty years."[27] But paradoxically, as melodrama comes to be—and to be seen as—the dominant mode of television expression, its usefulness as a way of understanding a specific genre such as soap opera becomes more and more limited.

In "Melodrama Inside and Outside the Home," Laura Mulvey traces the development of what she variously calls the "melodramatic style" and the "melodramatic aesthetic" from the eighteenth- and nineteenth-century stage through Hollywood cinema and finally "to its death in the television-dominated home."[28] In its stage incarnation, melodrama is characterized by exaggerated gestures and a plot more dependent on fate than on individual heroic action, while Hollywood film versions focus on women and the home, sexuality, repression, and a conflict between the individual and an intrusive community. Finally, says Mulvey, in television, "the long-standing tension between inside"—home, sexuality, emotion—"and outside is resolved": melodrama, which originally depended on public theatrical expressions of private emotions, becomes totally absorbed into the home when it is consumed via the domesticated medium of television.[29]

Mulvey seems to imply that television melodrama is essentially impossible, its necessarily public character canceled out when it is consumed in the home. But according to Lynne Joyrich, we can instead see melodrama as "the preferred form for TV."[30] Joyrich points out daytime and prime-time serials' employment of specific stylistic markers associated with melodrama, such as "the use of music to convey emotional effects" and the heightening of dramatic moments through "concentrated visual metaphors" (p. 131), but she argues that melodrama "so dominates [television's] discourse that it becomes difficult to locate as a separate TV genre" (p. 131). Although she draws on Thorburn's argument, her claim here is quite different from his sweeping generalizations, resting as it does on an analysis of postmodern consumerism and the ways in which the personal and domestic framework characteristic of film melodrama has come to enclose a wide range of television forms, from made-for-TV movies to police dramas to the stories on the evening news. Still, she admits that, "as it spreads across a number of TV forms . . . melodrama loses its specificity, becoming diffuse and ungrounded in its multiple deployments in the flow of TV" (p. 135).

Joyrich's argument is extremely persuasive, and several of the traits she assigns to melodrama will be important later in this essay—among them the externalization of internal conflicts, the perpetuation of the myth of the total legibility of meaning, an intense concern with gender, and the way that framing a story in exclusively personal terms allows the framer to evade its ideological implications. Yet the essay raises a serious problem for work on television genres that have traditionally been considered melodramas, for the increasing diffuseness Joyrich describes applies as much to the usefulness of the *concept* of melodrama as to its presence on the program grid. If melodrama is seen as TV's dominant mode of address, its dominant aesthetic, or the meta-genre that subsumes the majority of television genres—and I think it may be all of these at once—then there is limited value in discussing specific genres such as soap opera primarily in terms of their melodramatic nature. In other words, even if almost all of television is melodramatic, we still need to distinguish soap opera from the other melodramatic genres that fill the airwaves. An understanding of melodrama must certainly inform any serious discussions of soap opera, but we are still left with much the same question we have always needed to ask: how is soap opera different from other television genres?

At the same time, melodrama's very pervasiveness reminds us once again of the necessity of questioning the extent to which we can usefully employ filmic (or theatrical or literary) concepts in discussions of television. In its heyday from the 1930s to the 1950s, after all, film melodrama was only one of a number of different cinematic forms. Although some, such as film noir, were inflected by it, few film genres were actually transformed *into* melodrama, as so much of television has been.[31] At the very least, as Robyn Wiegman insists in her analysis of TV's presentation of the 1991 Gulf War, "melodrama must be understood, in its televisual deployment, as a 'contaminated' genre: cutting, mixing, and otherwise transforming the representational strategies we associate with it from the study of cinema."[32] Television *takes up* melodramatic strategies, as it takes up strategies employed by other film, stage, and literary traditions, such as the domestic novel, the mystery, vaudeville, the film musical, and so on. But rather than simply being transplanted to television, these features are adapted and transformed into specifically televisual strategies; while never wholly severed from other media, they follow a specific developmental trajectory within television.

In fact, there may be good reason to question even a broad equation of soap opera with melodrama. Christine Gledhill has drawn attention to the ambiguous historical and theoretical relationships between the two, tracing the ties between melodrama and a variety of "women's" fictions, including the domestic novel, film melodramas, and both radio and TV soaps.[33] She argues that soap opera's emphasis on dialogue undermines melodrama's dependence on gestural and metaphoric expressions of emotion, while serialization is antagonistic to what she describes as melodrama's "deus-ex-machina resolutions" (p. 113). Although Gledhill acknowledges that the forms share a number of mechanisms—including a heavy reliance on stories involving coincidence, mysteries about parentage, and the reappearance of long-lost characters—she suggests that melodrama and soap opera actually constitute separate narrative strategies for dealing with the realm of the personal. One of her most intriguing insights is that soap opera's much-publicized ability to deal with social issues is the result of a kind of handoff from melodrama to strategies specific to soaps: "once melodrama has put the problem on the agenda, soap opera's diagnostic technique of conversation will frequently dissipate the melodramatic charge as characters chew over . . . the emotional, moral, and social implications and consequences of the event" (p. 121).

Questions of genre necessarily also raise questions about the complex relationship between a medium and its audience and about the site(s) at which meaning is produced. In the case of television studies, the reluctance to dwell on genre definitions is probably connected to the fact that much contemporary criticism and theory developed in reaction both to social-science-based audience studies organized around issues of "influence" and to textual analyses growing out of film and literary studies. The resulting work has emphasized the notion of active viewers who make meaning through their encounters with polysemous television texts, and has shifted attention away from textually based studies. As I suggested in my discussion of Christine Geraghty's functional approach, this acknowledgment of viewers' role in the production of meaning has some clear implications for defining soap opera in particular. Yet, since one of the major projects of genre study is to group individual texts according to their shared formal characteristics, texts must necessarily be the basis of any notion of genre.

This is an especially vexing problem in television studies, for many theorists agree that what Robyn Wiegman calls television's "permeable borders . . . make difficult the isolation of any unified, singular televisual text."[34] In her discussions of the notion of "good" or "quality" TV, however, Charlotte Brunsdon defends retaining the concept of the television text while also taking seriously the difficulties inherent in identifying such an object. She acknowledges a diversity of viewing practices, yet she insists that such strategies can represent "defining features" of television as a medium only "if we choose not to pay attention to what is on the screen."[35] Instead, Brunsdon points to "the symbolic necessity of the audience, its varied inscription throughout the television text," the ways in which "the audience is called on, and constructed by television, as its main source of legitimation" (p. 120). She argues that, far from proving the nonexistence of such a text, critical approaches that focus on the audience or that emphasize television's intertextuality actually prove "that the choice of what is recognized as constituting 'a' text . . . is a political as well as a critical matter" (p. 123). (Thus, for example, critics may attempt to "redeem" an otherwise ideologically suspect media product—Madonna's videos, say, or maternal melodramas—by shifting the focus from the text itself to the various strategies through which viewers construct a preferable reading.)

In claiming that it is not television as a medium, but critical and theoretical approaches *to* television that undermine its textuality, Brunsdon concludes that,

> difficult as it may be, we have to retain a notion of the television text. That is, without the guarantees of common sense or the authority of a political teleology[,] with the recognition of the potentially infinite proliferation of textual sites, and the agency of the always already social reader, in a range of contexts, it is still necessary—and possible—to construct a televisual object of study—and judgment. (p. 125)

However, just as, in Brunsdon's view, soap opera presents a paradigm of television as a whole, so too it offers a particularly extreme demonstration of the difficulty of identifying such an "object of study." There are special problems attendant on defining the soap opera "text," problems that go well beyond the predictable difficulties involved in defining any text—or, indeed, in reaching a critical consensus about the possibility or desirability of identifying "a" text at all. For some, the genre's apparently total lack of closure means that, "in the instance of soap opera, there is no such thing as a text . . . , since the stories in question have no end."[36] This is by no means the only ground on which critics and theorists deny the existence of the soap opera text. The sheer volume of episodes of an individual television soap opera—the fact that some programs have been broadcast five days a week since the early 1950s—makes it hard for a critic to describe, much less recapture, a program's broadcast history. In contrast, even the longest-running situation comedy or drama, aired only once a week, can more easily be reviewed in its entirety.

In fact, the irretrievability of the complete record of a long-running soap has led Robert Allen and others to claim that such a text can never be defined with any certainty. Allen has argued that there is something about soap opera's narrative form that removes it from the realm of traditional aesthetic objects, making it impossible to describe it as a "text" in any meaningful way. He describes soaps as "narratively anomalous," contending that they "cannot be said to have a 'form' in the traditional sense."[37] Even if we accept the possibility of locating a specific television text, we cannot watch a "complete" soap opera, says Allen, so it is therefore impossible to define it as a text. Significantly, this conclusion is based not only on the predicted lack of series closure—viewers' expectations that an individual program will go on forever—but on the assumption that a particular program's *origins* are also inaccessible:

> I would argue that the soap opera as text can be specified only as the sum of all its episodes broadcast since it began. Hence what we are dealing with is a huge meta-text ... which [in the case of a 30-year-old program] ... would take 780 hours ... to run.... But even at the end of this marathon screening, the critic could still not claim to have "read" the entire text of the soap, since during the 32.5 days of continuous viewing, 16 additional hours of textual material would have been produced.[38]

The idea that what Allen calls the soap opera "meta-text" is ultimately irretrievable, however, overlooks several significant factors. First of all, there certainly exist viewers who have experienced the entire broadcast run of particular programs, whether these are older ones who remember *Guiding Light*'s 1952 move to television or viewers who have watched *The Bold and the Beautiful* or *Santa Barbara* since the far more recent beginnings of these shows in the 1980s. Indeed, for some programs, begun in the 1970s or 1980s and canceled within a decade (such as *Ryan's Hope, Generations, Texas, Santa Barbara,* and *Capitol*), there exist viewers who have consumed entire series, from beginning to end. Even if such viewers have missed occasional individual episodes—and in these days of VCRs, we need not assume even that gap—their position would in no way resemble that of Allen's critic, who sits down with a collection of unviewed videotapes representing 30 years of broadcasts. As a matter of fact, we might argue that the viewing experience of Allen's critic would bear so little resemblance to that of a regular viewer as to constitute a different practice entirely, and that it would thus yield few insights into the process by which soaps are actually consumed.

Equally problematic from a theoretical standpoint, however, is the implication that we cannot speak meaningfully about a program as a "text" unless we have consumed it in its entirety. Allen's own work demonstrates that the impossibility of reviewing the entire run of these programs in no way prevents the development of a sophisticated analysis of the form. But even more important, the lack of this kind of total retrievability is part of what marks television's specific difference from print, the medium whose "repeatability" implicitly forms the basis for any theory that presumes the critic must "read" an entire work in order to consider it as a text. Irretrievability also marks television's difference from film, whose discrete individual units—single films—can be endlessly reviewed in a way that television series cannot.[39]

Other differences between television and film or literature also have clear implications for the concept of the TV text, as well as special importance in understanding soap opera. Heath and Skirrow pointed out what is perhaps the most important difference in 1977: Television is characterized by an "immediacy effect ... supported by the experience of flow: like the world, television never stops, is continuous," and this effect is in turn inflected by "the overall definition of television as 'live.'"[40] Building on this insight, Jane

Feuer contends that "notions of 'liveness'" apply as much to taped or filmed and edited programs as they do to events broadcast at the moment of occurrence,[41] and that television's capacity to transmit events as they happen has led to the application of "an ideology of the live" (p. 14) to all television transmissions—regardless of the actual temporal relationship between an event and its televisual presentation. Thus all television transmissions are in some sense presented, consumed, and understood as if they were live.

The concept of television's perpetual liveness will come up again in connection with soap operas' multiple weekly installments, but for now I want to underline the fact that this "liveness" is at the root of some of TV's central differences from film. Feuer points to the conflation of the "live" with the "real"—if something is happening as we watch it, it must "really" be happening—as well as to the way that television seems "real" in the sense of being "an entirely ordinary experience" (p. 15). She also emphasizes the processes by which the "circuit of address" on genuinely live programs "propagates an ideology of 'liveness' overcoming [the] fragmentation" of television's ordinary segmented flow (p. 17). These observations have special meaning in the case of soap operas, where the apparent liveness of television is augmented by the programs' manipulation of time. By promoting the fiction that viewers' and characters' time passes at the same rate, soaps present themselves as "real" in both of the senses Feuer employs. The fact that many soap opera events take the same amount of time they would occupy in viewers' lives makes their depictions especially "realistic," while the frequent coincidence between "real time" and both diegetic time and the time that elapses between episodes lends an air of immediacy to events within the programs.[42]

These differences between television and film or literature suggest that soap operas, which exemplify so many television traits, may demand an entirely new conception of "text," one that allows for the kind of viewing habits that actually characterize the experience of their regular audience members. In this connection, the notion of soaps as an "indefinitely expandable middle"[43] may be useful, although that notion's usual association with the programs' lack of closure will be problematic. Putting aside, however, the question of whether or not soap operas ever achieve closure, viewers' consumption of them certainly has an identifiable beginning. Regardless of whether or not that beginning coincides with the first broadcast episode of the program, it constitutes the beginning of the viewing experience, and thus a point that we can at least provisionally identify as the beginning of a text.

Audience research suggests, in fact, that viewers think of the soap opera "text" in just this way. Ellen Seiter and her colleagues, for instance, have noted that their "informants were aware of the impossibility for a single person to grasp fully the text of a soap opera," largely because they could not watch every single episode.[44] Nevertheless, these same viewers assembled "a condensed version of the text" through selective viewing, consultation with other viewers, and speculation based on their own "expert textual knowledge" (p. 234). The authors therefore "identified the text with the experience of soap operas as our viewers described it on the basis of their individual exposure to the genre" (p. 232).

Clearly, however, there is more at stake here than questions about whether or not one can define a program without seeing it from its beginning to its end. Allen's concern over the impossibility of reviewing the complete broadcast history of a particular soap opera, for example, is ultimately based on a critique of the very notion of genre. Rather than defining soap opera in traditional generic terms, he prefers to consider it as the intersection of the three different discursive systems used by the industrial, critical, and viewer communities.[45]

Yet it is not necessary, as Allen seems to imply, to choose between rigid genre categories and no genres at all. Instead, we can follow theorists like Steve Neale, who understands genres as "systems of expectation and hypothesis," as processes that involve both producers and consumers of the programs that comprise them.[46] This is particularly appropriate in the case of soap operas, for, as audience studies have demonstrated, regular viewers bring very specific kinds of expectations to their viewing experience. While they may not talk explicitly about soap operas or soap-opera-like programs in terms of genre, they understand the series they watch as following a set of dramatic, narrative, ideological, and moral rules and conventions in which certain sorts of developments are permitted and others are unlikely or impossible.[47] This is actually a crucial component of audience pleasure, and competent soap viewers play a constant game of speculation and anticipation with regard to future story and character development. In a form whose viewers often draw on years of detailed expertise regarding specific programs and soap operas in general, the relevance of an understanding of genre as a relationship between producers' texts and consumers' expectations seems clear.

Let me return now to the definition I proposed at the beginning of this chapter:

> A soap opera is a continuing fictional dramatic television program, presented in multiple serial installments each week through a narrative composed of interlocking storylines that focus on the relationships within a specific community of characters.

As I have already indicated, each element in this definition can be found in other categories of contemporary U.S. television, and any regular TV viewer will be able to name programs that are not soap operas but that still incorporate many of these same traits. The serial format, for example, characterizes *Hill Street Blues*, *St. Elsewhere*, *L.A. Law*, *Wiseguy*, *Dallas*, *Dynasty*, *Knots Landing*, and, through the use of multipart story arcs and cliffhanger episodes, certain situation comedies as well (e.g., *Cheers*, *Murphy Brown*). Multiple and often interlocking storylines are a major structural feature, not only of the dramatic programs I've listed, but of *Hotel*, *Fantasy Island*, and *The Love Boat* as well. Personal relationships within a self-contained community dominate shows like *Northern Exposure* and *thirtysomething*, as well as more traditional series, such as *The Andy Griffith Show*, *M*A*S*H*, and *Emergency*.

Despite their individual appearance across a range of genres, however, certain of these characteristics are firmly associated with soap operas: Any program that presents an intense mesh of personal stories that continue, serial-like, beyond a single episode, is likely to be called a soap. While the term has long been used as a sweeping derogatory equivalent for "trash TV" or "melodrama," it is now broadly applied not only by cultural critics, but by journalists and even industry promotion departments, and no longer inevitably signals a specific negative evaluation of an individual program.[48] But it is this specific combination of characteristics, the idiosyncratic mix of these familiar elements that distinguishes a soap from a program that simply employs some of them. As Stephen Neale writes, "Generic specificity is a question not of particular and exclusive elements, however defined, but of exclusive and particular combinations and articulations of elements."[49]

In order to understand how these characteristics combine to create a unique television genre, then, let us look at the elements individually. *A soap opera is a continuing fictional dramatic television program*: By using the word "continuing," I mean to distinguish soaps, which are presented as first-run episodes 52 weeks a year, from the more limited runs of conventional television series aired according to industry "seasons," as well as from shorter miniseries, multipart made-for-television movies, and so on. (Thus, while sharing many traits with U.S. soaps, the *telenovelas* of Latin America do not qualify as continuing dramas in this sense, since they usually have a limited, if lengthy, run.)

Soap operas' fictional status may seem self-evident, but the May 1992 debut of MTV's nonfiction series *The Real World*—described in its own network promotions as "a real-life soap opera"—suggests otherwise. We need to be careful to distinguish fictional television programs from those that are unscripted and may be "performed" by nonactors, as in the case of *The Real World* and its precursors, the 1973 PBS series *An American Family* and Fox's 1991 *Yearbook*. Although such programs are elaborately mediated and constructed through highly selective editing and other practices, their allegedly nonfictional status puts them into a different category of television genres.

I also distinguish dramatic from possible comedy and parody series—*Soap* and *Mary Hartman, Mary Hartman*, for instance—to emphasize the fact that, while soap opera performance may involve a high degree of self-consciousness and may even be overtly camp, the programs themselves are essentially unironic. While it was possible to follow the storylines of *Soap* or *Mary Hartman* as one would a traditional serial, both programs offered preferred readings of themselves as parodies.[50] Soap operas, on the other hand, take themselves and their conventions seriously; indeed, it is that very seriousness that permits certain audiences to perform what Jane Feuer has called "camp decodings" of the programs and that makes possible the parodies that represent the ultimate ironic reading of them.[51] While Feuer insists that the decodings performed by gay male viewers are actually among *Dynasty*'s preferred readings, I am obviously suggesting just the opposite: that they exist in contrast to the dominant readings proposed by the program itself. It may also be true, however, that prime-time serials such as *Dynasty* offer, or at the very least make space for, easily accessible alternative, oppositional, camp, and/or comic readings as a function of their attempt to appeal to the broadest possible audience—a goal that characterizes U.S. prime-time far more than daytime television.

According to my definition, soaps are presented *in multiple installments each week*; in the United States, that means five days a week. Although many elements separate daytime from so-called "prime-time soaps"—including the prime-time emphasis on business and financial power—in my view these are secondary to the far more basic differences that arise from five-day-a-week versus weekly broadcast. In fact, what we might call soaps' "dailiness" has significant consequences both for the programs' structure and style and for regular viewers' experience of them.

Early theorists like Tania Modleski argued that the specific narrative structure of soap operas, particularly their cycles of interruption and repetition, closely resembles the daily lives of conventional housewives and therefore makes the experience of watching soap operas especially appealing, as well as easy to reconcile with the interruptions that supposedly characterize their days.[52] Others have contended that it is the domestic content of the programs that makes soaps both interesting and relevant to women viewers whose attention is traditionally focused on the personal.[53]

I would argue, however, that the intimacy that seems to characterize the experience of watching soap operas results at least as much from viewers' daily exposure to the programs as it does from the specific content and structure of the episodes themselves, or from particular camera work and other production choices.[54] The relatively brief interval between episodes permits the act of watching them to become part of a regular routine—part of "viewers' daily rituals"[55]—constructing a uniquely intense viewing experience and investing it with a status quite different from that of programs consumed weekly or even less frequently. While audience studies acknowledge that many fans miss occasional episodes or even watch irregularly, the same research suggests that they also watch with the assumption that daily viewing of the programs is the ideal.[56]

"Dailiness" functions on the levels of both production and consumption, and is connected to the "ideology of liveness" that has dominated and defined U.S. (and British) television from the outset. As Jane Feuer indicates in regard to *Good Morning America*, the construction of liveness, whether actual or artificial, allows a particular program "to insinuate itself into our lives."[57] Habitual daily viewing intensifies this process in the case of soap operas, and the notion of *repetition* may be useful in beginning to understand why. Charlotte Brunsdon has pointed out that, while researchers have concentrated on the consequences of the fact that women often watch soap operas in groups, a more thorough understanding may come from work that distinguishes "between modes of viewing which are repeated on a regular basis and uncommon or unfamiliar modes of viewing."[58] This seems to me to point to a potentially crucial way of understanding the television viewing experience. Although many recent theorists have called attention to television's penchant for repetition, it has often been made secondary to the notion of interruption, as in John

Caughie's claim that, like the "novelistic" in general, "the television novelistic is organized around interruption."[59] Caughie makes this point as a way of linking television to a long narrative tradition, to which television's "definitive contribution" is the development of "a narrative form built on the principle of interruption and therefore organizing expectation and attention to the short segments which will soften the disruption of being interrupted."[60]

But while it is important to consider the narrative effect of the constant interruption that characterizes commercial television, an argument like Caughie's ignores viewers' habit of returning to these "interrupted" television narratives on a weekly or, in the case of soaps, daily basis. The experience of watching an individual television program may indeed be marked by disruption, as the episode's forward movement is repeatedly broken by the intrusion of commercials and other forms of promotion, and Raymond Williams's notion of "flow" captures the extent to which an evening of viewing can be seen as consisting of a loose assembly of such fragments. But if we step back to take a wider perspective of, say, a week, a month, or a year of viewing, we can also see a pattern of repetition in which much of the audience returns again and again, not only to specific programs, but to particular day-parts (such as early morning or prime-time). As Heath and Skirrow maintain in their revision of Williams, "the 'central fact of television experience' is much less flow than *flow and regularity*; the anachronistic succession is also a constant repetition."[61]

Although nonfiction genres like talk, news, or game shows may operate on a similar schedule, soap operas are the only fictional examples of first-run daily telecast on U.S. television. This therefore puts soaps in a unique position as paradigmatic, not simply of the extent to which television narrative is built on constant interruption, but of the concomitant expectation that the interrupted narrative will resume. Indeed, as I will argue shortly, each soap opera episode presents in miniature both the "flow" and the pattern of return typical of television.

One question raised by my insistence on multiple weekly installments as a defining characteristic of soap opera is whether some threshold number of episodes must air each week in order for a program to qualify as a soap. For instance, in contrast to the U.S. standard of five episodes per week, British serials such as *Coronation Street* and *EastEnders* broadcast only two or three, usually with an omnibus installment on the weekend. The question of how these programs' multiple episodes fit into my definition is here complicated by the fact that, while U.S. daytime TV serials have always aired five days a week and had completely replaced radio serials by the 1960–61 season, their British television counterparts have had a far more varied broadcast history, including the fact that radio serials still continue to air alongside them. Thus, although the expectations and consumption patterns of U.S. soap opera viewers have been shaped by the kind of "dailiness" I am describing, British viewers may have quite a different set of expectations. Similarly, from the production side, U.S. soaps are inevitably structured around the demands of five-day-a-week broadcast, while the narrative and story development of British programs may be organized to meet quite different demands.[62]

These differences remind us of the crucial role played by local viewing (and production) conditions. As Sean Cubitt points out in his book on video culture, "the importance of the local . . . helps to circumscribe the generalisation of arguments to universal values, geographically or historically. . . . Programmes or programme formats in world-wide distribution are viewed differently in various cultures, even within the same culture, or by the same person viewing at different times."[63] Cubitt is arguing here that, while the widespread use of VCRs has changed British viewing habits in fundamental ways, the fact that communal, real-time viewing still dominates in many other parts of the world makes it difficult to extrapolate from British experience to the experience of viewers elsewhere. But his remarks are relevant for all areas of TV, including the exportation of the U.S. soap opera format (and of actual programs) to other cultures. Despite a shared set of televisual conventions and the long-standing exchange of specific individual programs, both the production and the consumption conditions of British and U.S. television differ considerably.[64] (Among the most obvious and influential differences is the historical development of U.S. television as primarily commercial and privately owned, versus the British model of noncommercial government monopoly.)[65] Thus, while the overlap between the two systems allows us to use examples from one to illuminate the other, we must do so with great care, for conclusions based on the experience of U.S. television may not apply smoothly to the British, and vice versa.

The emphasis on multiple episodes provides a perfect example of the complications that may arise when we ignore the differences between television cultures, not least because an individual program acquires its significance within the context of the larger televisual landscape. Five-day-a-week U.S. programs such as soap operas are explicitly marked as different from weekly ones, and watching them is therefore necessarily a different experience from watching those that appear once a week. Since U.S. television currently has no programs scheduled to air two or three times a week, the primary differences are between five-day-a-week and weekly broadcast. (I am speaking here of first-run episodes, rather than programs that are scheduled for one original and one or more repeat airings during a single week—a common practice on many local PBS affiliates, as well as on MTV, CNN, HBO, and other cable services.) In the United Kingdom, however, where programs may air anywhere from daily to weekly, the difference is somewhat more complicated. We might argue, therefore, that, in any television system that relies mainly on a *weekly* programming rotation, it is the experience of *multiple* episodes during a single week that is marked as different and therefore significant. Thus, the British practice of airing, say, three weekly episodes of a serial would generate many of the same patterns of expectation, including an incorporation of a particular series into viewers' regular routines similar to that generated by the five-day-a-week broadcast of U.S. soap operas.[66]

My emphasis on "dailiness" also raises an interesting question about another category of programs, series that are "stripped," or aired five or even seven days a week through syndication: Can a series designed to run weekly "become" a soap opera simply by moving into five-day-a-week syndication? In most cases the answer is no, since a sitcom or a traditional crime drama stripped daily still fails to meet the other criteria that define a soap opera. But the situation alters considerably when we consider dramas that closely resemble soaps in their use of interlocking storylines and their emphasis on personal relationships. Series such as *thirtysomething* and *L.A. Law*, which focus on the relationships within a small, essentially closed group of friends and relatives or coworkers, beg for comparison with soap operas. *L.A. Law*'s tendency to leave problems unresolved at the end of an episode and *thirtysomething*'s obsession with questions of gender, romance, and family, as well as the degree of viewers' emotional involvement with both series and their characters, make it particularly tempting to classify them as soaps.[67]

I have been arguing that, among other things, daily viewing allows audience members to incorporate a program into their lives in a way quite different from programs that recur on a weekly basis. If I am correct about this effect, then the intensity and intimacy created by daily involvement with a dramatic series do not depend on the specific structure of the narrative itself. Nor are they dependent on the particular purpose—daytime or prime-time scheduling, weekly or daily rotation, broadcast or cable setting, domestic or foreign consumption—for which it was originally designed. But the fact that I have been invoking the concept of "dailiness" primarily in terms of its effect on viewers does not mean that the prospect of five-day-a-week broadcast has no influence on story development, narrative structure, characterization, or other features of the production.

For instance, writers, directors, actors, and other participants in the production process who have five days a week in which to develop a story, explore a character, express an idea, consider a social issue, and so on, can employ a degree of detail unavailable to those who produce a weekly series. Soap opera stories proceed at what inexperienced viewers may see as an excruciating pace, but because of its attempt to imitate the rate at which events transpire in "real life," this pace contributes to the fiction of the programs' "liveness," the sense that the events depicted are actually happening as we watch them. Once again, the phenomenon of "dailiness" and television's "ideology of liveness" inflect each other through soaps' construction of time.

There are also specific negative consequences for production and performance style. Soaps' year-round five-day-a-week broadcast schedule requires a five-day-a-week production schedule, which means that actors have limited rehearsal time. This in turn results in what many viewers recognize as characteristically unpolished performances, exacerbated by a limited use of retakes, along with editing and production values that tend to be judged by nonfans as considerably "lower" than the more lavish ones of most prime-time television. In some ways, the fact that actors flub lines or improvise when memory fails them may contribute to soaps' apparent realism, since characters' conversations often seem no smoother than viewers'. At the same time, however, the impossibility of creating the perfect performances and camera work typical of prime-time programs also contributes to the low esteem in which nonfans hold soap operas.

If we were to arrange TV dramas along a continuum ordered in terms of their increasing likeness to soap opera—with, say, completely freestanding episodic series at one end and prime-time serials at the other—and then consider the impact of daily cable- or broadcast on each of them, we would find that, by the time we got to the daily syndicated airing of a series like *Dallas*, we would have reached a viewing experience nearly indistinguishable from that of a "real" soap. The possibility that a series originally designed as a weekly prime-time drama can seemingly be transformed into a soap opera also serves as yet another reminder of the importance of developing a comprehensive definition of the genre. In this case, soaps can be distinguished from other programs that might air daily by the fact that they take *serial form* and are generally characterized by episodic nonclosure, which manifests itself through the postponement of individual storyline resolutions and the use of major and minor cliff-hangers in place of the more definitive conclusions typical of traditional episodic television.[68] John Ellis claims that the serial form is actually characteristic of television narratives of all sorts, including episodic series, in which the essential problematic that powers a program remains unresolved across episodes.[69] Precisely because this brings us back once again to the idea that television is marked overall as much by repetition and return as by interruption, we need to be careful to distinguish between true serial form and the "serialness" of TV in general.[70]

This open-endedness is one of the most discussed aspects of soap operas' narrative form, forming the basis for many theories about soaps' narrative structure. Some theorists have discerned ties between irresolution and a specific kind of female viewing pleasure, while others have argued that nonclosure undermines the traditional narrative trajectory. Soap opera closure is a complex issue, yet while it is arguable that soaps do not attain traditional narrative closure at many levels—both at the levels of individual episodes and, as a rule, at the level of the program as a whole—they do achieve it in a number of other important ways. In addition, occasional individual episodes actually end with the explicit resolution of a specific problem, often a question of identity, and thus resemble a traditional television episode.

Still, there can be no doubt about their basic serial nature, an element that, as Robert Allen and others have documented, has its roots in the form's commercial origins. And like the airing of multiple episodes each week, soaps' serial format enhances the ease with which viewers can incorporate the programs into their regular routines. As Christine Gledhill contends, seriality is an "initially accidental but ultimately defining feature," one that lends "solidity" and "three dimensional reality to a tale that runs in parallel to its [viewers'] lives."[71]

Closely connected to their serial nature is the fact that soap operas' narrative is composed of multiple, *interlocking storylines*. The adaptation of the form from radio to television and the shift over the years from 15- to 30- and then to 60-minute episodes allowed storylines to multiply from the two or three that characterized radio and early television serials to the dozen or more ongoing stories that can be found in current programs. In contrast to more conventional storytelling practice, however, soap operas have from their beginnings featured plural storylines, and this has had a very specific consequence for their narrative development. Rather than following the linear path of a single story, organized around the exploits of a single (heroic) character, soap opera narratives necessarily proceed in what is at most only a quasi-linear fashion, with each story's forward progress constantly interrupted by the eruption of the latest events in another one. Typically, programs will cut among three stories in a single episode, allotting each only one scene at a time before moving on to another story. This means that soap operas offer an extremely complex form of storytelling, one that requires viewers to follow several stories at once and to suspend their interest in one temporarily when events from another intervene.[72]

As I suggested earlier, however, the multiplicity of soap opera storylines also imitates the "flow" of (commercial U.S.) television itself, in which regularly recurring programs constantly interrupt each other. In a week in which a habitual *Roseanne* viewer watches only a few other prime-time programs, for instance, she may be required to remember what distinguishes the individual members of the Conner family from one another, while paying equal attention to the intervening episodes of *Melrose Place*, *Seinfeld*, *Murphy Brown*, and *NYPD Blue*, and trying all the while not to be distracted by ads for a variety of products, as well as promotions for programs in which she has no interest. In the case of soap operas, of course, these interventions occur *within* as well as *between* individual episodes, and while an hour-long episode typically features events from only three or four storylines, a typical week may present developments in three or four times as many, most of which in turn assume viewer memories of earlier stories. Once again, then, soaps can be seen as a paradigm of U.S. television's overall form, making precision about their operations even more important.

Each story's indirect movement toward a climax or resolution is further complicated by the fact that individual soap opera storylines are all in some way connected to one another. That is because, to return to my definition, all of them *focus on the relationships within a specific community of characters*. The construction of this community plays a crucial role in the organization of soap opera narrative, particularly in the programs' obsession with characters' exchange of private information. But the important fact is that soaps take place within closed communities and that they emphasize the personal relationships among members of those communities rather than, for instance, their political or work lives, or the connection between a particular community and the larger world.

Such overlap between characters' lives and among the storylines that depict them must be distinguished, however, from what occurs on a program in which multiple storylines are linked merely by the fact that their protagonists share a law partnership or cruise-line employment. Although individual *L.A. Law* or *Love Boat* storylines may resonate with each other, for example, developments within each of them tend to be relatively autonomous.[73] In contrast, soap opera characters are diegetically entangled by their past, present, and potential future ties of kinship and romance, blood, marriage, and friendship. They are narratively entangled by the fact that their economic, political, and other "public" relationships are subordinated to these personal ties. Thus, the intimate connections among soap opera characters mean that events in one storyline inevitably have consequences in others.

The domestic, personal, and emotional emphasis of soap opera has received a considerable amount of critical and theoretical attention, most of it attributing the programs' focus to the fact that the form was designed—and still functions—to target a predominantly female audience, presumed to be interested in personal relations. While there are many ways in which soap opera expresses what Charlotte Brunsdon has identified as the "ideological problematic" of the genre, "personal life in its everyday realization through personal relationships,"[74] I simply want to point out the necessity of understanding this interest in the personal as a defining characteristic of the genre. Although the melodramatic strategies increasingly being adopted by U.S. television have given the personal a new prominence across genres, it is important to distinguish here between, for example, police or medical stories framed in personal terms and dramas that have the personal as their primary obsession. On a melodrama-inflected series like *Hill Street Blues* or *NYPD Blue*, for instance, major storylines about crime are often framed by the personal concerns of the police officers (or, less frequently, the criminals or lawyers) involved, but the relationships among characters, their positions within the program, and the implications of individual story resolutions are couched primarily in terms of public issues such as the crumbling criminal justice system. In contrast, on a soap like *Another World*, which regularly features storylines about crime, the "public" aspects of such stories are subordinated to the personal by being couched almost entirely in terms of the familial, romantic, and emotional relationships between characters. And while those characters may have other ties, they are connected to each other primarily by personal rather than public bonds.

My definition omits a number of characteristics that are commonly considered to be central to soap opera narrative and style. The major missing element, of course, is nonclosure, but other traits of narrative, production, and performance style have also figured prominently in critics' attempts to outline what constitutes a soap opera. I do not mean to suggest, however, that the nonlinear narrative strategies that advance soap operas' interlocking storylines are unimportant, but instead that their nonlinearity is a function of the fact that they are intertwined in such a complex manner. Nor would I claim that the programs' almost exclusive use of interior sets, their obsession with close-ups, their glossy "look," and the cosmetic, costuming, and decorative excesses usually associated with current soap opera production are trivial factors in constructing a soap's televisual style. What I do want to argue is that these are not necessary characteristics of the genre, but rather, stylistic elements that *serve* soap opera structure and format rather than *defining* them. The distinction I am drawing here is between those elements that define soap opera as a genre and the characteristics that merely mark them, a category that also includes what Robert Allen has called their "subliterary" production features, such as authorial anonymity and "industrial assembly-line methods."[75]

Some of these elements are more easily identified as secondary than others. As proof of the dispensability of the current "look," for example, we need only turn to programs from the days of black-and-white broadcast. Early episodes look grim and dowdy in comparison to today's colorful glossiness, yet no one would seriously claim that their lack of high-fashion glitz means that the 1950s or 1960s incarnations are not "really" soaps. British serials' focus on working-class life and the obvious "ordinariness" of their mise-en-scène also suggest how wide a range of "looks" might be possible within the genre. At the same time, the fact that genres like the variety, talk, and game show—and to some extent the whole range of current U.S. prime-time programming—are characterized by glamorous costumes, implausible hairstyles, and elaborate sets should demonstrate that excessive style alone is not enough to make a program a soap opera.

Similarly, a serious consideration of the whole range of programming available on U.S. TV reveals that the specific settings (domestic interiors) and camera work (close-ups) familiar to soap opera viewers actually characterize many genres. Situation comedies, for example, tend both to take place in the home or workplace and to employ a limited number of indoor sets, just as soap operas do. While prime-time family dramas (*Family, The Waltons, Little House on the Prairie*) make more frequent and more sophisticated use of outdoor locations, they, too, tend to share with soaps a focus on domestic settings. So, too, the intense close-ups that seem to provide soap opera viewers with such intimate knowledge of individual characters' affective lives serve the same function in a variety of film and television genres. Soap operas may rely more heavily on such shots, but the practice was well-established long before the rise of television.[76]

Among the other major features with a claim to defining status, some writers have identified soaps' emphasis on dialogue over action. Christine Gledhill, for instance, claims that "soap opera constructs a feminine world of personal conversation," while Robert Allen describes soaps as "in a sense, 'about' talk."[77] There is certainly no doubt that soap opera narrative moves forward more through the discussion of events than through their direct on-screen representation, yet I have chosen not to identify this as a basic defining trait because I think it has more to do with the *content* of the programs than with their essential form. That is, I see the primacy of talk, the telling and retelling of stories, as a function of the programs' concentration on personal relationships and their continual efforts to construct a particular kind of community.

Another characteristic of soap operas that may seem essential to the genre is its commercially motivated targeting of a predominantly female audience. As Allen and others have shown, the form originated in advertisers' desire to reach women consumers, making soap operas perhaps the most transparently commercial of all broadcast genres.[78] But the fact that commercial radio and television exist primarily to deliver audiences to advertisers means that the genre's history is not unique, but merely extreme. Furthermore, television producers' practice of aiming specific programming at increasingly narrow demographic groups means that soap operas are only one among many genres and subgenres designed for a specialized audience. Adult women are extremely desirable viewers because of their control of household purchasing power, and in recent years we have seen their importance acknowledged by network programming strategies such as CBS's famous Monday night lineup of "women's" shows, rooted initially in a desire to attract female viewers uninterested in ABC's *Monday Night Football*. The success of that strategy has reinforced faith in what has come to be called "boutique" programming, to the point where some network executives have begun to dismiss the traditional race to be number one in the overall ratings, insisting instead on the greater significance of high ratings among "quality" viewers. At the same time, increasing pressure from cablecasters, Fox Broadcasting, and the videocassette market has made the targeting of reliable, if small, audiences a standard television practice, particularly among beleaguered Big Three network programmers.[79]

A genre definition that assumed women as the primary audience would also forestall the possibility of soap operas designed to be watched by other target audiences. Yet there is reason to believe that many other potential soap opera audiences exist, such as the ones for which *Swans Crossing* and *Paradise Beach*—nationally syndicated five-day-a-week serials launched, respectively, in June 1992 and June 1993 and aimed at teens and preteens of both sexes—were designed. Serials have also been developed in college video production classes, on community-access cable stations, and elsewhere, often with fairly specific audiences (students, gay and lesbian viewers) in mind, and it is easy to imagine projects aimed at other population groups or subcultures. Although soap operas have traditionally been a "women's genre," we do not need to assume that genre rules demand that soap operas be aimed at women.

Still, I agree with Charlotte Brunsdon's argument that the cultural competence required to make sense of soap operas consists, not merely of experience of the television genre, but of a particular kind of social knowledge. Writing of the British serial *Crossroads*, Brunsdon has maintained that the program—and, by implication, the genre as a whole—"textually implies a feminine viewer to the extent that its textual discontinuities, in order to make sense, require a viewer competent within the ideological and moral frameworks (the rules) of romance, marriage and family life."[80] Although conceived in a British setting, her words apply equally to the U.S. context, but it is crucial to recognize that she is using the notion of a "feminine viewer" to represent, not a biological female or even a gendered female social subject, but a set of knowledges and skills normally associated with women in patriarchal culture. Only if we understand the "feminine viewer" in these terms is it reasonable to identify the soap opera audience as *necessarily* "female."[81]

Annette Kuhn has pointed out the importance of distinguishing between *spectators*—the viewing subjects "constituted in signification, interpellated by the ... TV text"[82]—and the actual social audiences that consume particular texts. Although Kuhn regards both of these groups as primarily discursive concepts, her terms are still helpful in separating the audiences targeted by, say, a particular soap opera producer from the viewers who actually watch that program. Still, I also have not included as a defining characteristic of the genre the fact that, to some extent apart from industry and advertiser intentions, soap opera audiences are in fact predominantly female. Ratings demonstrate gender differences in viewing across television genres, often corresponding to the most stereotypical ideas of what interests women and men.[83] Thus, to affirm soap operas' uniqueness on the grounds that they offer a special viewing opportunity for women is to overlook the fact that, at least in the United States, differences in viewing habits are quite often defined by gender.[84]

Finally, I have another reason for not defining the genre primarily in terms of who consumes it. Because viewing patterns may change over time (for instance, more men now watch daytime soap operas than did during, say, the 1950s and 1960s), a definition that depended on the identity of current viewers would be inherently unstable. For many theorists, this very instability would be an advantage, reflecting the inherent instability of the television text and underlining the role viewers play in constructing the programs they consume, and therefore in defining specific TV genres. But as I indicated in my introduction, I am drawing on a different notion of the viewing process, one that depends at least as much on the existence of an identifiable, if difficult to describe, television text as it does on viewers' active participation in the construction of that text.

NOTES

1. For example, Mary Ellen Brown lists the following as general characteristics of the genre:
   1. serial form which resists narrative closure;
   2. multiple characters and plots;
   3. use of time which parallels actual time and implies that the action continues to take place whether we watch it or not;
   4. abrupt segmentation between parts;
   5. emphasis on dialogue, problem solving, and intimate conversation;
   6. many of the male characters portrayed as "sensitive men";
   7. female characters often professional or otherwise powerful in the world outside the home;
   8. the home, or some other place which functions as a home, is the setting for the show.

See "The Politics of Soaps: Pleasure and Female Empowerment," *Australian Journal of Cultural Studies* 4, no. 2 (1987): 4.

2. Ellen Seiter, Hans Borchers, Gabriele Kreutzner, and Eva-Maria Warth, "'Don't Treat Us Like We're So Stupid and Naive': Toward an Ethnography of Soap Opera Viewers," in *Remote Control: Television, Audiences and Cultural Power*, ed. Ellen Seiter, Hans Borchers, Gabriele Kreutzner, and Eva-Maria Warth (London: Routledge, 1989), p. 234.

3. Charlotte Brunsdon, "Text and Audience," in Seiter et al., *Remote Control*, p. 123.

4. Robert C. Allen, *Speaking of Soap Operas* (Chapel Hill: University of North Carolina Press, 1975), p. 3. Social scientists like Muriel G. Cantor and Suzanne Pingree may add more details, but they still describe soap opera as "a form of serialized dramatic television broadcast daily over the three commercial television networks . . . usually during the afternoon," *The Soap Opera* (Beverly Hills: Sage Publications, 1983), p. 19. Even a guide for would-be scriptwriters, Jean Rouverol's *Writing for the Soaps* (Cincinnati: Writer's Digest Books, 1984), never actually defines soap operas, but assumes its readers' familiarity with the genre and its conventions, and offers instructions on the production process and hints about how to break into the business. Among the other writers who have specifically tried to define the form is Christine Geraghty, "The Continuous Serial—A Definition," in *Coronation Street*, ed. Richard Dyer, Christine Geraghty, Marion Jordan, Terry Lovell, Richard Paterson, and John Stewart (London:

British Film Institute, 1981), p. 926. While her essay contains many important observations about the serial structure, however, Geraghty explicitly confines her discussion to British programs. Other recent attempts to define the genre within a U.S. context include Martha Nochimson, *No End to Her: Soap Opera and the Female Subject* (Berkeley: University of California Press, 1992), and Carol Traynor Williams, *"It's Time for My Story": Soap Opera Sources, Structure, and Response* (Westport, CT: Praeger, 1992), especially pp. 61–70. For a brief review of other critical attempts to define the genre, see Robert C. Allen, "Bursting Bubbles: 'Soap Opera,' Audiences, and the Limits of Genre," in Seiter et al., *Remote Control*, pp. 44–55.

    5. Among examples from the popular media, *Twin Peaks* has been called a "soap noir" (*New York Times*, May 5, 1991, section 2, p. 1) and a "prime-time soap" (*Entertainment Weekly*, no. 8 [April 6, 1990]: 6). In his book *Three Blind Mice: How the TV Networks Lost Their Way* (New York: Random House, 1991), Ken Auletta groups *Dynasty* and *Hotel* together as "prime-time soap operas" (p. 45). *TV Guide*, which runs a weekly page of soap opera plot summaries confined entirely to daytime serials, is less precise on other pages, calling the ensemble drama *Homefront*, for instance, "ABC's post-WWII soap" (July 18, 1992, p. 2), and *Soap Opera Weekly*'s editor, Mimi Torchin, devoted her November 11, 1992, column to her conflict with *Homefront*'s producers over the series' status as a soap opera (p. 4). Fan magazines regularly blur genre boundaries by including prime-time programs, from *Knots Landing* to the revived *Dark Shadows* and *Twin Peaks*, in their plot summaries and treating actors from those series as part of the community of soap performers. *Soap Opera Digest*'s special issue, "Looking Back At: 60 Years of Soaps" (Winter 1991) featured a "comprehensive" list of TV soaps that included not only the predictable prime-time serials, but the public television broadcasts of *The Forsyte Saga* and *Upstairs, Downstairs* as well. In *From Mary Noble to Mary Hartman: The Complete Soap Opera Book* (New York: Stein and Day, 1976), Madeleine Edmondson and David Rounds document the fan-magazine debate over the correct genre categorization of *Mary Hartman, Mary Hartman*, pp. 173–85.

    Among scholars, the subtitle to Ien Ang's book *Watching Dallas: Soap Opera and the Melodramatic Imagination*, trans. Della Couling (London: Methuen, 1985), is only one of many such references. Lidia Curti, who includes both *Dallas* and *Dynasty* in the category, has gone so far as the formulation, "Women's television, that is, soap opera"; see "What Is Real and What Is Not: Female Fabulations in Cultural Analysis," in *Cultural Studies*, ed. Lawrence Grossberg, Cary Nelson, and Paula Treichler (Champaign: University of Illinois Press, 1992), p. 142.

    6. Cantor and Pingree, *The Soap Opera*, p. 26; Ang, *Watching Dallas*, p. 55. Despite her disclaimers, however, Ang's usage throughout the book indicates that she considers *Dallas* and programs like it to be soap operas of some kind.

    7. Jane Feuer, for example, stresses "the similarities between daytime soaps and the prime-time continuing melodramatic serials," arguing that they "share a narrative form . . . [and] concentrate on the domestic sphere," "Melodrama, Serial Form and Television Today," *Screen* 25, no. 1 (January–February 1984): 4.

    8. Gabriele Kreutzner and Ellen Seiter, "Not All 'Soaps' Are Created Equal: Towards a Crosscultural Criticism of Television Serials," *Screen* 32, no. 2 (Summer 1991): 156. See also Feuer, "Melodrama, Serial Form and Television Today," p. 5.

    9. Christine Geraghty, *Women and Soap Opera: A Study of Prime Time Soaps* (Cambridge: Polity Press, 1991), p. 4.

    10. Geraghty, *Women and Soap Opera*, p. 5.

    11. Lynn Spigel discusses this phenomenon throughout *Make Room for TV: Television and the Family Ideal in Postwar America* (Chicago: University of Chicago Press, 1992), e.g., pp. 113, 116–18, 139. See also Laura Mulvey, "Melodrama Inside and Outside the Home," in her *Visual and Other Pleasures* (Bloomington: Indiana University Press, 1989), pp. 63–77.

12. For a suggestion of the breadth of work done under the banner of cultural studies and the ways that individual viewers attempt to make personal meanings out of mass-produced media products, see Grossberg et al., *Cultural Studies*, especially the essays by Rosalind Brunt, Lidia Curti, John Fiske, and Constance Penley.

13. See Gloria-Jean Masciarotte, "C'mon Girl: Oprah Winfrey and the Discourse of Feminine Talk," *Genders* 11 (Fall 1991): 81–110.

14. Geraghty, *Women and Soap Opera*, p. 3.

15. Mimi White, "Television Genres: Intertextuality," *Journal of Film and Video* 37, no. 3 (Summer 1985): 41.

16. Jane Feuer, "Narrative Form in American Network Television," in *High Theory/Low Culture: Analysing Popular Television*, ed. Colin MacCabe (New York: St. Martin's Press, 1986), p. 111. Among discussions of the genre mixing that seems increasingly to characterize television, see White, "Television Genres," and Todd Gitlin's discussion of "recombinant" TV in *Inside Prime Time* (New York: Pantheon Books, 1983), pp. 77–81.

17. See for instance E. Ann Kaplan, *Rocking around the Clock: Music Television, Postmodernism, and Consumer Culture* (New York: Methuen, 1987), esp. pp. 143–53; and her edited collection, *Postmodernism and Its Discontents: Theories, Practices* (London: Verso, 1988).

18. John Fiske, *Television Culture* (London: Methuen, 1987), p. 112.

19. John Caughie, "Adorno's Reproach: Repetition, Difference and Television Genre," *Screen* 32, no. 2 (Summer 1991): 128.

20. See Thomas Schatz, *Hollywood Genres: Formulas, Filmmaking, and the Studio System* (Philadelphia: Temple University Press, 1981), p. 6.

21. Cf. John Caughie's remark in "Adorno's Reproach" that, "With *Twin Peaks*, the fascination is in watching, with mounting incredulity, the parodic games of multiple genres and thoroughly cliched conventions" (p. 149); and Jim Collins's discussion of *Twin Peaks* as an example of the "policing" of the boundaries between "high" and "low" art in "Television and Postmodernism," in *Channels of Discourse, Reassembled: Television and Contemporary Criticism*, 2nd ed., ed. Robert C. Allen (Chapel Hill: University of North Carolina Press, 1992), pp. 341–49. See also Richard Dienst's discussion of *Twin Peaks*, in *Still Life in Real Time: Theory after Television* (Durham: Duke University Press, 1994), pp. 89–99.

22. Caughie, "Adorno's Reproach," p. 149.

23. Patricia Mellencamp, *High Anxiety: Catastrophe, Scandal, Age, & Comedy* (Bloomington: Indiana University Press, 1990), p. 240.

24. Caughie, "Adorno's Reproach," p. 127. See for example Fiske, *Television Culture*, pp. 109–15; John Tulloch, *Television Drama: Agency, Audience and Myth* (London: Routledge, 1990), pp. 58–86; and Jane Feuer, "Genre Study," in Allen, *Channels of Discourse, Reassembled*, pp. 138–60.

25. Among the earliest theoretical explorations of this difference is Stephen Heath and Gillian Skirrow, "Television: A World in Action," *Screen* 18, no. 2 (Summer 1977): 7–59.

26. Feuer, "Narrative Form in American Network Television," p. 101.

27. David Thorburn, "Television Melodrama," in *Television: The Critical View*, 4th ed., ed. Horace Newcomb (New York: Oxford University Press, 1987), p. 631.

28. Mulvey, "Melodrama Inside and Outside the Home," p. 65, See also Peter Brooks, *The Melodramatic Imagination: Balzac, Henry James, Melodrama, and the Mode of Excess* (New Haven: Yale University Press, 1976).

29. Mulvey, "Melodrama Inside and Outside the Home," p. 76.

30. Lynne Joyrich, "All That Television Allows: TV Melodrama, Postmodernism and Consumer Culture," *Camera Obscura*, no. 16 (1988): 130; subsequent references cited in text.

31. Sec Thomas Schatz's discussion of the family melodrama in *Hollywood Genres*, pp. 221–60.

32. Robyn Wiegman, "Melodrama, Masculinity, and the Televisual War," paper presented at the first annual conference, Console-ing Passions: Television, Video, and Feminism, April 1992, Iowa City, Iowa, p. 7. See also Caren J. Deming's discussion of TV melodrama in "For Television-Centred Television Criticism: Lessons from Feminism," in *Television and Women's Culture: The Politics of the Popular*, ed. Mary Ellen Brown (London: Sage Publications, 1990), pp. 53–58.

33. Christine Gledhill, "Speculations on the Relationship between Soap Opera and Melodrama," *Quarterly Review of Film and Video* 14, no. 1–2 (1992): 103–24; subsequent references cited in text. See also her statement in the introduction to *Home Is Where the Heart Is: Studies in Melodrama and the Women's Film* (London: British Film Institute, 1987) that "soap opera is commonly seen as the last resort of melodrama. But soap opera, like the woman's film, has an affiliation with women's culture, the elision of which with melodrama should not be assumed" (p. 2).

34. Wiegman, "Melodrama, Masculinity, and the Televisual War," p. 8.

35. Brunsdon, "Text and Audience," p. 119; subsequent references cited in text. See also her "Problems with Quality," *Screen* 31, no. 1 (Spring 1990): 67–90.

36. Jerry Palmer, *Potboilers: Methods, Concepts and Case Studies in Popular Fiction* (London: Routledge, 1991), p. 7.

37. Allen, *Speaking of Soap Operas*, p. 14.

38. Robert C. Allen, "On Reading Soaps: A Semiotic Primer," in *Regarding Television: Critical Perspectives—An Anthology*, ed. E. Ann Kaplan (Los Angeles: University Publications of America/American Film Institute, 1983), p. 98. See also Dennis Porter, "Soap Time: Thoughts on a Commodity Art Form," *College English* 38, no. 8 (April 1977): 782–88, especially his claim that a soap opera's "beginnings are always lost sight of" (p. 783).

39. John Caughie contends that television actually continues the tradition of "novelistic" discourse that film, with its single-sitting pattern of consumption, interrupts, "Adorno's Reproach," p. 141.

40. Heath and Skirrow, "Television," p. 54. For the original conception of television's "flow," see Raymond Williams, *Television: Technology and Cultural Form* (New York: Schocken Books, 1975), pp. 86–96.

41. Feuer, "The Concept of Live Television," p. 19; subsequent references cited in text.

42. See Geraghty, "The Continuous Serial," p. 10; and Dorothy Hobson, *"Crossroads": The Drama of a Soap Opera* (London: Methuen, 1982), pp. 34–35. Examples of the coincidence between characters' and viewers' time include the soap's regular celebration of holidays and their frequent allusions to actual days of the week or month. Soap time does not, however, pass in a consistent manner, but is manipulated for diegetic purposes. The classic example of this practice is the aging of child characters, who may pass miraculously from infancy to adolescence to adulthood. Some writers have identified the passage of time on soap operas as itself a basic feature of the genre. For example, in *The Soap Opera*, Muriel Cantor and Suzanne Pingree call the programs' pace "very slow" (p. 23) and explicitly contrast the rate of story development with the "much more rapid" pace of the prime-time *Peyton Place* (p. 27).

43. Porter, "Soap Time," p. 783.

44. Seiler et al., "'Don't Treat Us Like We're So Stupid and Naïve,'" p. 233; subsequent references cited in text.

45. Robert C. Allen, "Bursting Bubbles," p. 45. See also Jane Feuer's position that, at least in the case of *Dynasty*, "the reading formation *is* the text," "Reading *Dynasty*: Television and Reception Theory," *SAQ* 88, no. 2 (Spring 1989): 458.

46. Steve Neale, "Questions of Genre," *Screen*, 31, no. 14 (Spring 1990): 46, 56.

47. See Brown, "The Politics of Soaps"; Seiter et al., "'Don't Treat Us Like We're So Stupid and Naive'"; and Elihu Katz and Tamar Liebes, "Decoding *Dallas*: Notes from a Cross-Cultural Study," in Newcomb, *Television*, pp. 419–32.

48. Some critics have closely interrogated the deployment of the term "soap opera," pointing out the ways in which it has come to be associated with commercialism (versus "real" art), low quality, and even to stand for U.S. television and culture. In "Text and Audience," for instance, Charlotte Brunsdon calls this "a little connotational string: soap opera—television—commercial—American" (p. 117).

49. Stephen Neale, *Genre* (London: British Film Institute, 1980), pp. 22–23.

50. Although their humor obviously depends on at least some knowledge of the original, the fact that parodies can be appreciated even by viewers with relatively little experience of soap operas demonstrates how far knowledge of the genre's conventions pervades the culture. The general outlines of the form are so widely recognized that written parodies may appear in publications that cannot necessarily assume their readers' familiarity with specific soap operas. One example is Ian Frazier, "Have You Ever," *The New Yorker* 68, no. 1 (February 24, 1992): 34–35.

51. Feuer, "Reading *Dynasty*," pp. 447, 456; and "Melodrama, Serial Form and Television Today," p. 9. See also Caughie, "Adorno's Reproach," pp. 150–53.

52. Tania Modleski, *Loving with a Vengeance: Mass-Produced Fantasies for Women* (New York: Methuen, 1984), pp. 85–109.

53. Charlotte Brunsdon, "*Crossroads*: Notes on Soap Opera," in Kaplan, *Regarding Television*, pp. 76–83.

54. Modleski, for instance, argues that "soap opera stimulates women's desire for connectedness . . . through the constant, claustrophobic use of close-up shots," *Loving with a Vengeance*, p. 99.

55. Tulloch, *Television Drama*, p. 211.

56. Seiter et al., "'Don't Treat Us Like We're So Stupid and Naive,'" pp. 230–31. There is also evidence that some of these viewers think of the time they spend watching soap operas as a regular respite from their responsibilities in the home. Cf. Janice A. Radway's description of Gothic romance readers in *Reading the Romance: Women, Patriarchy and Popular Literature* (Chapel Hill: University of North Carolina Press, 1984), pp. 86–118.

57. Feuer, "The Concept of Live Television," p. 19. See also John Ellis's contention that "the intimacy that broadcast TV sets up is . . . made qualitatively different by the sense that the TV image carries of being a live event," *Visible Fictions: Cinema, Television, Video*, rev. ed. (London: Routledge, 1989), p. 136.

58. Brunsdon, "Text and Audience," p. 125. Cf. Andrew Ross's distinction between "*everyday* life . . . [and] *everyweek* life. For most people there is no such thing as everyday life, but rather weekly cycles of work and leisure, both in and out of the home," "All in the Family: On David Morley's *Family Television: Cultural Power and Domestic Leisure* and Philip Simpson's (ed.) *Parents Talking Television,*" *Camera Obscura*, no. 16 (January 1988): 169.

59. Caughie, "Adorno's Reproach," p. 141.

60. Caughie, "Adorno's Reproach," p. 145. In the context of the soaps themselves, cf. Martha Nochimson's contention that "the dailiness of the gap [between episodes] insures a less hierarchical, less linear relationship among story lines," *No End to Her*, p. 35.

61. Heath and Skirrow, "Television," p. 15. See also Williams, *Television*, pp. 89–96; and Tulloch's claim that "television drama texts are defined as much by the regime of watching as by their conditions of performance, production and circulation, and have effect as part of the domestic routine," *Television Drama*, p. 228.

62. Dorothy Hobson discusses this same issue in *Crossroads*, pp. 26–32.

63. Sean Cubitt, *Timeshift: On Video Culture* (London: Routledge, 1991), p. 27.

64. The export of U.S. soaps to Europe and of British serials to the United States is well known, but Alessandra Stanley describes a less familiar example of cross-cultural soap watching in "Russians Find Their Heroes in Mexican TV Soap Operas," *New York Times* (March 20, 1994): A1, 8.

65. See Raymond Williams, *Television*, pp. 32–43. See also John Hartley's comment that "the semiotic allegiances of the viewer ... are both local and global," *Tele-ology: Studies in Television* (London: Routledge, 1992), p. 13; his discussion of viewer demand for locally produced soaps in the essay "Local Television," in the same volume, p. 195; and Edward Buscombe, "Nationhood, Culture and Media Boundaries: Britain," *Quarterly Review of Film and Video* 14, no. 3 (1993): 25-34, especially his remarks on "supra-national" versus locally and regionally produced and oriented programming (pp. 25–26).

66. For another point of difference between British and U.S. serials, see Christine Gledhill's discussion in "Speculations on the Relationship between Soap Opera and Melodrama" of the BBC's specific choice of the realistic over the melodramatic mode when developing its first serials, p. 117. See also Allen, "Bursting Bubbles."

67. For discussions of these series, see Sasha Torres, "Melodrama, Masculinity and the Family: *thirtysomething* as Therapy," *Camera Obscura*, no. 19 (January 1989): 86–106; Elspeth Probyn, "New Traditionalism and Post-Feminism: TV Does the Home," *Screen* 31, no. 2 (Summer 1990): 147–59; and Judith Mayne, "*L.A. Law* and Prime-Time Feminism," *Discourse* 10, no. 2 (Spring–Summer 1988): 48–61. On viewers' intense investment in them, see "Why We Are Still Watching 'thirtysomething,'" *Entertainment Weekly*, no. 12 (May 4, 1990): 78–87; and Lewis Cole, "The Stuff of Real Life," *The Nation* (April 29, 1991): 567–72.

68. Geraghty, "The Continuous Serial," pp. 13–16.

69. Ellis, *Visible Fictions*, pp. 154–59.

70. Raymond Williams cautions in *Television* against confusing "the cultural importance of the serial, as an essentially new form," with the high-culture "ratification" it receives when, in contrast to its frequent use in soap opera, it appears in such series as *Masterpiece Theatre* (p. 61).

71. Gledhill, "Speculations on the Relationship between Soap Opera and Melodrama," pp. 112, 122.

72. For some critics, this cycle of interruption is part of what marks soap opera as a peculiarly "feminine" form of discourse. See for example Brown, "The Politics of Soaps," and Mary Ellen Brown and Linda Barwick, "Fables and Endless Genealogies: Soap Opera and Women's Culture," *Continuum* 1, no. 2 (1988): 71–82. In contrast, Deborah D. Rogers argues, in "Daze of Our Lives: The Soap Opera as Feminine Text," *Journal of American Culture* 14, no. 4 (Winter 1991), that "the fragmented form of soap operas enhances audience receptivity to conservative messages that reinforce stereotypical behavior in women" (p. 29). Other considerations of "feminine discourse" on television include Jackie Byars, "Reading Feminine Discourse: Prime-Time Television in the U.S.," *Communication* 9, no. 3–4 (1987): 289–303; and Fiske, *Television Culture*, pp. 179–97.

73. Judith Mayne analyzes this resonance in "*L.A. Law* and Prime-Time Lesbianism," paper presented at the first annual conference, Console-ing Passions: Television, Video, and Feminism, April 1992, Iowa City, Iowa.

74. Brunsdon, "*Crossroads*," p. 78.

75. Allen, *Speaking of Soap Operas*, p. 15.

76. Porter, "Soap Time," p. 786.

77. Gledhill, "Speculations on the Relationship between Soap Opera and Melodrama," p. 114; Allen, *Speaking of Soap Operas*, p. 74.

78. It may also be one of the most successful, as Allen contends in *Speaking of Soap Operas*. "In the soap opera advertisers and broadcasters have found the ideal vehicle for the reinforcement of advertising impressions and the best means yet devised for assuring regular viewing" (p. 47).

79. For comments by various industry executives on the notion of "appointment television" and the declining importance of being number one in the overall ratings, see Thomas Tryer, "The Fall Season: Network Preview," *Electronic Media* 10, no. 35 (August 26, 1991): 16, and Thomas Tryer and William Mahoney, "Sagansky: CBS Poised for a No. 1 Season," p. 30; and Bill Carter, "NBC Thinks Being No. 1 Is Too Costly," *New York Times* (January 20, 1992): C1–2.

80. Brunsdon, *"Crossroads,"* p. 81.

81. Cf. Meaghan Morris's contribution to the "Spectatrix" issue of *Camera Obscura*, no. 20–21: 241–45. See also Mimi White's discussion of soap operas in her *Tele-Advising: Therapeutic Discourse in American Television* (Chapel Hill: University of North Carolina Press, 1992), pp. 15–18.

82. Annette Kuhn, "Women's Genres: Melodrama, Soap Opera and Theory," in Gledhill, *Home Is Where the Heart Is*, p. 343.

83. During the 1991–92 season, for example, ABC's *Roseanne* was frequently the number one show among both male and female viewers aged 18 to 49 (and the number two show overall, behind *60 Minutes*). While only special broadcasts like the Academy Awards pushed the sitcom out of first place among those women, sporting events televised on one of the major commercial networks regularly ranked number one among men in the same demographic group. During the week of April 6 through April 12, 1992, for instance, *Roseanne* had a Nielsen ranking of number one among women aged 18 to 49, while CBS's broadcast of the NCAA Basketball Championships and the related special, "Prelude to a Championship," ranked number one and number two among men aged 18 to 49. See "Prime-time Demographics for April 6–12," *Electronic Media* 11, no. 16 (April 20, 1991): 40.

84. Cf. Christine Geraghty's claim that "in their themes and presentation," the programs she identifies as soap operas "seem to offer a space for women in peak viewing time," *Women and Soap Opera*, p. 2.

The International Telenovela Debate and the Contra-Flow Argument: A Reappraisal

Daniël Biltereyst and Philippe Meers

INTRODUCTION

In the 1960s and 1970s the debate over unequal international communication flows and structural inequalities was often held in terms of dependency and media imperialism. These concepts referred to a complex set of neo-marxist, analytical approaches and tools with the common belief that, as Tomlinson (1991: 7) put it, "a form of domination exists in the modern world, not just in the political and economic spheres but also over those practices by which collectivities make sense of their lives." Over the past few decades, however, it has become clear that these critical concepts in the powerful centre of the world communication system were often turned into too deterministic models of unilateral cultural flow, meaning and impact. In the field of television for instance, one saw a prolific development of local production industries in some Third World countries; an ever more complex pattern of international programme flows, with strong examples of contra-flow from the South to the North, including dependencies in the North; and the arrival of some Third World programme providers who became huge players in the global market. The general diagnosis was, as Golding and Harris (1997: 5) wrote in their polemic introduction to the reader *Beyond Cultural Imperialism*, that "the term cultural imperialism began to limit rather than illuminate discussion" over dependencies of the post-colonial periphery. Referring to one critic of the cultural imperialism frame, Golding and Harris (1997: 5) summarized some key shortcomings of this critical frame in practice:

> Firstly it overstates external determinants and undervalues the internal dynamics, not least those of resistance, within dependent societies. Secondly, it con-

flates economic power and cultural effects. Thirdly, there is an assumption that audiences are passive, and that local and oppositional creativity is of little significance. Finally, there is an often patronizing assumption that what is at risk is the 'authentic' and organic culture of the developing world under the onslaught of something synthetic and inauthentic coming from the West.

One of the most frequently cited examples in this deconstruction of the cultural imperialism thesis has been the case of Latin American television fiction programmes, especially telenovelas.[1] For many authors in the field of global communication, this typical Latin American version of daily soap grew into an illustration of the potential of Third World cultural industries for resistance, alternatives and even contra-flow (for example, Tomlinson, 1991: 56-57; Reeves, 1993: 64-67; Sreberny-Mohammadi, 1993: 121, 130; Sinclair et al., 1996: 13). The hard facts of increasing production, the huge local success and the worldwide exports of telenovelas gave rise to what could be called an evolving international telenovela debate. On the one extreme of the debate some scholars claimed a revision of the cultural imperialism and dependency thesis, even going as far as launching ideas about a "reverse cultural imperialism." For other, especially critical scholars, such a revisionist framework tended to overestimate the range of the changes in global production and contra-flow. At this extreme of the debate, critical arguments stressed the remaining validity of the dominance thesis, notwithstanding the changing global media.

In the first, more theoretical part of this article we examine the main arguments in the international telenovela debate, presenting them at different analytical levels and within theoretical frameworks. In the second, empirical part we concentrate on the range of the contra-flow argument, presenting a telenovela flow study to the European television market of the mid-1990s.

THE INTERNATIONAL TELENOVELA DEBATE

In the international telenovela debate many conflicting arguments have been used to assess the validity of the original cultural imperialism thesis. The debate deals with hard structural and political economic arguments about the control of the local broadcasting system as well as with ideas about local resistance to foreign products or the success of telenovelas. Depending on the ideological framework, different interpretations or arguments are given at various levels of the debate. In the following theoretical overview we would like to discuss the range of these contrasting arguments at six analytical levels within two polarized frameworks (critical vs revisionist) (see Table 1). It has to be acknowledged that these frameworks represent extreme positions while in the actual discussion mixed, nuanced positions have to be identified.

One of the key problems in the whole debate is that many arguments often refer to different levels, provoking a lack of analytical clarity. On the one hand, arguments from a more revisionist framework tend to stress the levels of local production and reception and exports, while a more critical framework emphasizes the U.S.-inspired and controlled broadcasting system. A related problem deals with the rapidly changing global and regional Latin American communication context. This implies that the strength and range of certain arguments

TABLE 1
Main arguments of polarized critical and revisionist frameworks in the international telenovela debate

Levels of analysis	Critical frame	Revisionist frame
Broadcasting system	Copy of U.S. commercial model	Commercial drive of local entrepreneurs
Structural control	Historical strong U.S. capital control Recently: renewed U.S. participation, competition and concentration	Withdrawal of U.S. control Growth of Latin American media concerns Latin American participation in U.S./European companies
Local production/ inflow of foreign (U.S.) fiction	Historical huge U.S. inflow Substantial inflow in "small" countries Recently: renewed U.S. import	Substitution and replacement by Latin American production
Programme format and ideology	Copy of U.S. consumerism and capitalism Instrument for social status quo Recently: neutralization of L.A. values in telenovelas for export	Roots in Latin American melodrama tradition Localized genre
Reception	Passive audience Illusory relief Recently: audience studies obscure underlying power analysis	Active audience Creative decoding
Outflow of Latin American programmes	Marginal contra-flow Recently: possible decline of export success	Substantial contra-flow Reverse cultural imperialism

must be evaluated within their specific historical context. In the following discussion of the various levels we try to include this historical dimension.

Before treating the various arguments on the levels of software import and export, it is necessary to deal with broad structural influences, one level being the *broadcasting systems in Latin America*. Authors such as Lee (1980: 93) and Sinclair (1990: 350) noted that the Latin American broadcasters' adoption of the commercial television system might be the biggest U.S. influence of all. Even revisionist authors recognize that the structure of the Latin American television and telenovela industry is clearly North American in style and organization (Antola and Rogers, 1984: 200). But equally they stress that the option for the commercial rationale behind the local broadcasting systems was not only the result of the historical dominance of the U.S. networks. Authors such as Straubhaar (1984: 222) repeatedly stressed that one should not underestimate the tremendous drive for profit maximization of the local entrepreneurs since the 1950s. The nature of the broadcasting industry which evolved was a result of the overall domestic forces of each country (Fox, 1997a: 130).

A second structural level relates to *capital control over the Latin American television industry*. Since the 1970s there has been a structural withdrawal of Northern American networks and other corporate organizations in the sector so that their political economic influence gave way to, as Sinclair (1986: 98) put it, "a general Latin American pattern of initial US-investment and subsequential withdrawal." Even severe critics such as Muraro (1987: 18) recognize the structural change in the direction of a *latinoamericanización* with big Latin American corporations and investors controlling local cultural industries. It is generally acknowledged that telenovelas as a genre function as the key engine of their economic growth and success (for example, Marques de Melo, 1988). In addition, big Latin American corporations such as Globo and Televisa took the structural expansion one step further, developing foreign structural strategies. These international exporters tried to sustain their programme distribution by gaining direct control over or participation in foreign broadcasters, even in Western countries such as Italy, Portugal, Spain and the United States. Televisa and Venevisión, for example, participate in Univisión, a U.S. television network targeting the Spanish-speaking population. For Televisa this was in fact a re-entry into the United States since they initially founded the network (Sinclair, 1996: 53-54).

Since the late 1990s, however, new developments in the Latin American market have called for a reassessment. Several U.S.-based global channels, providing satellite and cable services in Spanish or Portuguese, have entered into competition with Latin American companies—successfully crossing the language barrier—and thus affecting the comparative language advantage of the Latin American concerns. In their international ventures, Latin American corporations such as Televisa are equally confronted with foreign partners (Sinclair, 1998: 7-11). An emerging pattern could be, as Fox (1997a: 3; 1997b: 39) recently predicted, the decline in economic power of the domestic Latin American media monopolies.

The *inflow of foreign programmes* constitutes a third level in the discussion. Several authors reported how, in different Latin American countries, the growth of national and regional television industries led to the substitution (Straubhaar, 1984: 229-34; also for example, Antola and Rogers, 1984) or even complete displacement of U.S. imports (Straubhaar and Viscasillas, 1991). In this respect, it has been claimed that Latin America is probably the only large region in the world where the huge television flow from the United States has been reduced substantially, and where local entertainment is so successful in dominating prime time. This is mainly the case in Brazil and Mexico, where huge corporations such as TV Globo and Televisa rely on an industrial base for (fiction) production in many ways similar to North American examples, and where they have been able to exploit the comparative language advantage of (respectively) Portuguese and Spanish (Sinclair, 1996). Nonetheless, smaller countries with a less developed television production industry still rely heavily upon U.S. imports. USA-based corporations have been (Varis, 1985) and clearly remain the most important non–Latin American programme suppliers for the region, especially in the wake of the 1990s explosion of U.S. satellite channels (Fox, 1997c: 187).

A fourth, more difficult, level deals with ideological questions about local *programme format, its norms and content*. Here quite contrasting arguments have been raised about the cultural values and authenticity of the telenovela texture. On the one hand, several critical authors have repeatedly indicated how the telenovela as a genre is inspired by U.S. soap models, and how it is deeply permeated by Western capitalist values such as consumerism and the embellishment of class conflicts (Muraro, 1987). Oliveira (1990: 119) looks at the creolization of local culture as a negative concept, referring to the imperialist effects of Western capitalist (production) values on the style and content of Third World cultural products. Telenovelas are seen as commercial fiction programmes inspired by U.S. soap models, spiced up with Third World decorum. Oliveira (1990: 129) claims that in "most Brazilian soaps the American lifestyle portrayed by Hollywood productions reappears with a brazilianized face." The external cultural imperialism has been replaced by an internal one, led by local military and political economic elites, which are keen to justify the social status quo. This quite dogmatic critical analysis has been revised by a long strain of authors, who argue that telenovelas are deeply rooted in historical forms of authentic local fiction. It goes from Straubhaar (1984: 221), who speaks of a "Brazilianization" of television content and values, to Martín-Barbero (1993) describing it as the television version of the traditional Latin American melodrama, to, more recently, Trinta (1997: 284) claiming that the telenovela is a "creative version of a possible Brazilian national story." Recently however these claims about authenticity in telenovelas have been challenged by new critical voices on the telenovela "made for export." Several authors point here to the hybridization and neutralization of the telenovela content for export objectives. Its contingent cultural and national characteristics tend to dissolve into a universal export-formula (Mazziotti, 1996: 113).

This discussion on the format has been intensified by the wave of research on the *audience reception of telenovelas* in their home countries.[2] A wide stream of audience-oriented studies emerged, displacing earlier critical assumptions about passive, alienated audiences (for example, see Oliveira, 1990: 119), and stressing the importance of local and oppositional creativity. Vink (1988) is a well-known scholar among those who drew upon audiences and their daily use of telenovelas. Stressing the possible subversive character of the telenovela production, text and the reception of it, Vink refutes the ideas of alienation and status quo. He concludes that "novelas might offer the working-class audience models of social change, at any rate of resistance to repression" (1988: 247). In their overview of studies about telenovela audiences, McAnany and La Pastina (1994) draw attention to methodological insufficiencies, which might make telenovela audience studies susceptible to more fundamental critiques on optimistic views about the emancipatory value of telenovelas. In more general terms it has been claimed that an overemphasis on reception studies can obscure the analysis of the underlying power structures (Hallin, 1998: 164). For critical scholars such as Oliveira (1990: 122, 125) the historical analysis that audiences would find the telenovela only an illusory relief from the harsh reality of daily life, remains quite valid.

The final and one of the strongest arguments in the deconstruction of the dominance thesis deals with the *worldwide export of telenovelas*. The pattern in which mainly Mexican and Brazilian television industries expanded their activities over their national boundaries, was raised as the ultimate disproof of the traditional critical frames. In the early 1980s for example, TV Globo became an important exporter of telenovelas, distributing its entertainment programmes to over 50 countries around the world. For Straubhaar (1984: 237) it is clear that "while dependency theory offers a useful perspective," it fails to "look closely at the internal dynamics of the Brazilian situation to see how factors once contributing to dependency may have changed to favour greater autonomy for Brazilian television broadcasters and programmers." Similar arguments have been often repeated by other scholars such as Vink (1988: 31), for example, who argued that Globo's export success disproved "one of the main arguments of the cultural imperialism thesis, which views the Third World countries as innocent victims of Hollywood invasion." This export argument has been strengthened by the audience success of these programmes in foreign countries such as (then) communist Poland, where some 28 million or 85 percent of the national audience followed the adventures of the slave girl *Isaura* (Mattelart and Mattelart, 1987: 15). In Spain, the Venezuelan telenovela *Cristal* broke all the rating records in the history of public broadcaster TVE in 1990 (RTVE, 1990: 281), while in Portugal a session of the parliament was interrupted to allow the members to watch *Gabriela* (Mattelart and Mattelart, 1987: 15).

One of the earliest and most provocative refutations of the cultural imperialism concept in analysing Latin American television industries came from Rogers and Antola (1985). These scholars launched the explicit concept of "reverse cultural imperialism," albeit without a thorough theoretical argumentation. This concept has often been criticized in academic circles, especially as a case of ideological revisionism in international communication research and theories. A prolific writer here has been Sinclair (for example, 1993, 1996, 1998) claiming that the new contra-flows from countries such as Brazil and Mexico must be seen in the fullness of global communication realities. Concentrating on Globo's international activities and on Televisa's exports to the United States, Sinclair (1993: 131) came to the conclusion that:

> The suggestion sometimes made that Televisa's incursion in the US-market or Globo's export to Portugal and Italy are forms of reverse cultural imperialism is a canard, based on cynicism at worst or ignorance at best.

Sreberny-Mohammadi (1993: 130) has raised similar concerns against the "reverse cultural imperialism" concept and the contra-flow argument. Putting Globo's activities in a global perspective, she wrote that "the exemplar of Rede Globo and Brazilian cultural production as a counter to 'cultural imperialism' as a net exporter of cultural products is cut to size." The point is that contra-flow from the (so-called) South to the North, and other revisionist arguments, tend to put too much weight on marginal contra-movements so that the real power structures in global communication may be disguised. For critical scholars such as Schiller (1991: 22) and Roach (1990: 295-96) the whole revisionist question is even part of a larger ideological project or political agenda to undermine the idea of capitalist expansion.

The actual developments of the Latin American television landscape in the late 1990s, as indicated by Fox (1997a, 1997b) and Sinclair (1998), tend to put the optimistic voices into a new perspective. The future of the telenovela export might very well be less bright than foreseen. Growing competition on the home front with U.S.-based companies, and the increasing concentration of delivery systems for the Latin American region (for example, the merger of the U.S.-based satellite hardware manufacturer Hughes Electronics Corporation and satellite system operator Panamsat) tend to affect the comparative language advantage (Sinclair, 1998: 11) and "erode the bargaining power of Latin America's TV exporters" (Fox, 1997b: 39). This weakened position on the international television trade market might very well result in a decline of telenovela exports.

One of the major flaws in the international telenovela debate, however, concerns a primary shortage of empirical data in the range of the contra-flow, especially the flow to Europe. It is also difficult to determine the validity of the data, especially when they originate from Globo's and other corporations' marketing files. In the second part of this article we will draw upon a large-scale comparative flow study of Latin American fiction exports to Europe, in order to shed some new light on the telenovela debate.

THE RECEPTIVE EUROPEAN TELEVISION SCENE AS A CRUCIAL CASE

In this second, empirical part, we examine the export of Latin American fiction to Europe as a crucial case in demonstrating contra-flow movements in global communication. This case is important because the European television scene has been a huge, highly receptive and economically important market for Latin American production centres. The available literature on the European activities of such producers as the Brazilian Globo and Bandeirantes, the Mexican Televisa or the Venezuelan Venevisión and RCTV is relatively poor, but it indicates that the United States and Europe are by far the two most important core export markets (for example, Marques de Melo, 1988; Sinclair, 1990; Mazziotti, 1996; de la Fuente, 1997). Globo's European adventure began in 1975 with the export of the successful series *Gabriela* to Portugal, and since that time it has used Latin southern Europe as the attractive entrance to the rest of Europe. In the 1980s for example, the export figures for Globo grew from U.S. $3 million in 1981 to some U.S. $15 million four years later. More than half of it came from Globo activities in Italy, France and Portugal (Marques de Melo, 1988: 45; Mattos, 1993: 65). The Mattelarts (1987: 15) might be slightly overestimating the inflow when they claim that "in Europe [in 1983] only Albania and the [former] Soviet Union did not programme telenovelas." Nonetheless, Globo and Televisa managed to penetrate most of the Western European countries. Belgium, the Netherlands, Germany, the U.K., Ireland, Denmark and Iceland are among the countries where, at least at some point in the 1980s, telenovelas appeared. This means that also historically, Europe has been an important market for the globalization activities of Latin American audio-visual corporations.

The influx of telenovelas clearly gained momentum in the 1980s, when the Western European television scene went through the paradigmatic shift of the demolition of public broadcasting monopolies, all under the umbrella of more competition, rational management and straight commercial influence. The central programming category in this all became, more than ever, long-running fictional material with the capacity to attract a large audience for a longer time. If possible, cheap foreign, mostly U.S., material was used. It is in this (by now) historical context of European broadcasters confronted with an expanding broadcasting time and tied by financial restraints, that Latin American telenovelas entered the wider Western European market. The telenovela corresponded well to the profile of cheap serial entertainment, perfect to fill new afternoon or early evening time slots (Mazziotti, 1996: 40). As de la Fuente (1997: 45) recently argued, telenovelas became the programming executive's dream come true, especially in emerging or growing markets, because they were relatively inexpensive while they held a captive audience for an extended period of time. A case in point has been Eastern Europe, where telenovelas were only sporadically broadcast in the 1980s, with the exception of Poland and Yugoslavia. It is remarkable how, since the fall of the Iron Curtain and the former communist regimes, commercial considerations have dominated most of the broadcasting policies (Jakubowicz, 1994: 13). This emergence of commercial television boosted the demand for serial entertainment, including growing telenovela imports.

Besides historical and economic reasons in relation to telenovela exports, Europe has also been an important case in relation to efforts in gaining structural influence on a foreign market. Several big Latin American media concerns tried for some time to gain a foothold in Europe through their participation in broadcasting projects—as a strategy to secure a steady outlet for programme sales. Since 1992, Globo has participated in the Portuguese commercial broadcasting company SIC. Televisa has been present in the European market since the end of 1988 through its satellite channel Galavision, and as such has been active all over Europe, albeit with an emphasis on the Spanish market. In Spain the Mexican company is also one of the main partners of Plataforma Digital, a project for digital television.

Another trend indicating the special attention of the Latin American media concerns for expanding strategies towards Europe, is situated at the level of co-production. This strategy has been well co-ordinated since the 1990s, especially towards Spain and Italy (Akyuz, 1994: 21). Fadul (1993: 20) even speculates about the intense influence of the telenovela formula on the local production in these countries.

The latter also converges with the fact that in several European countries within the Latin language and cultural sphere, there has been a positive cultural connotation stimulating the purchase and scheduling of telenovelas. In France for example, the "Journées de la Télévision Brésilienne" (Days of Brazilian Television) were held in 1985 in the prestigious Parisian cultural temple, the Centre Pompidou. Screenings and debates were organized in the presence of the progressive French Secretary of Culture Jack Lang. These events were seen by the press as a significant cultural labelling and legitimation of the telenovela (Bouquillion, 1992: 102). In Spain, where telenovelas gave rise to lively press debates, cultural personalities like Gabriel García-Márquez were brought into the arena (Guaderrama, 1993: 10).

All this means that European television has been an important market for Latin American fictional material for historical, economic and cultural reasons. However, while regional telenovela flows have been well documented (for example, Antola and Rogers, 1984; Varis, 1985), it is difficult to find empirical material for investigating the intercontinental flow of Latin American television products—crucial for the question of contra-flow from the South to the North. There have been several national case studies on the telenovela export success and activities in specific European countries,[3] but overall data are barely available.

In this article we present data about the flow of Latin American fiction programmes to Europe in 1995. Using a questionnaire sent to the research, purchase and programming departments of public and private television broadcasters in the wider Europe, we draw the map of telenovela imports. The data in this article relate to 71 companies (48 public and 23 private) in 30 countries, including Northern (for example, Sweden, Norway), Central and Eastern (here referred to as Eastern, for example, Bulgaria, Russia), Southern (for example, Greece, Spain), Northwestern (for example, Germany, the Netherlands) and Celtic–Anglo-Saxon European countries (for example, Ireland and the U.K.). Using these questionnaires, we not only examined the volume and quantitative importance of the Latin American contra-flow to Europe, we also tried to find out how these fiction programmes were scheduled, what kind of audience response they received, and why exactly they were purchased.

Marginality and cultural boundary

Studies about programming trends since the onset of multi-channel competition indicate how fiction has become an extremely useful, time-absorbing and multi-functional programme category. Besides the role of the attractive prime-time block-buster, it functions as an appetizer in the early evening, or even as a cheap filler during off-peak periods (for example, morning, afternoon, late evening). As such, it has been acknowledged that extending drama purchases could bring in foreign, even exotic, narratives other than those produced by local and U.S. cultural industries. Although this did happen in a first period of deregulation with huge imports from Japan, Australia and Latin America, the main trend, however, is one of bipolarization. This means that in (Western) Europe, most local broadcasters tend to produce more domestic drama, while they increase U.S. purchases. These main tendencies also come through the data in our survey.

The key question in this article, however, deals with the issue of the South-North contra-flow in relation to Latin American fiction. From an overall European perspective, several indicators show the limited and, in some European regions, even absent contra-flows. First of all, there is the poor overall flow of Latin American fictional material. Its share of 3.2 percent is nothing compared to the enormous flow from the United States (58%). Of course it is important to differentiate among the European regions. As such, Southern Europe is by far the top region for telenovelas with an import rate of 8.2 percent, followed by the emerging Eastern European market (4%) and Northwestern European broadcasters (2.3%). With the exception of Latin countries such as Italy, Spain and Portugal, these are indeed quite marginal figures.

As such, telenovelas may be considered a minor or in many regions and countries even a negligible category. However, it is quite remarkable that Latin American drama producers did succeed in covering a lot of European countries. In general, the Latin American production centres were able to sell their products to more than one third of the broadcasting companies under survey. In total some 79 telenovela series appeared on European screens in 1995, mostly broadcast by public service companies. But, in Northwestern, Northern and Celtic–Anglo-Saxon countries telenovelas seem to have disappeared; when they survived, they maintained a marginal position. The ten stations which have been scheduling telenovelas in these regions limited themselves to one telenovela each. The few telenovelas that were broadcast, in addition, were often reruns of series bought in the 1980s.

Also, the variety in telenovela series is limited with a striking predominance of Brazilian material. Out of 76 telenovelas, 43 originate from Brazil. Mexico and Venezuela follow each with only 12 productions. The media concerns from the three major production countries thus supply almost 90 percent of the telenovelas to Europe. Moreover, in Northern and Northwestern Europe Globo is the only producer present. It is also remarkable that popular Globo productions of the 1980s such as *Sinha Moça* (in Belgium, Portugal, Hungary and Croatia) and *Isaura* (in Portugal and the Slovak Republic) still remain at the top in West and East.

Besides the mere quantity in hours, shares and the number of telenovelas, it is also important to look at how telenovelas were scheduled. Were they prime-time material or just fillers in low-rate time slots? If we assume that this distinction might roughly indicate the strategic importance of a programme type (Varis, 1985), it is safe to say again that the Latin American share was relatively unimportant. The survey indicated that the vast majority of telenovelas were shown during the week, and only in a few cases continued during weekends. In 1995 they were generally broadcast in morning, noon, afternoon or late evening time slots. In most regions they were shown during the usual soap time slots, mostly in hours with low audience ratings. While some telenovelas did appear in Southern Europe in prime-time slots, they were never broadcast in the evening in Western and Northern parts of the continent. Not surprisingly, this marginality in the schedule is reflected in the market share in Northwestern Europe.

These quantitative indicators only underline the relativity of the "reverse cultural imperialism thesis" or other claims dealing with a substantial, growing contra-flow from Latin America. Especially in the economically most powerful parts of Europe, in the Northwestern, Northern and Celtic–Anglo-Saxon countries, telenovelas faced marginal attention. The reasons for their scarce success on these fronts are quite diverse, mostly referring to a mixture of cultural boundaries, commercial and programming strategies. Following

TABLE 2
Number of telenovelas (series) by company in Europe (1995)

Country	Company	Number telenovelas	Percent
Belgium	BRTN	1	1.3
Austria	ORF	1	1.3
Switzerland	DRS	1	1.3
	TSR	1	1.3
Germany	NDR	1	1.3
	BR	1	1.3
	ARD	1	1.3
	WDR	1	1.3
	MDR	1	1.3
Finland	YLE	1	1.3
Spain	TVE	10	12.7
	ETB	2	2.5
Portugal	SIC	15	19
	RTP	12	15.2
Greece	Megachannel	1	1.3
	ERT	3	3.8
Turkey	TRT	2	2.5
Lithuania	TELE3	1	1.3
Estonia	TV3 Estonia	2	2.5
Moldavia	TVMoldavia	1	1.3
Hungary	Magyar TV	4	5.1
Slovenia	RTV Slovenia	1	1.3
Slovak Rep.	Slovak TV	6	7.6
Bulgaria	BNT	1	1.3
Croatia	HRT	3	3.8
Rumania	Rumanian TV	5	6.3
Total		79	100

the responses by programming and purchase directors there is, first of all, the cultural distance, in particular the language boundary, the lack of cultural proximity and knowledge of the world of telenovelas. This relates to the aversion for subtitled or dubbed programmes. This reason is often mentioned as a key factor for not purchasing and scheduling telenovelas, especially among Celtic–Anglo-Saxon companies such as the Welsh S4C, responding that the "audience in Wales shares the general British lack of enthusiasm for dubbed or subtitled popular programming."

The language problem and the preference for fiction with a higher degree of cultural proximity, not only illustrate the importance of cultural distance in television programme flows. They are also closely related to the commercial rationale, often translated by scheduling executives as the ruling adage of "giving the people what they want." The German commercial channel Sat 1 bluntly claims that "our studies show that national, European and American formats are more popular," while their public service competitor ZDF even mentions that "if at all we broadcast foreign fiction they [sic] come from the USA." Other stations are more subtle in their strategies to cope with foreign, non-U.S. material, such as the Norwegian TV Norge, responding that they "are a commercial station so we opt for American and British films, no other international film unless it was a big success at the movie theatre."

So it seems that cultural differences, related to commercial strategies, the preference for culturally closer material and the aversion for dubbed or subtitled fare are a major obstacle to the telenovela's commercial success in most parts of Europe. It is clear that, especially in the Northern, Northwestern and Anglo-Saxon countries, telenovelas suffer from the harsh competition from major local and U.S. production centres. Since the 1990s there has been a clear trend in all Western European countries to refocus on domestically produced and U.S. soap series. It also seems that the eulogies from Latin American authors on the outstanding narrative and visual quality of telenovelas (for example, Marques de Melo, 1988: 57) are no longer valid for most European programming executives.

CULTURAL PROXIMITY IN QUESTION

Marginality or absence, however, is not the general pattern. It is clear that Southern Europe shows a different picture. Many indicators show the importance of Latin American fiction for the stations in these countries. In fact, more than half of the Latin American imports in Europe in 1995 were broadcast by Southern European stations. Nearly half of them (46.8%) are shown by three stations, that is, the Spanish TVE (n = 10), the Portuguese SIC (n = 15) and RTP (n = 12). It is notable that Brazilian companies are the major programme providers (55.6 percent) with twice as many telenovelas as Mexican and Venezuelan companies. The information on Italy is scarce but we do know, as the RAI notes in the questionnaire, that commercial channels like Mediaset, Rete4 and some smaller commercial stations regularly did (and still do) broadcast telenovelas (see for example, de la Fuente, 1997).

Besides the huge quantities of imported telenovelas, it is clear that these programmes also obtained a strategically important spot in the schedules. Although in Spain Latin American series were often scheduled in lower rating time slots (for example, morning, afternoon, late night), they used to appear quite frequently during prime time in Portugal. Our 1995 data are in line with other findings, such as those reported by Akyuz (1994: 16-17) about Spain and Italy, where in 1994 6 out of the 10 top soaps were telenovelas.

Asked for the reasons for purchasing and programming telenovelas, the executives mostly refer to cultural factors—in this case in an affirmative manner. Here language and cultural proximity are seen as important factors for commercial choice. The language factor is clearly illustrated for Portugal, where we find almost exclusively Brazilian programmes (22 out of 27). The Portuguese public broadcaster RTP scheduled telenovelas "for cultural reasons; it appeals to the same values of the Portuguese, because of the same Latin roots," while the Greek commercial Megachannel was said to be satisfied with its purchase because of "the similar culture and mentality with the Greek."

Cultural proximity also relates to the commercial rationale of audience success, as examples in Spain and Portugal in the 1980s and early 1990s clearly showed (see above). This euphoria, however, is not completely reflected by the 1995 data. On the southern channels TVE and Megachannel the ratings are low. In Portugal they are likely to be much higher since SIC claims in the questionnaire to reach 60 percent of the market in prime time with telenovelas, where "since 1975, it's the most popular programme for the Portuguese TV-audience." The financial attractiveness of the cheap telenovelas can be an argument as well. The Basque channel ETB schedules them "to fill the schedule at a low price."

However, there are indicators that the Latin image or the cultural advantage shows some cracks. For Antena 3 spokeswoman, Françoise Sabbah (in Akyuz, 1997: 52), "telenovelas are no longer seen as culturally relevant to the Spanish public." This seems to indicate that Spanish commercial companies have explicitly chosen U.S. material above Latin American and no longer engage in co-productions. In Italy co-productions continue, although the popular home channel of the telenovela, Rete 4, has substantially reduced its telenovela programming (Akyuz, 1997: 52).

A key reason for others not to purchase telenovelas is the poor quality. The Italian RAI, for example, categorically refused telenovelas and did not find them fit for the demanding image of a public service broadcaster. The Spanish regional channel Telemadrid does not purchase them because most of them are mere "culebrones" (Spanish nickname for telenovelas meaning snakes, but obviously with a connotation of tearjerkers).

Emerging markets in the East and the commercial rationale

A completely different picture arises when we look at the Eastern part of Europe, where the fall of the Iron Curtain and the introduction of the free market system quickly changed the broadcasting system, heralding well-known tendencies such as demonopolization and commercial programming strategies. One of the most astounding findings of our enquiry refers to the successful introduction of telenovelas in many of these former communist countries. In fact, the study shows that more than half the Eastern European channels (9 out of 15 in the enquiry) have telenovelas in their programme schedule, and that they are well distributed in it. In these countries telenovelas are clearly more than a flash in the pan, while most of these channels (for example, the Hungarian Magyar TV, the Croatian HRT or the Rumanian RTV) carried three or more telenovelas. The Slovak public broadcaster STV scheduled six series of Latin American origin. In fact, nearly one third of all telenovela imports in Europe (30.4 percent, or 24 series), are shown in these markets.

The situation in Eastern Europe clearly illustrates the commercial strategy of Latin American producers, who are keen to respond to the higher demand for cheap entertainment. Globo, for example, explicitly chooses to gain a presence with telenovelas in these opening markets; though not profitable in the short term, they prove to be highly profitable in the long run (Mazziotti, 1996: 45). Programming and purchase departments in these parts of the continent most often referred to the low price or the economic value as the main argument to schedule telenovela series, followed by their seriality and scheduling opportunities, technical qualities and content. As evidenced by what happened in Western Europe in the 1980s, it is clear that telenovelas are not the star prime-time category, but serve as cheap fillers for the expanding broadcasting time.

The Eastern European case once again illustrates that commercial considerations dominate the international flow of fiction. Following the U.S. patterns of exploitation of international television markets, telenovela producers sell their products at differential rates. This explains why a telenovela series costs approximately U.S. $50 per hour in Estonia, compared to U.S. $1500 in Switzerland and almost U.S. $3000 in Turkey. Given the precarious economic situation in many Eastern European countries, telenovelas are mostly cheaper than other types of foreign fiction. This market opportunity was reported by most channels, especially by those in smaller countries such as Estonia (TV3) or Lithuania (Tele3).

Eastern European purchase of telenovelas relates to an economic argument dealing with the capacity to capture audiences for a longer time in specific marginal time slots. This function is perfectly reflected in the performance of these programmes with the audience. Given the off-peak broadcasting time slots, the telenovelas' ratings are usually quite low, although their market shares tend to be often quite satisfactory. In several Eastern European countries, telenovelas manage to attract a good part of the viewers in low audience time slots, with the ultimate example of the Brazilian series *O Pogador de Promessas* reaching an audience share of 80.7 percent in Hungary. In their written comments, channels such as the Lithuanian LNK-TV summarized that "the quality does not satisfy but it attracts the audience and advertising." The Estonian TV3 refers to "good ratings" too, while the Bulgarian BNT mentions "high ratings, audience interest, good prices, alternative for soap opera." And Tele3 from Lithuania summarizes: "High ratings, popularity among the audience and good sales of adtime."

But again, one should be careful about the future of telenovelas in Eastern Europe, given the parallels with Western European programming tendencies of the 1980s. The main question here is whether the Latin American wave will last or disappear in the East too, given the further commercial development of the broadcasting scene and the subsequent rise of U.S.- and domestically produced fiction.

CONCLUSION

This article started with the observation that Latin American telenovelas can be seen as a test case in international communication theory and research, illustrating alternatives in global communication flows. Since the mid-1980s an interesting debate has been developed around the meaning of telenovelas, especially in their worldwide exports, for the analysis of global cultural change. On the one hand, optimistic voices were raised about the end of "cultural imperialism," while others responded by questioning the range of these revisionist arguments.

Drawing upon an empirical comparative enquiry of Latin American fiction flows to Europe in 1995, this article supports the relative weakness of the contra-flow argument. The overall European pattern of telenovela imports has been related to marginality, or even, in some parts of Europe, dehydration. Mainly in the North and Northwest of Europe telenovela series are not scheduled at all or have disappeared since the beginning of the 1990s. The central argument here is that the audio-visual industry in those countries was first keen to use telenovelas as mere fillers for the expanding broadcasting time. But since the 1990s, competition has increased so much that programmers have tended to avoid "exotic" material and have fallen back on proven fiction programming.

Telenovelas were relatively well represented in other parts of Europe. In Southern countries we referred to broad cultural arguments dealing with language and a sense of proximity with the world depicted in the telenovelas, while in Eastern parts the success of telenovelas was due to their relative cheapness. But here again, the enquiry draws attention to the fact that in these cases the telenovela phenomenon should not be overestimated and that its future is not secure. A significant indicator in this direction may be that Spanish commercial channels declared themselves to be no longer prepared to schedule telenovelas at all, referring to their weaker quality standards and poor audience performance. It seems that in these cases Latin American fiction is defeated by material from the United States and from other big Western production centres. Telenovelas may soon face the same hard competition in the vibrant Eastern European television markets.

In the 1980s and early 1990s Europe was the most promising market for telenovela exporters. Globo and other Latin American corporations, however, appear to be less present in Europe than euphoric voices might have expected. In the mid-1990s oversaturation and competition with U.S. fiction urged Latin American media concerns to redirect their efforts to new markets such as Asia and, in particular, Japan (Mazziotti, 1996: 41; de la Fuente, 1997: 45). But Latin American fiction is still more important in Europe than, say, Japanese or Australian imports. A key reason that may help telenovelas to stay in the (near) future is the importance of Mexican and Brazilian programme producers in their respective (huge) language regions. This position has been intensified on a structural level because these corporations are attempting to encroach upon the broadcasting system in countries such as Portugal and Spain.

Returning to our theoretical opening, this article empirically supports the analysis of scholars who firmly reject the thesis that the international activities of Televisa or Globo could be considered as a form of reverse cultural imperialism (for example, Sinclair, 1993: 131). Of course, the new complex realities of the 1990s can no longer be analysed with former tools and concepts, often leading to dichotomous views about global cultural flow and influence.

Although international television flows no longer fit in Nordenstrengs and Varis's metaphor of a "one-way street" (1974) and seem to make up a kind of "patchwork quilt" (Tracey, 1988: 24; Sinclair et al., 1996: 5), it is important to emphasize that they still are culturally influenced and both politically and economically regulated. In this sense, the European findings hardly justify euphoric arguments about a more balanced flow. The issue of the worldwide flow of Latin American television programmes has strongly complicated research and theories on global communication and dependency, but one may not overemphasize its range. We should not forget that "the coming of age of many Third World media producers and the localization of some media production" are important, but as Sreberny-Mohammadi (1993: 121-22) continues, "at the same time even stronger tendencies toward greater globalization and conglomeratization can be discerned."

In this sense it becomes clear that in the international telenovela debate we have to disentangle the international activities of private communication companies from their national governments' interests. The frequently assumed equivalence between them constitutes, as Sinclair (1990: 351) stated, "a nationalised distortion of the transnational character of contemporary cultural industries." As a result, the telenovela phenomenon should not (only) be treated as a case in the traditional North-South dialogue, but should equally be firmly located in the debate around globalization strategies of late-capitalist cultural industries. Here we can refer to the striking parallels between U.S. and major Latin American corporations' strategies to conquer overseas markets. In many respects, Globo and other commercial production centres use quite similar strategies in producing, distributing, selling and marketing their products as their Northern American competitors (for example, López, 1995: 273), while their success also rests upon the huge home market and the language advantage (Sinclair, 1996).

Another caveat in discussions about the success of telenovelas and other Third World media products, mostly stressing export arguments, is that various other analytical levels should be taken into account. Reflecting upon our own case study, it must be underlined that it relates to the outflow level, refuting former optimistic voices within a revisionist framework. As indicated in the theoretical overview, however, one cannot escape the idea that certain revisionist arguments at other levels are challenged by recent developments too. A key issue in the debate will be how Latin American audiences and concerns will face the strategies of and the harsh competition from other global (U.S.) concerns.

NOTES

The authors wish to thank the Research Department of the VRT (Flemish Public Broadcasting Company) for their financial and logistic support, with a special thanks to Brigitta Parisis and Daniël Poesmans. They also thank Jay G. Blumler and Caroline Pauwels for their stimulating remarks.

1. In Latin America this rewriting of the critical frame was paralleled by an interesting theoretical revision of the twin concept of dependency/dominance in the work

of cultural critics such as Martín-Barbero (1993) and García-Canclini (1995). See also Schlesinger and Morris (1997).
2. For an overview and discussion, see McAnany and La Pastina (1994).
3. See for example, a special issue of *Intercom. Revista Brasileira de Comunicação* (1990, issue 62/3) with case studies on the export of Brazilian telenovelas to countries such as Spain, Yugoslavia and Belgium.

REFERENCES

Akyuz, G. 1994. "Soaps Make a Clean Sweep." *TV-World* 7-8: 16-22.
Akyuz, G. 1997. "Heart of the Community." *TV-World* 1: 49-54.
Antola, L., and E. M. Rogers 1984. "Television Flows in Latin America." *Communication Research* 11(2): 183-202.
Bouquillion, P. 1992. "La Réception des Télénovelas Brésiliennes en France." *Intercom* 15(1): 98-117.
de la Fuente, A. M. 1997. "Endless Love." *TV-World* 1: 45-47.
Fadul, A. 1993. "Telenovela y Cultura en el Brasil," paper presented at the Primeras Jornadas Internacionales de la Telenovela Latinoamericana, Universidad Autónoma de Barcelona, April.
Fox, E. 1997a. *Latin American Broadcasting: From Tango to Telenovela*. Luton: John Libbey.
Fox, E. 1997b. "The Rise (and Fall?) of the Telenovela Abroad." *Intermedia* 25(4): 37–39.
Fox, E. 1997c. "Media and Culture in Latin America," pp. 184–205 in J. Corner, P. Schlesinger and R. Silverstone, eds., *International Media Research: A Critical Survey*. London: Routledge.
García-Canclini, N. 1995. *Hybrid Cultures: Strategies for Entering and Leaving Modernity*. Minneapolis: University of Minnesota Press.
Golding, P., and P. Harris, eds., 1997. *Beyond Cultural Imperialism: Globalization, Communication and the New International Order*. London: Sage.
Guaderrama, M. 1993. "La Telenovela en la Prensa Española," paper presented at the Primeras Jornadas Internacionales de la Telenovela Latinoamericana, Universidad Autónoma de Barcelona, April.
Hallin, D. 1998. "Broadcasting in the Third World," pp. 153–67 in T. Liebes and J. Curran, eds., *Media, Ritual and Identity*. London: Routledge.
Jakubowicz, K. 1994. "The Audiovisual Landscape of Central and Eastern Europe," pp. 13-21 in K. Jakubowicz and P. Jeanray, eds., *Central and Eastern Europe. Audiovisual Landscape and Copyright Legislation*. Antwerp: Audiovisual Eureka, Maklu.
Lee, C. C. 1980. *Media Imperialism Reconsidered*. Beverly Hills, CA: Sage.
López, A. M. 1995. "Our Welcomed Guests: Telenovelas in Latin America," pp. 256–75 in R. C. Allen, ed., *To Be Continued... Soap Operas Around the World*. London: Routledge.
McAnany, E., and A. C. La Pastina. 1994. "Telenovela Audience." *Communication Research* 21(6): 828–49.
Marques de Melo, J. 1988. *As Telenovelas da Globo: Produção e Exportação*. São Paulo: Summus.
Martín-Barbero, J. 1993. *Communication, Culture and Hegemony: From the Media to Mediations*. London: Sage.
Mattelart, M., and A. Mattelart. 1987. *Le Carnaval des Images. La Fiction Brésilienne*. Paris: INA.
Mattos, S. 1993. "Un Perfil de la Televisión Brasileña: 40 Años de Historia (1950–1990)." *Comunicación y Sociedad* 16–17: 45–74.
Mazziotti, N. 1996. *La Industria de la Telenovela. La Producción de Ficción en América Latina*. Buenos Aires: Paidós.

Muraro, H. 1987. *Invasión Cultural, Economía y Comunicación*. Buenos Aires: Legasa.
Nordenstreng, K., and T. Varis. 1974. *Television Traffic—A One-Way Street?* Paris: Unesco.
Oliveira, O. S. 1990. "Brazilian Soaps Outshine Hollywood: Is Cultural Imperialism Fading Out?" pp. 116–31 in K. Nordenstreng and H. Schiller, eds., *Beyond National Sovereignty: International Communication in the 1990s*. Norwood: Ablex.
Reeves, G. 1993. *Communications and the 'Third World.'* London: Routledge.
Roach, C. 1990. "The Movement for a New World Information and Communication Order: A Second Wave?" *Media, Culture & Society* 12: 283–307.
Rogers, E. M., and L. Antola. 1985. "Telenovelas: A Latin American Success Story." *Journal of Communication* 35(4): 24–36.
RTVE. 1990. *Memoria*. Madrid: RTVE.
Schiller, H. 1991. "Not Yet the Post-Imperialist Era." *Critical Studies in Mass Communication* 8: 13–28.
Schlesinger, P., and N. Morris. 1997. "Cultural Boundaries: Identity and Communication in Latin America." *Media Development* 1.
Sinclair, J. 1986. "Dependent Development and Broadcasting: The Mexican Formula." *Media, Culture & Society* 8: 81–101.
Sinclair, J. 1990. "Neither West nor Third World: The Mexican Television Industry within the NWICO Debate." *Media, Culture & Society* 12: 343–60.
Sinclair, J. 1993. "The Decentering of Cultural Imperialism: Televisa-ion and Globo-ization in the Latin World." *Intercom* 16: 120–34.
Sinclair, J. 1996. "Mexico, Brazil, and the Latin World," pp. 33–66 in J. Sinclair, E. Jacka and S. Cunningham, eds., *New Patterns in Global Television*. New York: Oxford University Press.
Sinclair, J. 1998. "Geolinguistic Region as Global Space: The Case of Latin America," paper presented at the 21st Scientific Conference, International Association for Media and Communication Research, Glasgow, July.
Sinclair, J., E. Jacka and S. Cunningham. 1996. "Peripheral Vision," pp. 1-32 in J. Sinclair, E. Jacka and S. Cunningham, eds., *New Patterns in Global Television*. New York: Oxford University Press.
Sreberny-Mohammadi, A. 1993. "The Global and Local in International Communication," pp. 118–38 in J. Curran and M. Gurevitch, eds., *Mass Media and Society*. London: Edward Arnold.
Straubhaar, J. D. 1984. "Brazilian Television. The Decline of American Influence." *Communication Research* 11(2): 221–40.
Straubhaar, J. D., and G. M. Viscasillas. 1991. "Class, Genre, and the Regionalization of Television Programming in the Dominican Republic." *Journal of Communication* 41(1): 53-69.
Tomlinson, J. 1991. *Cultural Imperialism*. London: Pinter.
Tracey, M. 1988. "Popular Culture and the Economics of Global Television." *Intermedia* 16: 8-25.
Trinta, A. R. 1997. "News from Home: A Study of Realism and Melodrama in Brazilian Telenovelas," pp. 275–85 in C. Geraghty and D. Lusted, eds., *The Television Studies Book*. London/New York: Arnold.
Varis, T. 1985. *International Flow of Television Programmes*. Paris: Unesco.
Vink, N. 1988. *The Telenovela and Emancipation: A Study on TV and Social Change in Brazil*. Amsterdam: KIT.

Telenovelas and Soap Operas: Negotiating Reality from the Periphery

Christina Slade

INTRODUCTION

I begin with two anecdotes. In 1988, in Belgium, it was possible to watch the Australian soap *Neighbours* in English, Italian, Dutch, French, Italian and German in one week, delivered by CODITEL, the local cable company. From the periphery of the global communication network, an Australian soap was flooding the heartland of Europe. Images of Australians and the Australian way of life were shot through with the mores of a *Neighbours*-style community. My own neighbour, an aristocratic Belgian, sent her child in to borrow tomato sauce, explaining later that she knew that all Australians had tomato sauce, and all sent regularly to their neighbours for such things. A way of breaking the ice perhaps.

The other anecdote concerns a Mexican family travelling in Indonesia in the early 1990s. The young child of the family, María Mercedes, shared her name with the immensely popular Mexican telenovela starring Thalía (Ariadna Sodi Miranda). As the mother called to her child, crowds of normally restrained Javanese descended wanting to talk of the telenovela of Mexico and of love. They *knew* the name María Mercedes and knew the society from which the name came. The French-educated and somewhat restrained Mexican couple were taken aback.

Anecdotes like this are universal. Many are apocryphal. In one version it is the Romanian sitting of parliament which is delayed for the final episode of a Mexican telenovela, in others the Egyptian, or Russian senior leaders who pause for the show. What the anecdotes underline is the extraordinary success of the genre of soaps—or of the family of genres that includes soaps and telenovelas. It is interesting that they are produced in the periphery, not in the great centres of production in Europe or the United States.

Christina Slade: "Telenovelas and Soap Operas: Negotiating Reality from the Periphery," first published in *Media International Australia*, vol. 106, num. 2 (2003): 6–17.

A GLOBAL PRODUCT

The global success of Australian soaps is a familiar story. But the Latin American telenovela genre has also had its share of attention. In 1996 Ien Ang, quoting Vink (1988) and Mattelart and Mattelart (1990), cites the success of telenovelas as an instance of the localisation of global cultural products such as the American daytime soaps:

> Telenovelas became so popular in that part of the world that they gradually displaced American imports from the TV schedules and became an intrinsic part of local culture. (Ang, 1996: 155)

But that is the wrong way around. The major producers of telenovelas, Brazil and Mexico, chart their own paths and in neither country was the U.S. daytime soap the model. As Thomas Tufte puts it:

> The telenovela genre has developed as a complex cultural product with generic, social and cultural roots far back in Latin American history. (2000: 2)

He argues the case for Brazil. In Mexico, likewise, Televisa telenovelas were a home-grown product, and never replaced a diet of American daytime soaps. As the leading Televisa producer Gabriel Vazquez Bulman put it in an interview with Rosalind Pearson:

> If you go back to the origins of the telenovela, Mexico in the 1940s had a great tradition of comics and cheap cartoon books ... known as 'folletines' ... you didn't need to read to understand them. ... Later came the radionovelas which were directly descended from the folletine and later ... the telenovela. Telenovelas based on the same stories that were in the folletines years ago in the 30s and 40s, are called 'telenovelas de folletin'. That is why the Mexican telenovela is very distinct from the European or US soaps. (Pearson, 1999)

Mexican telenovelas created a form which was itself very exportable. The same was true to some extent in Australia. *Neighbours* was never a poor man's *Coronation Street*. Each national style has colonised the markets of the world in its own right. It is not that the global product has been localised, but that the local product of the periphery has invaded the global producers.

That was the insight underlying the conference entitled "Telenovelas and Soap Operas: Negotiating Reality from the Periphery." The conference took place at the Humanities Research Centre of the Australian National University in Canberra early in 2002. The premise of the conference was that it was worth examining the international success of the telenovela/soap opera industry in Latin America and Australasia. Australian soaps from *Neighbours* to *Home and Away* have had remarkable international success. Latin telenovelas, such as *Los Ricos también Lloran* (The Rich Also Cry), *Mirada de Mujer* (A Woman's View) and *Yo soy Betty la Fea* (I Am Ugly Betty), are shown across the Mediterranean.

In 1960 a formal legal structure was instituted in Mexico: La Ley Federal de Radio y Televisión. The law made explicit the public service role of television and distinguished between commercial and non-profit channels. In 1968, President Díaz Ordaz attempted to open the television market to competition, selling Channel 8 and Channel 13 to commercial competitors of the Azcárraga family. Channel 8 was bought by the Garza Sada family company Grupo Alfa de Monterrey. By 1972, however, Telesistema Mexicana (Channels 2, 4, 5) and Grupo Alfa (Channel 8) combined, and soon afterwards the son and heir of the family empire, Emilio Azcárraga Milmo, was able to buy out Grupo Alfa. This new monolith in the industry was named Televisa. Under President Echeverria, the Mexican government was far more interventionist, promulgating a law on 4 April 1973 which gave the state the role of approving content and allowed commercials on state and non-profit television. From this time on, government censors sat in through the filming of telenovelas. The very close links between Televisa and the presidency, however, meant that there was little friction.

In 1961 Telesistema Mexicana had expanded to San Antonio, Texas and the Spanish International Network (SIN) was set up. By 1976, the company now named Televisa was globalising, acquiring 20 per cent of the United States–based Spanish International Communication Corporation. SIN grew from controlling 16 U.S. channels in 1979 to 240 in 1983. In 1986 the FCC ruled that Emilio Azcárraga Milmo controlled SIN and, as he was not a U.S. citizen, he was forced to divest himself of the company. In 1988 he bought Galavisión International in Europe, in 1991 acquired 49 per cent of Megavisión in Chile and in 1993 bought Red Bolivia. By this time, Televisa was the largest Spanish-language network in the world. It rested, however, on immense borrowings which, with the financial crisis in Mexico in 1994, put pressure on the company.

In July 1995, there was a landmark meeting between the heads of the family television empires from the periphery, held in Mexico City. Emilio Azcárraga Milmo from Televisa, Rupert Murdoch of News Ltd and Fox Television and Roberto Marinho of TV Globo met together with a representative of the U.S. Cable company TCI to establish and divide up the cable business in Latin America (Fernández and Paxman, 2000: 455). This was the high point of the Azcárraga empire. By the end of 1997, Emilio Azcárraga Milmo had died and his empire, now in the hands of his son Emilio Azcárraga Jean, was divesting. By 1998, the Argentine television company Clarín (owned by another Latin media family named Noble) was the largest earning Spanish language net work.

Daniel Mato (2001) describes the process whereby Spanish-language telenovela production was moving to Miami, where a transnational Spanish style was emerging. The stories written on the periphery, in a language from the periphery and very often performed by actors of the periphery, have now so successfully invaded the centre that production has moved. Mato traces the fortunes of Televisa over the last years, and the rise of competitors not just in Miami but also in Colombia, where the highly successful comic telenovela *Yo soy Betty la Fea* was produced, and Venezuela. The heyday of Televisa's domination of the Spanish telenovela is over.

TELEVISA TELENOVELAS

The mainstay of Televisa was, from the very beginning, the telenovela. Valentin Pimstein, a Chilean expatriate producer, joined the younger Azcárraga, Emilio Azcárraga Milmo, in the 1950s. Colgate Palmolive signed on with Pimstein, and Proctor and Gamble with another of the young Azcárraga's offsiders, Ernesto Alonso. Pimstein developed the formulaic telenovelas based on the Cinderella, *Cenicienta*, plot line, which served to carry the advertising. Alonso began the habit of buying scripts: the first telenovela, *El Otro y Pecado Mortal* (1960), was written by a Cuban (Fernández and Paxman, 2000: 68). By the mid-1960s, the mini-microphone created by the technician Alberto Nolla Reyes in 1951 was small enough to be worn in filming. Rehearsal times were cut drastically. Televisa could produce in its studios and transmit up to five telenovelas a day. Twenty telenovelas were produced a year, with some 17 studios, 250 actors and 100 musicians on the permanent Televisa staff (Fernández and Paxman, 2000: 136).

Emilio Azcárraga Milmo was quite explicit about the role of the telenovela. He is quoted as saying:

> Mexico is a country with a large class of people who are screwed. Television's responsibility is to bring these people entertainment and distract them from their sad reality and difficult future. (Quiñones, 1998: 42)

Emilio Azcárraga Milmo's role as a gatekeeper of the production of Televisa telenovelas during the heyday of Televisa's power ensured that the lack of realism persisted in Mexican telenovelas long after it had disappeared in the soap operas of, say, Australia or Brazil. Emilio Azcárraga Milmo drew on a code of values originally made explicit by his father for the radio network: "la superación personal, la integración familiar y la unidad nacional"—personal improvement, family integration and national unity (Fernández and Paxman, 2000: 192).

The conventions governing the Televisa telenovela were very strict: no smoking, no poverty, no abortion, no politicians, no one of Indian descent, except as maids or labourers. One formula became known as the "María" telenovelas. Predominantly fair heroines, maids in the houses of the rich, played out Cinderella stories by marrying the son of the house. Another formula was first used by the telenovela writer, Fernanda Villeli, in the 1960 telenovela *Senda Prohibida*. It was a reverse fairytale. The younger mistress of an older man, typically a young woman who has come to the city from the pueblo, is finally rejected in favour of the wife (Fernández and Paxman, 2000: 77).

Throughout this period, Televisa was the largest producer of telenovelas in the world. From the actresses and crew through to the studios and the production houses, Televisa had complete control. It owned each stage of the process of producing and distributing telenovelas. It was an enormously profitable business. With a monopoly of commercial television in Mexico, cheap labour costs and an industry that was both horizontally and vertically integrated, Televisa's telenovelas were a cash cow. Indeed, Fernandez and Paxman (2000: 218-19) argue that it was on the back of the success of the telenovela *Los ricos también lloran* that the globalisation of Televisa was possible.

In 1993, the government under President Salinas sold two of its stations to Telelvisíon Azteca, which was to become an alternative commercial network. Televisíon Azteca, drawing on an independent production company, ARGOS, challenged the ratings of Televisa by producing soap operas of startling relevance. No longer reverential about government and politicians, the new telenovelas literally described what was happening in the country. Days after political events occurred, they appeared in a fictionalised form in telenovelas such as *Nada Personal*. Drugs, AIDS, teenage pregnancy and political assassination proliferated in plots. *Mirada de Mujer*, the story of a wealthy, respectably married woman of a certain age, María Inés (Angélica Aragón), who herself took a younger lover on being abandoned by her husband, was the most notable of the new wave of telenovelas.

Angélica Aragón, who attended the conference, spoke at the showing of *Mirada de Mujer* and talked on the directors' panel. She has worked in the telenovela industry both as one of Mexico's best-known actresses and most recently as a director. She talked of her experience in *Mirada de Mujer*. The importance of the telenovela was that it revealed social issues which were at the heart of the Mexican experience. Yet viewers, accustomed to the Televisa formulas, reacted violently. The direction of the plot was sometimes influenced by the fury of the public reaction. For example, when María Inés' elder daughter was pregnant, she decided to have an abortion, although this was still illegal in Mexico. The public reaction proved to be so violent during the week this was screening that the producers chose to let the daughter have a miscarriage instead.

The producer of the series, Epigmenio Ibarra, was well aware of the force of the telenovela and argued that this was as it should be. He said:

> [It] was envisaged as a 'mirror of society' . . . to talk of the disintegration of the family is not to foster disintegration, but to encourage discussion of the causes of disintegration. We hoped to initiate debate with the soap opera, to provoke polemic, reflections. (Reforma, 1997: 9E)

Angélica Aragón talked in her introduction to the showing of *Mirada de Mujer* of the immense power of the telenovela to structure social expectations. In her role as an independent woman, she was able to provide a model. But, as she explained later in the directors' panel, she has not been able to get funding for telenovelas with an explicit social message. The complexities of the industry, and its competing pressures, undermine the possibilities for social action.

THE WRITERS' AND DIRECTORS' PANELS

The panels reported in the three sets of transcripts drew on writers, directors and actors to talk of their experience of the industries in their countries.

It is illuminating to discover just how the interweaving of specific constraints and practices in the industry determine what is made, and how messages are delivered. For instance, in the writers' panel, Cuauhtémoc Blanco Arias, the head of the writing team for Televisa, explains how Mexican telenovelas are written. A single writer is responsible for the entire nine months of episodes, which are then adjusted and tweaked by producers, directors and actors. But the plot line is the responsibility of one writer. He explains the enormous burden of writing, but also the individual control each writer has. The industry in Brazil has a similar respect for writers. However, as Felicity Packard, a writer for *Home and Away* and *MDA* explains, the structure is quite different in Australia. A story editor works with a team to set out broad plot lines, and then freelance writers are contracted particular episodes to write. The parameters of writing, down to the number of location shots, the style of dress and the availability of particular actors, are set in advance.

Cuauhtémoc Blanco insists on the importance of fantasy in the writing. He argues that the stories which take the fancy of the middle classes and lower middle classes of Mexico—the serving women, the housewives—are essentially escapist. In a similar vein, Greg Haddrick, of the immensely successful *Home and Away*, showed an episode in which there was a marriage and explained that, while a long-running series like *Home and Away* cannot have too many weddings, they do create a marvellous feeling. He tells a cautionary tale about an attempt to create social relevance in the script, introducing a gay couple (carefully modulated so that the young viewer would think that they were just good friends); critics' views were overwhelmingly positive, but the viewers switched off. Social criticism simply does not sell.

A partial counter-example to this claim is given by Gillian Arnold, who talked of the SBS innovation *Going Home*. This "reality soap" is filmed on a train with daily commuters discussing real-life events from that day's newspapers. A mix of characters of ethnic groups, and of different types, react as a community in a commuter train. The mix of truth and fiction is heady, and in fact excellent television.

Peter Dodds from *Neighbours* explains just how restrictive production requirements are. The structures for pay for actors dictate that only a few actors can be used in more than two or three episodes a week. The cost of location shots puts a limit on the number of scenes that can be filmed outside the studio. The delay in production—three months between production and showing of episodes—means that the close political commentary of Mexican and Brazilian telenovelas is not possible.

Angélica Aragón describes a very different industry structure. Her actors are generally on contract, with filming schedules set up daily. Sets are built as required, with very short lead times. The ready availability of labour means great flexibility but, she argues, very little expertise in the production. She is attempting to imbue a greater sense of respect for actors and producers and to create what she calls a "holistic" approach to filming. That, of course, is costly: actors would stay for longer periods with space for developing characters. But some of the profits of telenovelas should, she suggests, be fed back into the industry.

THEORISING SPECIFICITY

While Jorge González Sánchez talks from a Mexican perspective, his central argument applies equally to the Australasian case. In order to understand the phenomenon of the telenovela, he argues, we have to see the institutional forms that are used in the production of melodrama. The particular institutional factors in the Mexican case—the dominance of Televisa, for instance, and the development of the nine-month format—determine how the melodramas and stereotypical characters are portrayed. These forms must then be seen in the complex social structures in which they are interpreted and read. He offers a model of the complex and layered interaction of production, text and social readings of telenovelas.

González traces the aetiology of difference in the soap operas and telenovelas, in the melodramatic traditions and the industry that produces them, and in the audiences that interpret them. With such difference, is there any value in analysing telenovelas and soaps under one umbrella? The Socratic question becomes urgent: what do they have in common? In Felicity Packard's words, talking of the shared project of Latin and Australian writers of telenovelas and soaps, they share an underlying trope: "to create order out of chaos." Perhaps we can do a little better: they share domestic settings, romance, extended story arcs, melodrama. But these are far more universal than the genre of soap, and the ways in which those features play out depend crucially on local cultures.

THE PLEASURE OF VIEWING

What is the pleasure of viewing, and how do we explain the global attraction of the soap and telenovela? For Martín-Barbero:

> The full meaning and pleasure [of telenovelas] are found not just in the text but more in the discussion of the family, neighborhood, work place and friend networks. (2000: 156-57)

He talks of the role of telenovelas in the collective imaginations of different groups of viewers, manifested in discussions between viewers or their role as the focal points in personal histories. My own argument is similar: soaps and telenovelas are part of the texture of daily discussions, and their attraction lies, I suggest, in the fact that we can use the fictional narrative as a sounding board for ethical issues that are difficult to discuss as first-person issues. Discussion about *Mirada de Mujer* certainly had this flavour. There is ample evidence of debate about Mexican telenovelas over the generations. The following short excerpts of dialogue, from a transcript of young Mexicans discussing telenovela, are typical:

M: I got up at seven in the morning, and set the alarm, to see [the soaps] and I could never see them from the beginning—I always stayed asleep. I don't know ... and we weren't allowed to watch—we went to a Catholic school, and telenovelas were forbidden, but my grandma was much more lax, and she lived nearby and ever since I could think I watched telenovelas and knew them by heart, and all my friends came here to see the telenovelas—which were absolutely forbidden, but tele was always very important...¹

Here M talks of the social importance and the allure of the telenovelas, and the social function, not only with her friends but also with a grandmother. The spice of the forbidden is also a common theme when kids talk of watching telenovelas. Later in the same discussion, the kids talk of a telenovela they had seen years before:

F: No, no, *Live a Little* was Angélica Aragón.
A: Who they put in gaol in Argentina
M: And who appeared 30 years later...
F: My brother watched all the telenovelas and was always acting and when he said something like in the novela... he was forbidden to watch for a month.²

The telenovelas are a basis for talk, for discussion of, say, historical events in Argentina. They also provide models of ways of behaving and talking—however unsavoury. Here the brother repeats a phrase which I have not attempted to translate, and was forbidden to watch for a month. Despite the range of myths about telenovelas, men can be as immersed in soaps as women even in Mexico. As the sister goes on to explain:

F: He became mad... he was mad about the telenovelas, and it was terrible... terrible, since he never liked football, he never went out. Now he is more sophisticated, but then he was always watching telenovelas.³

The attraction of telenovelas and of soap operas is at least in part the attraction of shared stories, of fiction which allows identification and which can be used as models, or as the basis of talk with friends. However, if this is true, why do Latin telenovelas and Australasian soaps travel so well? If soaps and telenovelas derive their attraction from the fact that they produce a sounding board for the lives and moral dilemmas of the viewers, as Martín Barbero and I argue, then it would appear to follow that the closer the narrative is to the familiar, the more successful it is. The rise of home-grown soaps in Taiwan and Eastern Europe would be readily explained, but the success of Latin telenovelas in Eastern Europe or Australasian soaps in Europe would be a mystery. An element in the success of the Latin telenovela and the Australasian soap seems to be precisely the very difference of the societies they depict.

Mato argues: "The success of telenovelas, to a great extent, depends upon the possibilities of audience identification with the characters, stories, actors and actresses." The localised forms of the genre allow such identification. But he goes on to note that the rise of the market in Miami shows the elision of local differences, of the marked regional accents of Mexican telenovelas, for instance. Yet he argues that the basis of production is national, and the local product is still immensely important. How is it that a localised product sells so well, if it is identification with the audience that drives the viewers to keep watching?

One answer can be found in Harrington and Beilby (1995), whose book about soap fans is subtitled *Pursuing Pleasure and Making Meaning in Everyday Life*. They argue that, far from being confused about the reality of soaps, fans make clear distinctions between the personal histories of the actors and actresses and of the characters they portray. Fans are interested in discussing both narratives: that of the soap and that of the real lives of characters. Fans develop a complex and active sense of agency as they discuss soaps and negotiate the rituals of fandom. Perhaps most telling is the remark in the conclusion:

> Viewers enjoy the fictional world of soaps not because they lack fulfilling lives themselves—the real and fictional are not so clearly separable. Instead, soap operas offer viewers the chance to stand on the boundaries between multiple worlds and see real life as connected to, and informed by, a variety of perspectives. (Beilby and Harrington, 1995: 180)

It is here that we find a clue to the extraordinary global success of the telenovela and the Australasian soap. Viewers become involved not so much by identifying with the characters of soap operas and telenovelas as by seeing their own lives through the lens of similarities and differences in the lives portrayed. We are accustomed to—and have analysed exhaustively—the pleasure of watching *Dallas*. The huge success of Discovery channel documentaries shows the attraction of the landscape and animals of distant countries. What the success of telenovelas and Australasian soaps shows is that domestic difference is also attractive. Telenovelas and soaps have succeeded in markets in which the lifestyle is utterly unfamiliar. The attraction is the mix of the different and the familiar.

To examine this claim properly, we need a thorough study of fandom across national boundaries. We need to examine how telenovelas and soaps from unfamiliar cultural backgrounds are discussed, as viewers talk of their own lives relative to the lives of the characters of the soaps. But this is another project.

NOTES

1. *M*: no yo me levantaba a las siete de la mañana ponía el despertador para verlo completo y nunca pude verlo desde el principio, siempre (risas) siempre me quedaba dormida, este . . . no sé como que, a mi de chiquita, a todas mis amigas, les prohibían la, iban en una escuela de monjas, les prohibían las telenovelas, yo tenía un abuelo demasiado consentidor, que vivía aquí arriba, que (risas) que desde que tengo uso de razón vi novelas y me las sabía de memoria, entonces como que, todas mis amigas venían aquí para ver las telenovelas, que estaba súper prohibido, pero si como que la tele siempre ha sido así, muy importante . . .

2. *M*: no, no, no . . . *Vivir un poco* era la de *Angélica Aragón*.

A: que la meten a la cárcel en Argentina

M: y que aparece 30 años después

F: oye, mi hermano veía todas las novelas y siempre actuaba y cuando le decías algo ponle te actuaba como novela, (modula la voz) 'maldito bastardo', mi hermano así me insultaba, 'maldito bastardo, malnacido' y mi hermano le prohibían ver novelas porque cuando se portaba mal le castigaban, ponle un mes sin ver novelas, entonces no podía ver.

3. F: se volvía fanático, mi hermano se volvía fanático de las novelas y era terrible y siempre como que mi hermano nunca le gustó el fútbol, ni salía, ni así y entonces ... ahora es todo culto pero antes veía novellas. Thanks to Daniela Rivera for permission to use all three extracts.

REFERENCES

Ang, I. 1996. *Living Room Wars: Rethinking Media Audiences in the Modern World.* Routledge, London.

Bielby, D., and C. Lee Harrington. Forthcoming. "Opening America? The Telenovelaization of US Soap Operas," in *Television and New Media*.

Dunleavy, T. Forthcoming. *"Coronation Street, Neighbours, Shortland Street:* 'Localness' and 'Universality' in the Primetime Soap," in *Television and New Media*.

Fernández, C., and A. Paxman. 2000. *El Tigre: Emilio Azcárraga y su Imperio Televisa.* Grijalbo, Mexico City.

Harrington, C. Lee, and D. Bielby. 1995. *Soap Fans: Pursuing Pleasure and Making Meaning in Everyday Life.* Temple: Philadelphia.

Martin-Barbero, J. 2000. "The Cultural Mediations of Television Consumption" in I. Hagen and J. Wasko, *Consuming Audiences? Production and Reception in Media Research.* Cresskill, NJ: Hampton Press.

Mato, D. 2001. "Transnationalización de la Industria de la Telenovela, Referencias Territoriales, y Producción de Mercados y Representaciones de Identidades Transnacionales," paper delivered at the XXII International Conference of LASA, Washington, 6–8 September.

Mattelart, M., and A. Mattelart. 1990. *The Carnival of Images.* New York: Bergin and Garvey.

Mazziotti, N. 1996. *La Industria de la Telenovela. La Produccíon de Ficcíon en América Latina.* Buenos Aires: Paidós.

Mejia Barquera, F. 1998. "Del Canal 4 a Televisa," in O. M. Martínez, ed., *Apuntes para una Historia de La Televisión Mexicana: Revista Mexicana de Comunicació*n, pp. 19–99.

Pearson, R. 1999. Interview with Gabriel Vazquez Bulman of Televisa. Mexico City, 20 May.

Quiñones, S. 1998. "Telenovelas: Sexy Soaps Reflect a Changing Mexico." *US/Mexico Business*, December, pp. 41–45.

Quiroz, M.-T. 1996. "Telenovela delirium." *Variety*, October, p. 61.

Reforma. 1997. "Encuentran sus 'miradas'," 17 September, p. 9E.

Sinclair, John. 1999. *Latin American Television: A Global View.* London and New York: Oxford University Press.

Tufte, T. 2000. *Living with the Rubbish Queen: Telenovelas, Culture and Modernity in Brazil.* Luton: University of Luton Press.

Vink, N. 1988. *The Telenovela and Emancipation: A Study on Television and Social Change in Brazil.* Amsterdam: Royal Tropical Institute.

Romancing the Globe

Ibsen Martínez

It was too late for Marimar. By the time she found out that her long-lost father wanted to leave her his vast fortune, she had fallen hopelessly in love with Sergio. The object of her affection was handsome, young, and rich—and the same man who had saved her from the lecherous Nicandro. But, sadly for Marimar, her lover's intentions were not pure; Sergio was using her to get back at his own family.

Marimar's saga, captured in the eponymous Latin American soap opera, kept millions of people around the world glued to their television sets for 148 emotionally charged episodes. Produced and originally screened in Mexico in 1994, *Marimar* became a global phenomenon. It helped propel Mexican pop artist Thalia Sodi, who played the lead role, to global stardom. In the Ivory Coast, it was reported that mosques issued the call to prayer early so that an enthralled population wouldn't miss an episode. When Thalia visited the Philippines, she was received by the president and attracted crowds that rivaled those for the pope.

The success of *Marimar* is far from unique. Accounts of the global impact of Latin American soap operas, or *telenovelas*, are now legion. In post-communist Russia, the Mexican hit *Los Ricos Tambien Lloran* (*The Rich Also Cry*) became the country's top-rated show; roughly 70 percent of the Russian population, more than 100 million people, tuned in regularly. Latin American telenovela stars often find themselves mobbed at airports in places as distant as Poland, Indonesia, and Lebanon. In postwar Bosnia, U.S. diplomats intervened to ensure that the Venezuelan show *Kassandra* could stay on the air in the midst of a tug of war between Bosnian Serb factions for control of the media. In Israel, the Mexican novela *Mirada de Mujer* (*The Gaze of a Woman*) was broadcast with both Hebrew and Russian subtitles to ensure that recent Russian immigrants wouldn't miss an episode. And in the United States, the Latin American shows have become top sellers on Spanish-language networks, which have themselves outpaced English-language networks in some major markets, such as Miami and Los Angeles.

Ibsen Martínez: "Romancing the Globe," first published in *Foreign Policy*, vol. 151 (Nov.–Dec. 2005): 48–56.

In all, about 2 billion people around the world watch telenovelas. For better or worse, these programs have attained a prominent place in the global marketplace of culture, and their success illuminates one of the back channels of globalization. For those who despair that Hollywood or the American television industry dominates and defines globalization, the telenovela phenomenon suggests that there is still room for the unexpected. Indeed, the success of telenovelas is often celebrated as an example of reverse cultural imperialism or, as one academic memorably called it, "Montezuma's Revenge."

But the story does not end there. Telenovelas have ridden the currents of cultural globalization to astonishing success. Now, they are experiencing the complications that come with being part of the cultural establishment. They have spawned local imitators, eager to put a familiar face on tried and true story lines. And their success is luring some of the world's largest entertainment companies.

TOBACCO AND TOOTHPASTE

It is ironic that telenovelas, one of Latin America's most successful exports, originated in what is now its most closed society: Cuba. But, in fact, the small island-nation played a vital role in launching the genre. At the end of the 19th century, Cuba was still a Spanish colony and cigars were a lucrative export. The budding cigar makers' guilds achieved a major improvement in working conditions by creating a new job, the *lector de tabaco*. A worker with a flair for the dramatic would, from a platform in the factory, read novels in installments during the tedious hours of filling, rolling, and shaping tobacco leaves. Nearly all the books were Spanish translations of European social realist novels: Victor Hugo's *Les Misérables*, Honoré de Balzac's *Le Père Goriot*, and Charles Dickens's *A Tale of Two Cities*.

With the dawn of the radio age, serialized melodrama soon took to the airwaves and became known as *culebrones* (serpents), an allusion to their habit of extending themselves indefinitely if they captured a big enough audience. It was only a matter of time before the "radio novel" expanded into the visual realms, and exiles from the Cuban Revolution helped transform the burgeoning taste for serialized novels into the modern telenovela. When Fidel Castro stormed to power in 1959, many Cuban producers, directors, actors, and writers scattered to Argentina, Brazil, Colombia, Mexico, Venezuela, and other parts of Latin America. It was a period of cultural ferment throughout the region. "People and scripts moved around Latin America in the 50s and 60s," says Joseph Straubhaar, a communications professor at the University of Texas. "It's been an export genre for a long time."

After a period of jostling, Televisa in Mexico, Venevisión in Venezuela, and Globo TV in Brazil emerged as the leading producers of telenovelas. During the 1960s, the novelas began to claim the top spots on national television stations. They replaced imported U.S. television shows and movies, turning huge swaths of the population into dedicated viewers. But it was only a partial declaration of cultural independence. U.S. companies sponsored many of the shows and sometimes even had a hand in drafting story lines and themes. Colgate tied a fabulously successful promotion to one of the first Brazilian novelas, *Em Busca da Felicidade* (*In Search of Happiness*), and the early Mexican show *Senda Prohibida* (*Forbidden Path*) was branded as "your Colgate novela." The persistent corporate influence led many Latin American academics to deride the shows as "agents for the creation of a capitalist and consumerist international global village . . . engineered by the U.S. and U.S-allied interests," according to Marina Vujnovic, a researcher at the University of Iowa.

Still, telenovelas were always distinct from U.S. soap operas, and most observers now see them as cultural hybrids. Unlike their North American counterparts, telenovelas have a distinct beginning, middle, and end. Most air daily for a period of between four and six months and culminate in a climactic episode that rights all wrongs. (In comparison, the U.S. soap opera *Guiding Light* first aired in 1952 and is now the longest story ever told on television.) A successful show might spawn a spinoff or sequel, but in most cases, audiences must regularly acquaint themselves with new characters and plotlines. And while U.S. soap operas air during daytime hours with women as their target audience, Latin telenovelas are often prime-time shows, aimed at the whole family.

Telenovelas share key ingredients with their North American cousins. Romance and intrigue are, of course, never in short supply. "There is always a Cinderella in a novela," says Helena Bernardi, director of marketing and sales for Brazil's Globo TV. Colombian telenovela producer Patricio Wills describes the genre as "a couple that wants to have a kiss and a writer who doesn't allow them to for 200 episodes." The physical allure of telenovela casts and the balmy locations where they film haven't hurt either.

But the context in which the romance, intrigue, and beauty play out is distinct from the soap operas of the United States. "It's the journey, it's the struggles, it's the obstacles," says Ramón Escobar, an executive at the Spanish-language network Telemundo. And often, those obstacles are poverty, class conflict, and institutional instability, something U.S. soaps ignore. "[U.S. soaps] do not have a historical, political, or social framework, like unemployment or inflation," says Globo's Bernardi. Indeed, one of the leading theories for the global success of novelas is their comfort with characters who are not affluent and are sometimes even poor. The place of struggling women, in particular, is a well-worn telenovela plotline. *Simplemente María* (*Simply Maria*), a classic telenovela that has been remade in several Latin American countries, features a poor girl from the countryside who arrives in the city and struggles to make a living as a seamstress. "*Simplemente María* is the founding myth," says Venezuelan telenovela writer Alberto Barrera Tyszka. "For many years most telenovelas were nothing but variations on its plot and themes."

That focus is not surprising given the poverty that is endemic among Latin American women. Almost half of the 90 million people in the region's female-headed households live in poverty. Women are more likely than men to fall on hard times, and they are more likely to make up the poorest of the poor. In urban areas, 48 percent of women lack their own income (only 22 percent of men do). And so characters such as Maria are often condemned by the scriptwriters to live in the most extreme poverty until a sudden twist of fate restores them to their rightful place. In many cases, the twist comes in the form of an unexpected inheritance, which is still seen as the way to get rich in most Latin American countries.

Plots that rely on such reversals of fortune resonate in cultures accustomed to economic uncertainty. Latin America is one of the more economically volatile regions in the world. Argentina's recent history provides ample evidence that losing everything is a persistent worry, even in relatively well-off societies. During that country's 2001 economic crisis, half the population went to bed as middle-class bank depositors and woke up all but destitute. In this environment, people rarely find succor from the government or the justice system. This institutional weakness in many parts of Latin America may explain why law and order themes—so popular among U.S. viewers—have limited appeal abroad and never took hold in telenovelas.

If novelas often draw on the harsh realities of life in parts of Latin America, their plotlines still generally devolve into sentimental fairy tales. Happy endings are all but certain. The emotion and melodrama of the genre beg the question of whether they are anything more than distractions for the disaffected. Telenovelas endure withering criticism from Latin American elites, who are often embarrassed to see them as one of the region's most successful cultural exports. Arturo Uslar Pietri, a prominent Venezuelan novelist and essayist, expressed what many Latin American elites still feel when he described telenovelas as "the opium of the poor."

Condemning the genre as a whole, however, glosses over what a tailored commodity it has become. As scripts and templates were swapped and sold within Latin America, local tastes and tolerances came into play. Over time, national producers developed their own distinctive styles that departed from or modified the traditional story lines. Mexican novelas became known for their melodrama. Brazilian novelas leaned toward hard-hitting social realism and even tackled contentious social issues, including biotechnology, sex, drug use, and ethnic relations. It was a style that didn't always go over well in other parts of the region. The edgy Globo TV novela *Angel Malo* (*Bad Angel*) underwent a thorough cleansing before appearing on screens in far more conservative Chile.

As the Latin networks hit their stride in the 1960s and 1970s, they began exporting content to the growing and relatively affluent Latino population in the United States—the richest Hispanics in the world. The U.S.-based network Univision, for example, has imported hundreds of telenovelas from Mexico, Brazil, Colombia, and Venezuela. In 2004 alone, it paid $105 million in licensing fees to the Mexican network Televisa. For its part, Brazil's Globo TV has exported dozens of novelas to networks in Portugal. Culturally, the success of Latin telenovelas with Spanish- and Portuguese-speaking communities was not surprising. But what happened next was a twist worthy of a novela script. Somehow, the often sneered-at melodramas leapt out of their cultural zones and raced around the globe.

CONQUERING THE EAST

When communism fell, television executives in Eastern Europe and the former Soviet Union faced a crisis. For decades, turning the television dial brought viewers nothing but state-approved programming. In other words, they had no shows that people actually liked to watch. Nor did these former communist-controlled networks have the budgets to purchase U.S. or European programming wholesale.

The makers of telenovelas saw an opportunity. "Telenovela producers were visionary enough to offer [eastern European] stations very good deals," says Patrick Jucaud, general manager of DISCOP, an organization that promotes telenovelas in the region. "These stations didn't have any money... and Latin American companies were the first ones to help them get started." The quality was relatively high given the price. Telenovelas, after all, attract the top acting talent in Latin America. Rather than being a résumé builder, as is the case with American soaps, a telenovela spot is often the apex of a Latin American actor's career. And recurring themes—rising from poverty, coping with economic hardship—seemed to resonate in countries struggling to emerge from state socialism. "When you're looking at countries that are rapidly industrializing, rapidly urbanizing, with all the attendant stresses and strains on the family and personal relationships, something produced in Brazil or Mexico may be a lot more relevant to Russians in the 90s than an American sitcom, which is frothy and all about L.A.," says Straubhaar, the University of Texas professor.

Telenovelas conquered Russia in a matter of weeks. Discussing the early success of *The Rich Also Cry*, the *Moscow Times* wrote "when the film started, streets became desolate, crowds gathered in stores selling TV sets, tractors stopped in the fields, and guns fell silent on the Azerbaijani-Armenian front." Without breaking a sweat, *Los Ricos* outperformed the imported U.S. soap *Santa Barbara*, which ran at the same time in much of Russia. Central and eastern Europe also fell to the novela charm. *A Escrava Isaura* (*Isaura, the Slave*), a historical Brazilian telenovela about the slave trade, received top honors in Poland. In some cases, telenovelas even sparked civic activism. Townspeople in the Serbian town of Kucevo—so overwrought that they hurdled the boundary between reality and fantasy—drafted a letter to the Venezuelan government pleading the case of the title character in the hit show *Kassandra*. In the Czech Republic, restaurants that did not have televisions reportedly emptied out when the Venezuelan show *Esmeralda* aired.

This large-scale expansion into central and eastern Europe represented a new leap forward for the industry. And as international revenue poured in, production at the leading studios became more lavish. In 1995, Brazil's Globo TV—which claims to have sold telenovelas to more than 120 countries—opened a brand new facility with Hollywood-quality technology. High-end Globo episodes can now cost as much as $100,000. The quality of the programs produced by the telenovela powerhouses has become a principal selling point.

The realization that telenovelas could succeed beyond their cultural spheres ramped up competition in the industry. Production companies that once focused on their national markets found themselves in competition for foreign-market share. Lesser-known telenovela producers dove into the export market in search of fast money, leading to occasional charges of unfair pricing and "dumping" of content. Brazilian and Mexican leaders Globo TV and Televisa, for example, were startled when Argentine and Colombian novelas met with international success.

Some themes covered in telenovelas, to be sure, have fallen flat outside of Latin America. The show *Clase 406*, for example, touched on issues including drugs and rape. "We could never put it on the air in [eastern Europe]—never. We really tried and we couldn't," said Claudia Sahab, Televisa's director of sales for Europe, at a recent industry seminar. The steamy sex scenes in some novelas have roused the censors in more conservative countries, forcing studios to produce edited versions. Program executives in Indonesia pulled the popular show *Esmeralda* off the air because a particularly devious character bore the name of the prophet Muhammad's daughter.

Some observers of the industry worry that shows deemed "too local" have been sanitized so as not to risk international revenue streams. But for the major telenovela producers, the domestic market is still the main course, and export revenue is gravy. "[Telenovela producers] get their investment back quickly on the domestic market which allows them to make money on the international markets," says Thomas Tufte, a European academic who studies the industry. The most serious challenge to the dominance of Latin telenovelas is not watered-down content but the hungry new players entering the market.

THE PRICE OF SUCCESS

"Local always wins," is a mantra of the entertainment industry, and producers in eastern Europe, Russia, and Asia are eager to prove it. Whereas five years ago overseas networks gobbled up ready-made telenovelas, many are now dropping that business model in favor of developing their own local productions for export. The Philippine network ABS-CBN, for example, exported its own telenovela-style dramas to Cambodia, Cameroon, Kenya, and Malaysia in 2004. Taiwanese novellas—often called "chinovelas"—have had success throughout Asia and have been particularly popular in the Philippines, where Spanish-language novelas had long ruled. "Now we have something to compare the Spanish novelas to," a Philippine professor told the local press. "These new shows deal with conflicts that Filipinos can relate to, like going out with friends and getting into trouble."

Some small networks in eastern Europe have opted to simply hire away scriptwriters from Latin America. Alicia Carvajal, who worked as a telenovela writer and director for almost 20 years, was stunned when the Croatian network HTV offered her a job. "Why me?" she asked. "I don't even speak Croatian!" But her success with the hit show *La Duda* (*Doubt*) convinced Croatian executives that she did speak the international language of melodrama. And so Carvajal, still based in Mexico City, went to work on *Villa Maria*, a show touching on the fall of communism in the former Yugoslavia. It aired simultaneously in Bosnia, Croatia, and Serbia and has already netted several honors.

In some cases, established Latin American producers enter into coproductions with local studios in an effort to foster local influences without forfeiting profits entirely. Brazil's Globo, for example, has reportedly considered forging ties with Indian producers, creating the possibility of an alliance between the developing world's two largest entertainment industries. In other cases, outside production companies pay licensing fees for the rights to a script, which can be adapted to the tastes of the local audience. The Colombian megahit *Betty la*

Fea (*Betty the Ugly*), for example, caught the eye of Michael Grindon, president of Sony Pictures Television International. He persuaded Sony's Hindi channel to license the program and air a local version. According to Nyay Bhushan, an Indian correspondent for the *Hollywood Reporter*, the remake "has spawned a merchandising and marketing bonanza." Sony also teamed up with a Russian studio to produce *Poor Anastasia*, based loosely on *Betty la Fea*.

Sony's emergence as a player in the telenovela world heralds the arrival of the entertainment industry's big guns—and a potentially important shift of cultural flows. "The biggest and most important producers in the world have become interested in the telenovela," says Carlos Bardasano, vice president of the Cisneros Group and president of Venevisión Continental. No longer willing to see Latin American production studios reap all the profits, major conglomerates have begun to produce their own telenovelas. In 2003, European giant FremantleMedia teamed up with NBC-owned Telemundo to film *La Ley de Silencio* (*The Law of Silence*) in Houston. Telemundo, the second largest Spanish-language network in the United States, has decided against importing shows from Latin America (as its competitor Univision does). "Now [telenovelas] move north to south," says Ramón Escobar, the Telemundo executive. "That's creating a tremendous amount of competition in the international market." The network is banking on the multinational flavor of its shows—it uses actors from all over Latin America—and the glimpses of Latino life in the United States that it can offer. Another hint that the cultural currents may be shifting is the success of ABC's *Desperate Housewives* in parts of Latin America. Argentine and Chilean networks are vying to make local versions of its provocative premise, and a half dozen other regional networks may soon follow.

For the moment, U.S. and European media conglomerates are still minor characters. Telemundo's novelas, for example, have not yet seriously challenged the Mexican novelas shown on Univision. Globo TV's reputation as the world leader in high-quality telenovelas is undiminished. But the industry is changing fast, and the entrance of the world's media giants into the fray may soon test the theory that the global appeal of telenovelas derives from the economic and cultural environment in which they were born. Is there really something unique about the Latin American experience—or can their success be duplicated by Hollywood studios? Will the Latin American networks maintain their hard-won empire, or will the rich relatives from abroad snatch away their success? Will the torrid affair between novelas and Czechs, Filipinos, and Russians continue? Or will the long-distance relationship fall apart? The story, as always, is to be continued.

Understanding Telenovelas as a Cultural Front: A Complex Analysis of a Complex Reality

Jorge González

The social phenomenon of televised melodramas, called telenovelas in Spanish, can be taken as a perfect example of a complex symbolic form in contemporary societies. Every day, all over the world, millions of people from all social groups watch Latin American telenovelas. There are a number of differences and nuances between Latin telenovelas and their electronic "cousin," the soap opera. Nevertheless, the two genres are closely related. In this brief paper, I will stress only some traits of a major theoretical and methodological framework that I call *cultural fronts* (González, 1997, 2001) which serves to analyse and bring into partial scientific visibility this global and local phenomenon.

The cultural fronts approach gives us a more detailed look at the sociocultural phenomenon of telenovelas. At least three interwoven social processes are involved. Telenovelas:

- construct *symbolic commonalities* between different social agents and cultures;
- create and re-create a set of different *possible worlds*;
- enact *symbolic struggles* for defining *elementary human* cultural elements within those possible worlds.

MELODRAMA AS A SOCIAL EXPERIENCE

Contemporary melodrama typically narrates tales in which, after a number of problematic events, misunderstandings and sufferings, the main character—a hero or a heroine (who is normally a good and tender-hearted

---

Jorge González: "Understanding Telenovelas as a Cultural Front: A Complex Analysis of a Complex Reality," first published in *Media International Australia*, vol. 106, num. 2 (2003): 84–93.

young woman)—comes to a happy ending. The audience are well aware of the outcome. But they want to know *how* that ending will be produced and delayed—what forms of suspense will delay the resolution of the problem until the very end. That has been the structure of melodrama throughout Latin American cultural history. At least in the twentieth century in Mexico, that cultural genre has taken and used several formats, from comic books to television, including music like the *corridos*, photo-novels, radionovelas, movies, popular theatrical plays and television. With the technical possibilities of electronic transmission and formatting, both of radio and then of television, there has been an evolution of the genre in terms of the length and the organisation of the production of these melodramas.

Telenovelas as serial melodramas have evolved particularly into a style of content that appeals to larger audiences. A normal melodramatic plot produced in a film can last at most two hours. A story sung and narrated through a *corrido* can last at most four or five minutes. In radio and television, the development and resolution of the plot can last six months or, in the case of soap operas, several years. This process implies the construction of an interesting relationship of *fidelity* with the audience. They follow every single detail of the slow development of the plot every day. Because of these specific historical traits, in order to understand telenovelas we have to deal with at least three main topics of interest: the process of their *production*; the specificity of the *discourse and texts* of telenovelas; and the process of *social reading and interpretation*.

It should be noted that telenovelas are a complete industrial product, produced by large and complex media corporations like Televisa (Mexico), TeveGlobo (Brazil), Venevisión (Venezuela), Caracol (Colombia), more recently TV Azteca (Mexico) and some others. Thousands of professionals (writers, actors, technicians, scene directors, musicians, editors, advertisers) work everyday in specialised production crews and corporate departments to create and sell telenovelas all over the world. Since 1970, the international market for telenovelas has grown. First it spread into the Spanish-speaking countries of Latin America, following the common cultural market of Spanish-narrated fiction, especially into the radio and music (1930s), cinema (1940s) and publishing (1950s) industries. Since then, the telenovela has spread to a wide range of countries and cultures.

Joe Straubhaar (1998) has studied different processes of "cultural proximity" behind the understanding of success of this kind. It is clear that the strongest single international market for Mexican telenovelas is the massive Spanish-speaking population of the United States (more than 20 million people). What is striking about this is that it is a rare example of an industrial global product coming from the periphery of the world system to be sold in the "centre." It is in part a slight counterbalance of the "normal" flow North-South of technology and industrial fiction as evidenced by the movie industries (Hollywood), music (MTV) and television series such as *Friends, South Park, National Geographic, Bay Guardians, Queer as Folk, The Sopranos* and Japanese cartoons. The development of first local and then global success by peripheral media industries is itself a major topic, as Sinclair (1998) has pointed out. Here we examine how very different tastes and symbolic ecologies have adopted and adapted a wide range of symbolic forms, especially the serial fiction of *possible worlds* provided by telenovelas.

Behind this phenomenon lies a complex process that leads us to consider communication as a complex cultural experience. As shown in Figure 1, we can identify at least two different strategies that link media corporations and social audiences. Strategies of *organisational anticipation* are confronted by and negotiated with *social strategies of multicontextual interpretation*.

Let us begin with organisational factors. It is necessary to deal with a multidimensional set of actions, interactions and representations that converge in different strategies of organisational anticipation. This kind of anticipation actually operates as a clear *symbolic vector*, oriented and specified before, during and after a complex internal process of conflict, struggle and negotiation occurring at different levels in the organisation. Anticipation is considered and produced as a *vector*—that is, a strength with specific institutional orientation—implying that there are a number of negotiations of power relationships within one organisation. In television, interest groups and specialised production areas such as News, Special Events, Magazines, Series and Sports are constantly struggling for the best programming time, advertising fares, merchandising and budgets, and for increasing the limits of tolerance of the *corporate risk* allowed to each area. If the production is not earning *enough* (that *"enough"* marks the fixed and negotiated limit into the corporation normally defined by quantitative ratings and share), that product is simply terminated.

It seems clear that this set of internal power relationships produces a number of micro resistances and micro strategies that finally have to be "tuned" in order to capture the precious *bio-time* of the audience. Under these conditions, there is room for almost any symbolic tactic to gain audience attention (nudes, violence, reality shows, sex, vivid colours, slang, easy listening and viewing, superstars, instant mosaics of forms, sounds, linguistic textures and fashions).

On the lower side of Figure 1, we can see an unranked cluster of arrows. Each arrow represents a rich variety, but not organised strategies of interpretation. Interpretation presupposes anticipation. The process of social interpretation can be understood as deriving from strategies of anticipation within the social networks. Audiences must be able to anticipate and recognise the selected symbolic form. The ability to do so is linked to social position, social trajectories, social networks established over time and so on. The very complexity of those factors, together with ethnicity, language and social conditions such as migration, make it almost impossible for the corporate vector to fit exactly with the audience anticipation. Hence a wide and variable zone of symbolic struggle and resistance emerges. Two processes can be identified: audience anticipation limits the specific symbolic forms that institutions can produce; on the other hand, there is a clash between corporate strategies and the rather disparate and non-convergent strategies used as people interpret the program.

The multidirectional arrows also represent diverse processes of non-organised social interpretation and elaboration of the symbolic vectors in society. Those forces should not be considered as vectors, because they do not

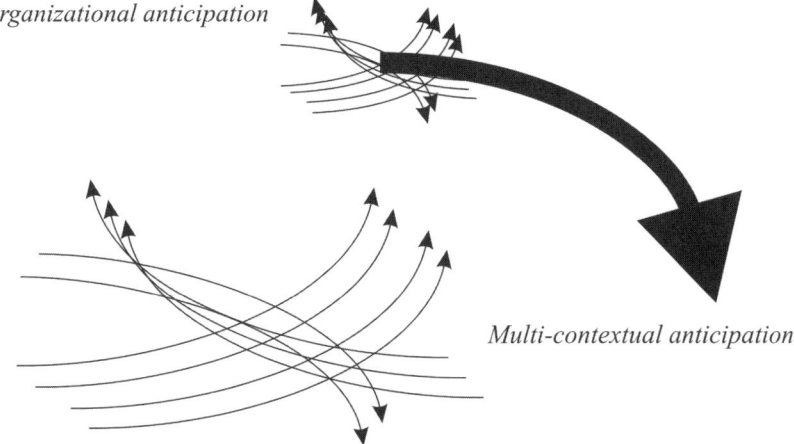

Figure 1: Communication as a negotiation of complex strategies

have any centralised direction, but anyway tend to create and re-create convergent social identities. Within the cultural fronts approach, we can relocate these two processes as strategies of centring and decentring social meanings and creating and re-creating commonalities between very different social positions in a given society. This is a complex process.

First, cultural fronts are *multidimensional*, rather than one-dimensional, objects. They are subject to an *infinite game of interactions* and retro-actions, instead of changes in a unique variable. Second, by grounding the model in *complexity*, we admit:

- the recognition of the *solidarity of phenomena*, instead of the isolation and separation of them;
- a *high degree of uncertainty* and fuzziness, instead of clear boundaries;
- confronting clusters of contradictions, instead of certainties.

The alternative *simplistic* picture implies:

- a view which reduces the factors and loses the multiplicity of levels of relationships and dimensions of connectivity of the object;
- poor elaboration that normally implies a *miscasting* of problems.

Again, I am not pretending to offer here a complete and documented view of the telenovela phenomenon, but only to point out some of the richness that lies beneath an oversimplistic (mis)understanding of this symbolic and complex process.

We consider three different levels and dimensions of telenovelas as a symbolic and complex form: telenovela production; telenovelas as complex texts; and telenovelas and their social readings and appropriations.

UNDERSTANDING TELENOVELA PRODUCTION: LEVELS OF ANALYSIS

We propose five levels of analysis implying five different sets of observables in the process of production of telenovelas:

1. *Professional producers.* Detailed ethnographic studies of different telenovelas production crews are required to identify the specificity of the professional tasks required for creating a telenovela. But, in order to describe this set of processes adequately, we need to identify another level of analysis that operates as the corporation link of all the single production crews.
2. *Production control.* In this stage, we need to identify the relationships that unify all the organisational production of telenovelas. Again, the ethnographic descriptions of this level should produce thicker descriptions of rules, limits, risks, assignments, reports, decision-taking, budget and resources distribution and the maintaining of a sort of *professional ideology* or "ethics" and constructed meaning of what represents a successful production from the corporation point of view.
3. *Organisational context.* We need historical documentary information and in-depth interviews with actual and former decision-makers to estimate the *relative weight* of telenovela production *vis-à-vis* broader television products.
4. *Cultural field of production.* We can focus first on *"popular" entertainment* and second on the complete field of *specialised cultural production*. Some of the most prevalent prejudices and myths against the telenovela phenomenon come as a result of claims of cultural agents and producers in specific socio-historical spaces, such as a nation.
5. *The world market of television fiction.* We identify different flows and export of telenovelas as against other forms of serial fiction bought by different companies or countries.

UNDERSTANDING TELENOVELAS AS A COMPLEX SYMBOLIC FORM

The very text of the telenovelas as a symbolic form necessitates discussion of four dimensions of its *form* and *content*. Telenovelas are always a human narrative and should be, at least, *plausible* and *believable* in real social life. The primary form of the telenovela is the script that must be interpreted by the director and actors with the help of a number of professional techniques and tools that define a fourfold scheme including narration, meaning, argumentative logic and proposed social actions. We will follow a classic exploration of the telenovelas as a symbolic form through its syntactic structure, its semantics, its argumentation logics and its pragmatic resolution of conflicts and interactions.

A *stylistic* analysis of telenovela television form tends to identify a certain *style of narrating* using an audio-visual language (two-shots, close ups, medium shots), including the kind of camera movements (zoom in and out, travelling, panning, dolly in), the accents and special marks (musical accents and themes designed for each character identification and for the enhancement and recognition of key scenes and parts, produced and codified for the anticipation of the telenovela's viewers). Over almost five decades of TV drama, there are some *rules* and *audio-visual grammar* that identify the genre.

A *semantic analysis* of the plot will give us a clear understanding of the processes and changes underlying the narration process. Using the tools of the semiotics of narration, we can identify the syntax and meaning of the transformations that are in the core of the story. Thematic and semantic roles are to be connected with the syntactic structures of the different elements of the specific telenovela story.

An *argumentation analysis* of the plot, including findings of the stylistic and the semantic levels, will give us the specific logic of arguments that are presented as meaningful in the plot. We will try to identify certain paths of *argumentation* presented in the telenovelas. Describing the key arguments and establishing their proposed connections will produce a configuration map in which all the argumentation logics of the telenovelas are displayed.

Using the tools of the *pragma-linguistic analysis* as a fourth approach to the specificity of telenovelas, we will describe the taxonomy of social situations (including at least actors, actions, time, space and goals) presented and narrated in the telenovelas. This analysis begins with a *demography of the fictional participants* and with an *ethnography of the social situations*. There is also a limited set of social situations "preferred" by telenovela writers: poor and beautiful but tender women, rich men, bad stepmothers, good priests, incidental doctors, faithful servants, decadent aristocrats, interacting in rich mansions, large haciendas, including limited classes of objects and social positions that can be perfectly described using the social tools of a demographic and ethnographic analysis. By identifying the social situations presented and solved in the plot of the telenovelas, we have a powerful tool for relating the three previous levels in order to produce and offer a thicker description of the specific symbolic form of the telenovelas. This in turn links to production decisions.

UNDERSTANDING SOCIAL INTERPRETATIONS OF TELENOVELA

Probably the most intriguing and fuzzy area of the telenovela phenomenon is the way in which social agents relate symbolically with this industrial and cultural product. The key point is to describe and identify at least part of these dispersed arrows that describe the social strategies of anticipation and interpretation of the social situations presented, narrated and solved in telenovelas. In order to attain that goal, we employed a twofold strategy. First, we undertook a quantitative study to establish features and properties of telenovelas in Mexican society. Second, an ethnographic study was carried out to examine the ways in which different Mexican households relate to television and telenovelas in their everyday life. Through a quantitative survey analysis, we produced a social description of the most elementary figures of the phenomenon. The first attempt was organised in six Mexican cities from the east coast to the west coast (Veracruz, Puebla, México, León, Guadalajara and Colima) (González, 1992).[1] Once we had a first sketch of the social relevance and distribution of the cultural practice of following telenovelas, we made a detailed ethnographic analysis of households in which watching television and telenovelas was a common practice of everyday life. We tried to determine the relative weight of the habits of watching telenovelas in the household routine. We devoted 10 months of detailed participant observation to that. One of our most important findings both in the survey and in the ethnography was that the cultural experience of the telenovelas does not "begin" with the episode and does not end with the the conclusion of the single daily showing. All the evidence points towards an *extended universe* of telenovelas.

That ubiquity of telenovelas showed the *cultural genre* as one of the most important symbolic forms used in everyday social life. The detailed observation of households found that viewing telenovelas was the most important time when the whole family was together. In spite of the normal prejudices held towards telenovelas, we found complex reactions. At times, people surrender to the intrigue and plot, and at others experience forms of critical distancing. We also found that many women who normally invest their lifetime in serving others treat watching a telenovela as a time that is sacred, untouchable and not negotiable. Moreover, they compared characters in the telenovelas with themselves in terms of emotional attitudes, dressing styles or manners. In effect, there are a number of processes of appropriation, social use, consumption, interpretation and shared meaning going far beyond the simplistic statements about this genre (Covarrubias et al., 1992).[2]

FIVE SOCIAL AND "SCIENTIFIC" MYTHS

As a result of the research, we challenge five myths about telenovelas, based on unconscious ideologies. The ideologies have led to the scientific invisibility, not only of telenovelas but of a number of key cultural practices. The ideologies have the following traits:

- *socio-centric*, claiming that the real culture is only the culture of a dominant social class. The lower classes have bad or no *taste* at all;
- *ethnocentric*, claiming that the only valid and prevalent values and behaviours are those of Western (European and American) lifestyles;
- *youth-centric*, disqualifying cultural practices of the elderly;
- *andro-centric*, claiming that the only valid attitudes and cultural practices are male-oriented.

Given this ideological framework, we can easily understand prejudices against telenovelas:

- *"Just for small towns and provincial taste."* Our study showed that telenovelas are watched in very big cities by just over half the population; as the size of the city diminishes, the preference percentages rise to almost 80 per cent. Telenovelas have an intense urban vitality.
- *"Just for women and aged people."* Forty per cent of men interviewed admitted to watching telenovelas; even those 60 per cent of men who denied watching knew a great deal about them.

- *"Just for lazy people."* Unemployed and retired people are those who watch fewest telenovelas. Fifty-five per cent of active students and almost half of professionals and employees are regular viewers.
- *"Low taste of the poor."* Sixty-three per cent of the interviewees of high-class status were constant viewers.
- *"Canned ideological food for the ignorant."* Our data showed that, although the less formally educated people are indeed the ones who watch most telenovelas, better-educated people are also watching.

From this evidence, it is clear that—at least in Mexico—telenovelas are a trans-class cultural phenomenon. We call them a *cultural front*, a space in which different social agents struggle to define and redefine specific commonalities: ideas about the meaning of love, good living, honour, fidelity, cruelty, betrayal, hate, fate, beauty and sexual relationships, all of them linked to different elaborations of basic elementary human drives and necessities. They provide the very core of constructed identity.

TOWARDS A MODEL OF DEEP INTERPRETATION OF TELENOVELAS AND SOCIETY

Our model for the study of telenovelas has prompted us to design and pursue a complex strategy for a complex object. Various and different levels of partial analysis and information inform the specificity of each area. We have identified the three main *elements* of the process, but now, in order to get a deeper understanding of the phenomenon, we have to work with the relations between each area.

Figure 2 shows the lines of relating our three different approaches to telenovelas in a model of deeper interpretation. Once we have identified variables of the three main areas of inquiry—that is, Production (P), Text (T) and Readings (R)—a Deep Interpretation (DI) can be constructed by defining the relationships and links between the elements (P, T, R).

Using that second-order relationship, finally we can establish a renewed and deeper gaze over the single elements (P, T, R) that integrate a higher level of interpretation of the object. We can follow those *second-order* relationships through a matrix of logic contingencies, as Figure 3 shows.

The first-order information defined the specificity of the three elements considered (PP) Production, (TT) Text and (RR) Social Readings. Now we can develop a set of six *second-order* levels of questions and observables:

1. PT: influences from *production to the text*.
2. PR: flows coming from *production* over the *social readings*.
3. TP: effects of the *text* over the *production*.
4. TR: constraints from the text to the *social readings*.
5. RP: retro-actions from the social readings to *production*.
6. RT: interactions coming from the *social readings* to the *text*.

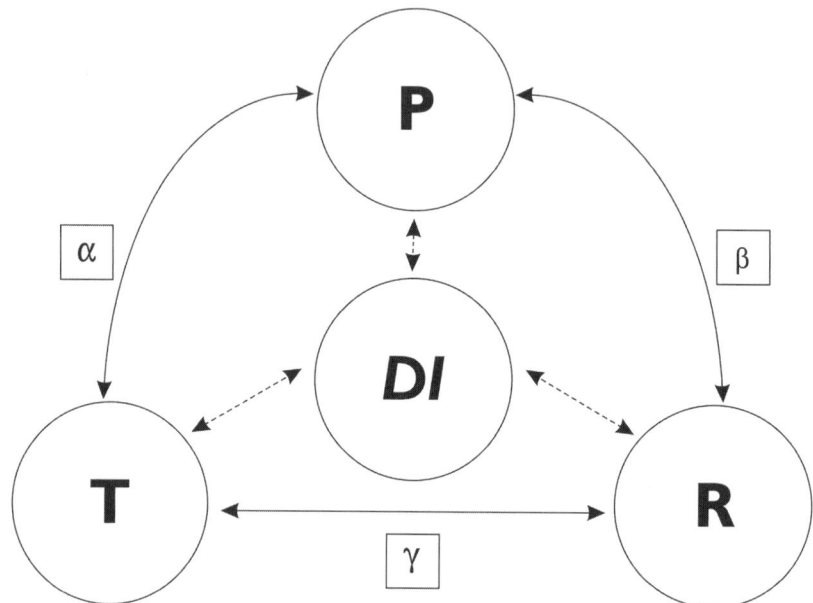

Figure 2: A model for deep interpretation of telenovelas

That framework can be further completed when we take a *third-order* level of inquiring by following the flows in triads between P, T and R like this:

1. PTR: threads from Production to Text yielding *Social Readings*.
2. PRT: threads from Production to Social Readings yielding *Text*.
3. TPR: threads from Text to Production yielding *Social Readings*.
4. TRP: threads from Text to Social Readings yielding *Production*.
5. RPT: threads from Social Readings to Production yielding *Text*.
6. RTP: threads from Social Readings to Text yielding *Production*.

	P	T	R
P	**PP**	*PT*	*PR*
T	*TP*	**TT**	*TR*
R	*RP*	*RT*	**RR**

Figure 3: Matrix of contingencies for deep interpretation of telenovelas

Through this model, we now have 12 different *logics*, or theoretical relationships, constructed over our first three elements. We can find empirical examples for any of these threads and by so doing will increase our abilities to question the object.

It is clear that we need to produce and facilitate a number of different resources and observables in order to completely fulfil the whole model. And probably we will never get all the information needed, but at least we can use the DI model to understand in a more complete and complex way a very complex and relevant socio-symbolic practice like telenovelas in society.

CONCLUSIONS: RETHINKING TELENOVELAS

We can identify a vital symbolic process in multiple social networks, constantly creating clashing flows and social appropriations of the telenovelas as a cultural experience. Some can be understood as *strategies of resistance* which yield the description of telenovelas as a cultural front. Telenovelas demarcate a *symbolic border* between cultures that points towards different appropriations of those meanings by social groups and classes. The social definitions of these common social meanings between contrasted social agents open the symbolic space of telenovelas as a struggling *arena* in which different social modes of interpretation are in a symbolic contest for defining and redefining common *social meanings* created and re-created by means of the elaboration of *transclass* symbolic formations. That struggle in a cultural front is always over a *symbolic occupied territory* that different social agents try constantly to reoccupy by means of their own elaboration of the commonalities present in the front. The clash and turbulences of different forces trying to void and re-fill a specific *symbolic occupied territory* mark the historic success or failure of more or less organised social agents. Following these guidelines, we can conclude for now that, in Mexico, the television industry has become the central "giver" of fame, charisma and social "visibility" (symbolic capital) in society. Telenovelas are a very complex reality that deserves a very complex, collective and comparative approach for understanding an interesting trait of twenty-first-century globalisation.

NOTES

1. It should be said that this first study, conducted in 1985, initially had no official support from Mexican research agencies, because by that time the subject was considered "not scientifically relevant." Later on, I will talk about the social prejudices that created a scientific invisibility of kind of objects.

2. More recently, during the 1990s and using an approach of discussion groups, a network of young scholars studied the changes in the format of Mexican telenovelas analysing the enormous success of a different telenovelas (*Mirada de Mujer*) produced by Argos and broadcast nationwide by TV Azteca. In that telenovelas, the main character (María Inés) and the whole plot showed a very different way of producing and understanding telenovelas, especially by contesting the "normal" roles assigned to married women. The study focused on the social representations from the readings and appropriation of Mexican women touched by this telenovelas (Covarrubias et al., 2001).

REFERENCES

Covarrubias, Karla, A. Bautista, and Ana Uribe. 1992. *Cuéntame, ¿en qué se quedó?, telenovelas y familias en México*. Mexico: Editorial Trillas.

——— 2001. "Hacia una nueva cultura televisiva: La telenovela Mirada de Mujer en la percepción de los públicos colimenses. Resultados de investigación." *Estudios sobre las Culturas Contemporáneas*, Epoca II, vol. VII, pp. 89–126.

González, Jorge. 1992. "The Cofraternity of (Un)finishable Emotions. Constructing Mexican Telenovelas." *Studies in Latin American Popular Culture*, vol. 11.

——— 1997. "The Willingness to Weave: Cultural Analysis, Cultural Fronts and Networks of the Future." *Media Development*, vol. 1, no. XLIV.

——— 2001. "Cultural Fronts: Towards a Dialogical Understanding of Contemporary Cultures," in James Lull, ed., *Culture in the Communication Age*. London: Routledge.

Sinclair, John. 1998. "Geolinguistic Region as Global Space: The Case of Latin America," paper presented to the IAMCR 21st conference, Glasgow, 26–30 July.

Straubhaar, Joseph. 1998. "Cultural Capital, Travel and Cultural Proximity in the Globalization of Television," paper presented at "Crossroads in Cultural Studies" conference, June/July 98, Tampere, Finland.

Opening America?
The Telenovela-ization of U.S. Soap Operas

Denise D. Bielby and C. Lee Harrington

The global market for syndicated television programming remains the focus of considerable debate by media scholars and policy leaders concerned with television's impact on national culture. A central theme in this debate is the dominance of the United States in the international marketplace (Nordenstreng and Varis 1974; Varis 1986). However, a burgeoning line of scholarship challenges the theoretical and empirical relevance of the cultural imperialism thesis for understanding the state of the television industry worldwide (see, e.g., Pool 1977; Antola and Rogers 1984; Hoskins and Mirus 1988; Sinclair, Jacka, and Cunningham 1996). According to Sinclair, Jacka, and Cunningham (1996), television's appeal is resolutely local, not global, and it circulates largely through exchange within geolinguistic regions. Moreover, they observe, as television programming crosses borders not only do audiences generate unanticipated meanings, the product undergoes a dynamic process of "cultural syncretism" that modifies genre conventions almost beyond recognition. "The resulting situation is not the passive homogenization of world television which cultural imperialism theorists feared, but rather its heterogenization" (Sinclair, Jacka, and Cunningham 1996, 13). A comprehensive understanding of these local adaptations calls for a middle-range theoretical approach (Cunningham and Jacka 1994) that foregrounds practices by the industry through which programming is made available to audiences.

The United States is the undisputed leader in exported television, and that fact has tended to suppress inquiry into the ways in which its dominance in the global arena is affected as the industry adapts its products for export (Bielby and Harrington 2002) and as the products are consumed by audiences in other countries (Sinclair, Jacka, and Cunningham 1996). Moreover, while research on the export of U.S. television programs has focused almost exclusively on their "one-way flow," relatively little scholarly attention has been devoted to the reverse: how programming from abroad fares in the United

---

Authors' Note: This article was prepared for publication in 2002.
Denise D. Bielby and C. Lee Harrington: "Opening America? The Telenovela-ization of U.S. Soap Operas," first published in *Television and New Media*, Vol. 6, Issue 4, 383–99.

States. As part of a larger project on the international market for exported television, our analysis examines the impact of Latin American *telenovelas* on the U.S. daytime soap opera genre. In particular, we consider how shifts during the past decade in the demographics of the U.S. population and changes in practices and tastes of television audiences have affected how the U.S. soap opera industry has adapted to competition from other countries. Our analysis contributes to the theoretical and empirical "opening up" of the cultural imperialism approach by considering how the U.S. television industry is influenced by program trends from abroad.

THE SOAP OPERA GENRE

Uniquely capable of drawing a large and loyal viewer base, serial narratives are argued to be a global cultural form in that they are "a narrative mode *produced* in a variety of countries across the globe" and are "one of the most exported forms of television *viewed* in a range of cultural contexts" (Barker 1997, 75). While Americans are most familiar with seriality in the form of daytime soap operas, there is such a diversity of serial forms worldwide that the genre itself is increasingly difficult to define. Most commonly, serials are divided into two main types based on the presence or absence of narrative closure. Open-ended storytelling is associated with serials produced in the United States, Great Britain, and Australia, while closed-ended serials are more characteristic of Latin America, India, Japan, China, South Africa, and elsewhere (Allen 1997, 112). Serials can also be divided thematically and/or structurally. O'Donnell (1999, 4–5) suggests that one type of serial engages primarily with emotions or melodrama (such as Mexican, Venezuelan, and U.S. serials) while others engage more explicitly with political and social issues (such as Brazilian and Colombian serials). Finally, Liebes and Livingstone (1998, 153) argue that three prototypical forms or models can be applied to different countries' soaps: dynastic soaps (focusing on one powerful family), community soaps (focusing on a number of equal, separate families and characters), and dyadic soaps (focusing on romantic entanglements, disentanglements, and re-entanglements).

These distinctions between forms or models do not imply, of course, that the serial genre (or any genre) has a fixed set of conventions or impermeable boundaries. Genres are not fixed and immutable. Rather, genres evolve and new ones appear "by transgressing the formulae of their predecessors" (Cunningham, Miller, and Rowe 1994, 14). Genres are socially constructed through relationships between artists and audiences in specific social, historical, and ideological contexts, and they are modified as they are produced and received (Fiske 1987; Griswold 1987; Taylor 1989).[1] Explains Gledhill, "we find a sliding of conventions from one genre to another according to changes in production and audiences. This sliding of conventions is a prime source of generic evolution" (1997, 357). In this article, we explore factors contributing to, and implications of, one such evolution: the "telenovela-ization" of U.S. soap operas.

WHY EVOLVE? THE U.S. INDUSTRY CONTEXT

U.S. daytime soap operas air five days per week, fifty-two weeks per year, are only rarely repeated by their home networks,[2] and can remain in production for decades.³ Since their transition from radio to television in the 1950s, soap operas have been a reliable source of revenue for the U.S. television networks. Despite their continued low cultural status (because they target the female audience and are regarded as women's texts), soaps' enduring popularity and resulting profit-making potential have consistently paid for other less popular or more expensive forms of network programming. Indeed, soaps have arguably been the single best "deal" in the history of American television, "serving large audiences at comparatively low costs and providing an impressive yield for its investment" (Matelski 1999, 2). During the past two decades, however, changes in the paid labor market, increasingly limited leisure time, expanded channel capacity, the growth of the Internet, and the growing fickleness of American viewers (among other factors) have contributed to rapidly dwindling domestic audiences for the genre (Allen 1996). The decline in viewership was particularly noticeable in the 1990s. Since 1991, soaps have lost 33 percent of their viewers, and there are 27 percent fewer women between the ages of eighteen and forty-nine (daytime soaps' target audience) watching today than in 1994 (Baldwin 1999).⁴ From an all-time high of nineteen soaps on the air in the 1969–1970 television season, there are currently only ten airing.

Initially, industry members responded to the slide by blaming factors outside the industry. A key target was the months-long, live coverage of the O. J. Simpson preliminary hearing and murder trial in the mid-1990s, which preempted most daytime serials for the duration of the proceedings. If not the O. J. trial, it was the explosion of daytime talk shows; if not talk shows, then the lure of the Internet was blamed for soaps' decline (Foulk 2000, 27). But as ratings continued to fall through the late 1990s, the industry recognized that the lost audience was not going to return and that new strategies were needed to restore its ability to generate revenue for the networks.

Some shows now market merchandise tied to storylines, others have developed online support, and almost all have slashed production costs.⁵ But perhaps the most significant adaptation of consequence to the genre is the courting of the Spanish-speaking audience as a way of bringing in additional revenue. *TV Guide's* resident soaps critic, Michael Logan, succinctly notes, "The Hispanic population has surpassed 35 million, and that vast audience, already nuts for telenovelas, has American soap programmers drooling" (Logan 2002, 36).

As has been well documented, the history of U.S. television is characterized in part by a strong resistance to foreign programming and is "informally closed" to television from other cultures (Allen 1996, 124; see also Barker 1997; Cunningham and Jacka 1994).⁶ Network television continues to be "resolutely monolingual," with virtually all programming directed toward an English-speaking audience (Allen 1996, 124). However, a viewing revolution has taken place in the United States during the past decade. Largely as a result of the expansion of the cable industry, the proportion of the television audience traditionally commanded by the major broadcast networks plummeted. In the 1970s, the share of primetime viewership held by ABC, CBS, and NBC stood at more than 90 percent; by August 1998, that percentage was around 47 percent (Lowry 1998). With the plethora of channels now comprising the multichannel media universe, American audiences have an astonishing array of special-interest networks from which to make viewing choices. The rise of Univisión as the largest Spanish-language cable network in the U.S. (with Telemundo as its chief competitor) is widely attributed to the long-standing neglect of Latino and Latina viewers by the major U.S. networks. Despite efforts to diversify programming in the past few years, telenovelas remain a staple at both Univisión and Telemundo, airing mornings, afternoons, and evenings, and earning consistently high ratings (Barrera and Bielby 2002; Lopez 1995). As such, U.S. networks' burgeoning attempts to woo Latino and Latina viewers face stiff challenge from Spanish-language cable channels.[7]

EVOLVING THE GENRE

The format of the U.S. daytime soap opera genre, which is structured as open-ended narratives that never achieve closure, has remained unchanged since its inception in 1930 (Intintoli 1984; Cassata 1985; LaGuardia 1974). Despite its well-defined characteristics, however, the genre is hardly static. While its basic narrative premise has not changed—soap storylines are structured around the creation, development, and dissolution of increasingly complicated social, familial, and romantic relationships (Allen 1985, 74)—it has undergone "distinct shifts in character, style, and setting" during the past decades (Patterson 1995, 104). Some of these changes have resulted in subgenres, such as soaps that specialize in medical dramas (e.g., ABC's *General Hospital* and the defunct *The Doctors*) or those that incorporate supernatural elements (e.g., NBC's *Passions* and the defunct *Dark Shadows*). Changes have also occurred in lighting and camerawork, such as the unprecedented "prime-time look" of *The City* (ABC) before its cancellation in the mid-1990s. Most notably, the overall focus of daytime soaps has evolved since their early days to celebrate heterosexual romance, marriage, and family life. Indeed, contemporary U.S. soaps have evolved into the best example of what Liebes and Livingstone (1998, 153) refer to as the dyadic model of the serial genre:

> a destabilized network of a number of young, densely interconnected, mostly unigenerational, interchanging couples, with past, present and future romantic ties, continually absorbed in the process of reinventing kinship relations.

Soaps' preoccupation with romantic coupling, decoupling, and recoupling has rendered them particularly resistant to depictions of "otherness" of any kind, whether racial, ethnic, sexual, or religious. As Allen notes, "The problem of including [differences] in soaps is not of working them into plot lines, but of dealing with the paradigmatic consequences of their entry into the community of the soap opera world" (1985, 7).

To understand the significance of the networks' current focus on wooing Latino and Latina viewers, some historical context is useful. Until 1980, the only racial groups represented on daytime shows were African Americans and whites (Cassata and Skill 1983). Although ethnically differentiated groups—such as Poles, Jews, and the Irish—were explicitly incorporated into *One Life to Live* (ABC) when it premiered in 1968 and *Ryan's Hope* (ABC) when it debuted in 1975, Latinos were not introduced as central characters until

1984, when the soap *Santa Barbara* debuted on NBC, with a Mexican American core family. In the 1990s, ABC's *All My Children* and *One Life to Live* introduced core Latino characters, families, and plots, a move that proved popular with the viewers. However, scholars and industry critics (as well as some audience members) considered the characters stereotypical, despite their expanded presence onscreen and best of intentions by head writers (see, e.g., Jenrette, McIntosh, and Winterberger 1999). From a production standpoint, as noted above, narratives that incorporate a multiracial or multiethnic tapestry of characters and plots make writing more complicated because of the added challenge of preserving authenticity in a multicultural context (Allen 1985). Without a demonstrable effect on ratings, then, such adaptations are rarely perceived as worth the expense and extra effort. From the industry's point of view, attempts at multiculturalism were not worth sustaining until the eroding economics of the daytime industry literally forced it to search for additional avenues to expand the audience.

The 2000 U.S. Census revealed that the Hispanic or Latino and Latina population grew by nearly 60 percent in the past decade, with more than 32 million Hispanics currently living in the United States. In total numbers, it has almost caught up with African Americans, the largest racial-ethnic minority group in the United States, and it is expected to surpass them by 2005. The rapid growth of the Hispanic population, half of which is younger than twenty-seven years old, has, in turn, attracted the attention of advertisers seeking to capture the purchasing power of the burgeoning Latino market (Hassell 2001). Responding to the gradual loss of daytime's key demographic audience (women between eighteen and forty-nine years old), at the present time, there are three notable, ongoing developments in network attempts to grow the Hispanic daytime audience.

First, NBC's *Days of Our Lives* and *Passions* began closed-captioning their shows in Spanish in July 2001 (*Soap Opera Digest* 2001a, 14). A second, more significant development is the simulcast of *Bold and the Beautiful* in Spanish and English, from May 2001. This marks the first time a network has used a secondary audio program (which provides Spanish translation) for a daytime serial; the move will make *Bold* available to almost half the Latino homes in the United States (Calvo 2001). *Bold*'s executive producer and head writer, Bradley Bell, made his intentions behind this development explicit when he stated in a recent soap fan magazine, "We're hoping to be the first to capitalize on introducing [the Hispanic] market to American soap operas" (*Soap Opera Digest* 2001c, 6).

The decision to simulcast the show in both English and Spanish coincides with the addition of a new central Latino character, "Antonio," who is tied to the core family through marriage to one of their daughters. Whether this character will truly amount to a breakthrough in nonstereotypic ethnic representation remains to be seen, but the critical reaction in some corners has been quite positive. For example, *Soap Opera Digest* Editor Lynn Leahy admitted in a recent column that while she was initially skeptical of the Antonio storyline, "It would appear that B&B, which has never tried to be more than a classy, highly entertaining diversion has found a way to remain that . . . and then some" (Leahy 2002, p. 22).[8]

The third and perhaps most significant development within the U.S. daytime industry has occurred on ABC's half-hour soap *Port Charles*, which debuted in 1997 as a spin-off of the network's popular and long-running *General Hospital*. Faring poorly in the ratings since its premiere, cancellation rumors were swirling when *Port Charles* shifted to a twelve-week story-arc format in March 2000.[9] The first "book," titled *Fate*, was told in three chapters: "Desire," "Deception," and "Destiny." When the second book, *Time in a Bottle*, debuted, the show had dropped the chapter format but offered something new to U.S. daytime television by thematically linking the story to popular musician Jim Croce's song by the same name. Subsequent books have also been named for popular songs—*Tainted Love* (sung by Soft Cell), *Secrets* (Madonna), and the current book, *Superstition* (with pop reggae band UB40)—with the songs featured in primetime promotional spots. According to one editorial, "Using musical themes was a brilliant marketing tool, that resulted in record downloads of the corresponding theme songs from MP3 song-swapping services" ("SOC Names Port Charles Best Soap of '01," www.soapcentral.com, December 20, 2001).

Although widely regarded as introducing the telenovela-ization of U.S. soaps, *Port Charles*'s twist on the genre was clearly driven by a need to stanch the declining daytime audience and its own poor ratings. In this instance, the change in format was an attempt to capture distracted, short-attention-span viewers with story arcs that capitalize on popular themes and remain apart from the overall show rather than an effort to adapt the genre to the traditional story interests of Latino and Latina viewers. Although Latin American telenovelas air complete narratives in 100 to 120 episodes, their storylines characteristically "tend towards the romantic and melodramatic with an emphasis on upward social mobility usually through romantic attachment, and they are expected to have a happy ending" (Patterson 1995, 105).[10] But *Port Charles* stories have been anything but tales of upward mobility, romance, and happy endings; the two most popular books to date, *Tempted* and *Tainted Love*, featured vampires, time travel, and other supernatural elements. After creating buzz within the industry and a guarantee to air at least through summer 2002 (Dawn 2002, 49), the latest ratings show that the short-arc format has helped *Port Charles*. As of February 2002, Nielsen ratings show a 10 percent improvement over last year in the key demographic of eighteen- to forty-nine-year-old women (Freeman 2002).[11] In regard to the telenovela-ization of the show itself, a nonscientific poll in *Soap Opera Digest* reported that 72 percent of viewers "loved" the story-arc format while 28 percent "hated" it (*Soap Opera Digest* 2001d, 58-59).

AUDIENCE CONSIDERATIONS: REVOLUTION OR COMPROMISE?

In 1997, when anticipating the shift to short-term arcs by *Port Charles*, former president of ABC daytime Patricia Fili-Krushel observed that "the best cure for the audience's attention deficit is also the oldest: compelling stories. . . . On the other hand, a plot can't move so slowly that frequent viewers get bored" (Schmuckler 1997, 13). In the same vein, Mickey Dwyer Dobbin, former head of CBS daytime, now executive in charge of production at Proctor & Gamble

Productions, stated, "Many people don't want to get hooked on a new show, so maybe we should be thinking about [the telenovela] form—doing a story over a thirteen- or twenty-six-week period" (Schmuckler 1997, 13). In what is perhaps a preview of how the entire ABC lineup will change as a result of *Port Charles*'s success with the short-term arc, Felicia Minei Behr, senior vice president for programming at ABC daytime, says that the network plans to bring the new format to all its shows in the coming year (*Soap Opera Digest* 2001b, 6). Indeed, on February 11, Ms. Behr announced that *One Life to Live* will be the next ABC soap to experiment with the novela format by year's end (Freeman 2002). However, the adaptation of the new format to the hour-long *One Life to Live* is expected to be more of a challenge because of the greater number of characters and subplots and its decades-long history (see below). With an eye toward those challenges, Ms. Behr and Angela Shapiro, president of ABC daytime, plan to withhold conversion of the other ABC hour-long serials, *All My Children* and *General Hospital*, until the waters are more fully tested with *One Life to Live* (Freeman 2002).

As for *Port Charles*, despite its increase in the key audience demographic of eighteen- to forty-nine-year-old women (Freeman 2002), it remains the lowest-ranked soap currently on the air. In still another attempt to avoid cancellation, the show recently shifted to a more cost-effective production schedule common to prime time—taping two episodes a day for six months and then going on hiatus for the rest of the year. While this will reduce production costs, it jeopardizes the show's ability to tweak story-lines in response to audience feedback as stories unfold, thus potentially undermining the established give-and-take relationship between the soap opera industry and its loyal and vocal audience (see Harrington and Bielby 1995). Shorter-arc storytelling does have an upside, however: "at least plots will be wrapping up every few months. So, if reaction is negative, viewers will not have to watch something they don't like for long" (*Soap Opera Digest* 2002, 10). Speculation about the possible cancellation of *Port Charles* is still widespread in the industry (*Soap Opera Digest* 2001e, 5; Pursell 2001).

Revenue problems aside, the adaptation of the telenovela format within the United States is predicted to have genre-altering consequences. These changes are not necessarily positive in the opinion of some industry observers and long-time audience members. Former *Soap Opera Weekly* critic "Marlena De Lacroix" (in real life New York University journalism instructor Connie P. Hayman) raised several concerns shortly after *Port Charles* debuted its telenovela format. As she put it, "It's apparent already that the people behind the show aren't so much revolutionizing the art of soap operas as they are compromising it" (De Lacroix 2001, 12). Hayman bases her criticism on considerations that are central to the U.S. serial format. One is that soaps' endless middle and five-days-per-week airing schedule allow stories to be told in real time. Says Hayman (or De Lacroix), "Since soaps are experienced day-to-day, they mimic real life, strengthening viewers' feeling that a soap's story is real" (p. 12). She argues that *Port Charles*' fast-paced plots feel "surreal," and viewers are "clobbered over the head with key turning points at least once a week" (p. 12). Traditionally, U.S. soaps incorporate key plot transitions once every thirteen weeks or so. A result of this slower pacing is that it holds the audience (and attracts new viewers along the way by word of mouth), which continues to watch to follow the incremental buildup to resolution. The payoff for the audience lies within that resolution, which entails multilayered significance through its outcome. But there is an additional benefit to the audience of the U.S.'s form of the genre, according to Hayman: "one of the aspects of traditional soap opera that keeps the audience coming back is consistency in both story and character" (p. 12). Hayman suggests that one of the compromises from the change in format for *Port Charles* has been the rewriting of history and of character to come up with "ubermelodramatic" events for the sake of story. Hayman continues, "Reinterpreting history is a writer's prerogative, but it has a serious downside: It makes viewers feel deceived" (p. 6). For long-term viewers, those most familiar and comfortable with the established conventions of the U.S. form of the genre, the modification of the traditional soap opera form might be a hard sell.

In addition, there are real costs and complications associated with introducing a different genre form into a long-running and established genre concept. One problem that may not have been fully anticipated by the industry is that character and plot developments of the short-term arcs need to be reintegrated with the long-term bible for the show, and continuity of character has to be balanced against the requirements of the short-term story. The editors at SoapCentral.com,[12] who proclaimed *Port Charles* the best soap opera of 2001, suggest that while storytelling in early books was disjointed and somewhat belabored (as Hayman argued above), later books maintain the story integrity and character consistency familiar to U.S. soap viewers:

> To assume . . . that every three months means something entirely new on *Port Charles* is a mistake. There are common threads that transcend each book and the continuity level is extremely high. New stories are set up during the course of each book so that by the time the next story arc rolls around, there's already a new story brewing, one that the viewer has already been lured into watching. (http://www.soapcentral.com/soapcentral/news/2001)

It is perhaps too early to say whether the telenovela-ization of U.S. soap operas is a genre adaptation or a new competing subgenre. Whether this genre form takes hold in the U.S. context depends, obviously, on whether network executives view it as a business success in terms of ratings and revenues. In the absence of clear markers of business success, the experiment in bringing telenovela-like elements into U.S. soaps will be abandoned. On the other hand, the networks can afford to alienate segments of the loyal viewership if the innovations bring in new audience constituencies in large enough numbers. It is a difficult balancing act for the networks, since critics and loyal viewers are invested in the genre and are closely monitoring any radical departures from established convention. Whether that segment of the audience is expendable cannot be known until after the fact, and it is especially difficult to introduce changes that both remain true to what established audiences seek and address the demands of a changing marketplace.

REFORMATTING PLEASURE AND THE PORTABILITY OF THE SOAP GENRE

There are at least two significant issues at stake with the widespread reformatting of U.S. soaps: one speaks to viewer/fan pleasure, and the other speaks to the global market for exported television programming. First, we believe a move to short-term story arcs requires scholars to retheorize the meaning of pleasure in open-ended serial narratives. Our concern is not so much with casual soap viewers but with long-term dedicated fans of the genre. As we argued in "Soap Fans: Pursuing Pleasure and Making Meaning in Everyday Life" (Harrington and Bielby 1995), viewer and fan must be understood as conceptually distinct categories; fans make an affective investment in the genre that speaks to central issues of play, creativity, and personal identity. A key source of pleasure for dedicated U.S. fans is soaps' ability to act as "transitional objects," allowing them to play with the boundaries between internal and external, between the "real" and the "nonreal" (Harrington and Bielby 1995).[13]

The U.S. soap industry—its directors, writers, actors, and fans themselves—have a long-standing investment in cultivating and maintaining this form of emotional boundary playing, which seems threatened by telenovelaization. The praise of *Port Charles* from the editors at SoapCentral.com (as noted above) is heartening in that it appears, to some viewers at least, that a relatively new show (*Port Charles* is only five years old) can switch to short-term story arcs without losing character and narrative consistency. But what about shows with a thirty-, forty-, or fifty-year legacy? To transform characters, communities, and narratives that were designed to go on endlessly (as real life does) into twelve-week segments risks a central source of pleasure and identity available to U.S. soap fans for more than seventy years. Without question, *Port Charles* has been an interesting experiment; the telenovelaization of *One Life to Live*, if it occurs as predicted, should give us greater insight into audience considerations surrounding genre reformatting.[14]

A second issue at stake with the proposed reformatting is its impact on the exportability of U.S. soaps to the global syndication market. One of the biggest drawbacks to the export potential of U.S. serials is their open-ended format. While providing a large pool of episodes for buyer selection, with long-running, domestically successful products, the text literally becomes unwieldy to export. How many episodes constitute the story? Importing markets prefer programs without a long history, and in the United States, this typically applies only to cancelled programs or recent entrees into the daytime lineup. Of soaps currently airing in the United States, CBS' *The Bold and the Beautiful* is by far the most popular globally. Not coincidentally, it has a relative short history in the U.S. context (first airing in 1987) and is a half-hour program. *Port Charles*, while still garnering fairly dismal domestic ratings, seems well poised to enter the global market: like *Bold*, it is a half-hour show, it has a very short history, and most importantly, its reformatting could allow each book to be exported as a self-contained package. We question whether the telenovelaization of *Port Charles* speaks to a recent trend in the U.S. daytime industry to prioritize global audiences over local ones. While a full discussion of this issue is beyond the scope of this article, there have been several indications that as a result of declining domestic profits, network decisions are increasingly oriented to the global marketplace. For example, in 1999, NBC debated whether to cancel *Sunset Beach* or *Another World* to make room in the schedule for its new show, *Passions*. While both shows drew low ratings, *Beach* had been on the air a mere two years, while *World* was one of the grande dames of U.S. daytime television, with thirty-five years on the air. NBC elected to cancel *World* but gave *Beach* a six-month extension before finally canceling it in December 1999. U.S.-based fans were outraged over this decision, confused as to why *Another World*, given its legacy, was not granted the extension. However, a major difference between the new shows was the substantial foreign sales of *Beach*, which NBC coproduced with Spelling Productions. NBC had no financial stake in *Another World*, which was owned by Proctor & Gamble.[15] A question for future research is, How might the reformatting of U.S.-based soaps enhance their export potential?

CONCLUSION

What makes opening America to imported programming or new programming concepts such a challenge? Hoskins and Mirus (1988) observed in writing about the cultural discount factor that in any given country, the audience's preference for familiarity is paramount. Our research conducted on the U.S. soap opera audience demonstrates clearly that storytelling that portrays emotional authenticity, that relies on elements of melodrama as a stylistic form, and that unfolds in "real time" is crucial to audience pleasures. Our research on the international market for television points also to the importance of technical quality, visual style, and other aesthetic considerations in attracting audiences. Another factor related less directly to audiences and more to the industry itself is the sheer difficulty of introducing innovation of any sort. In an industry where the costs of production are considerable and the commissioning or purchase of new programs is made in a business context of ambiguity and uncertainty, industry decision makers demand that any new product be framed as familiar or otherwise knowable in some way. Moreover, increasingly, because of industry deregulation that took effect in the United States in the 1990s, any imported series or concept competes with a network's ownership stake in its own shows and in keeping them on the air as long as possible to sell them to the domestic (and international) syndication market (Bielby and Bielby, 2003). In short, even when the genre properties of an import are familiar and production quality is excellent, the American television industry has its own interests at heart, which in this case is a bottom line in which revenue flows accrue to the established stakeholders. However, as we see with the telenovela-ization of U.S. soaps, even the otherwise closed American industry is willing to open up when confronted with opportunities it perceives as potentially improving the bottom line.

NOTES

1. Consensus between creators and audiences over genre boundaries is probably greater in television than in any other area of popular culture, in part because of the industry's aversion to the risks that accompany innovation and in part because of the

audience's preference for familiarity when seeking popular entertainment (Bielby and Bielby, 2003).

2. Networks will occasionally repeat so-called classic episodes when certain segments of the market anticipate scheduled preemptions, such as during NCAA basketball playoffs or during coverage of the Wimbledon tennis tournament (see Harrington 1998). SoapNet, the twenty-four-hour soap opera cable network launched by Disney/ABC in January of 2000, shows same-day repeats of all four ABC-owned soaps (*Port Charles, All My Children, One Life to Live,* and *General Hospital*), as well as NBC's *Passions* and CBS's *As The World Turns* and *Guiding Light*.

3. For example, ABC's *General Hospital* is currently celebrating its thirty-ninth year on the air, CBS's *As The World Turns* has been airing for forty-six years, and in June 2002, *Guiding Light* celebrated its fiftieth birthday on radio and television—the longest story ever told.

4. Despite declining ratings, however, soaps continue to be profitable in the domestic market. An average hour-long show costs $60 million per year to produce, and the most popular earn $150 to $200 million per year (McAvoy 1999).

5. In the past decade, for example, networks have begun licensing soap memorabilia, such as coffee mugs, T-shirts, key rings, and specially produced videotapes devoted to favorite villains or memorable weddings (Bellafante 1995, 74). They have also begun promoting soap operas on prime-time television in the hopes of attracting new viewers. *Port Charles* (ABC) premiered in a two-hour primetime movie-of-the-week format, and it is now typical for a show's twentieth or twenty-fifth anniversary to be commemorated with a prime-time special; such exposure would have been unthinkable even a decade ago. More recently, CBS increased exposure for its daytime lineup through an arrangement with American Airlines to feature CBS soaps in its in-flight magazine (Stanley 2000), and ABC's *All My Children* and Revlon have agreed to a deal "in which the cosmetics company will be the focal point of a three-month storyline in exchange for buying several million dollars' worth of advertising time on the show" (*Soap Opera Weekly* 2002, 5; see also Flint and Nelson 2002).

6. The lack of imports on U.S. television is typically blamed on American viewers' rejection of low(er) production values, slow pacing, unfamiliar settings and accents, and dubbing and/or subtitling (Allen 1996; Antola and Rogers 1984; Cunningham and Jacka 1994).

7. As Barrera and Bielby (2002) point out, while considerable scholarly attention has focused on the study of telenovelas within their countries of origin, far less is known about their reception in other cultural contexts. Through an analysis of interviews with novela watchers in the United States, they find that telenovelas are much more than "entertainment" for viewers. Rather, they "assist Latinos who reside in the United States in recreating and maintaining a strong cultural bond to Latin America" (Barrera and Bielby 2002, 13). Through the visual representation of Latin American styles, the use of the Spanish language, and the unique scenery and storytelling devices, telenovelas allow viewers in the United States to "remember" or "revisit" Latin America.

8. *Bold and the Beautiful* also hired Erik Estrada to play Antonio's father in fall 2001. Well known to American viewers for his role in the classic 1970s primetime series *Chips*, Estrada also appeared on the Mexican serial *Dos Mujeres, Un Camino* (see www.tv.com/erik-estrada/person/20070/appearances.html).

9. In a departure from the new model, the show's fifth story arc, which debuted December 3, 2001, was only four weeks long.

10. This is an overgeneralization, of course. As noted earlier, telenovelas differ significantly in theme, structure, and realism, depending on country of origin.

11. In fact, the soap genre as a whole is experiencing a small but promising rebound; ABC's overall soap lineup, for example, is up 3 percent during the past season in the eighteen-to-forty-nine demographic (Diliberto 2002, 30). These ratings are obviously

important to the network and to the stabilization of the industry more broadly, but they also point to networks' increasing success in appealing to the youth market. Says Felicia Behr of ABC, "*PC* [*Port Charles*] has grown enormously; I think it's [up] 340 percent in the last year in the 18-24 demographic.... We're interested in bringing in young viewers, because every day in the 18-49 demographic somebody reaches their 50th birthday and goes out of the demographic. So we're interested in bringing in somebody at the 18-year-old level to balance off the people that are falling out of that ever-precious demographic advertisers want" (quoted in Diliberto 2002, 31). The ability to appeal to the younger audience's taste may speak to an important transformation of the genre.

12. Founded in 1995, SoapCentral.com is one of the Internet's first all-encompassing Web sites for U.S.-based soaps.

13. Noted psychologist D. W. Winnicott (1971) proposed three realms of life: "internal" reality, "external" reality, and an intermediate realm of experience that keeps the inner and outer worlds separate yet interrelated. The intermediate realm is neither "inside" nor "outside," but in between. Winnicott links this realm to a specific stage in child development (between four and twelve months) in which infants first become capable of perceiving the self as both subject and object. This stage is characterized by the appearance of transitional objects, which the infant becomes emotionally attached to but is unable to realize are not fully "real" (such as a favorite blanket or toy). This intermediate realm, characterized by creative play and pleasurable affect, remains with us as adults, though we learn to experience it privately rather than openly. In *Soap Fans*, we proposed that soap operas are uniquely positioned to serve as transitional objects for adults: "While many genres aim at fictionalizing the real, serials are uniquely situated to offer a fictional community to viewers who then, quite knowledgeably, bounce the real off the fictional and the fictional off the real. If television programs can act as transitional phenomena [as Lembo and Tucker (1990) first proposed], then soaps are the easiest type of programming for us to use in this way" (Harrington and Bielby 1995, 135).

14. As noted earlier, another source of viewer pleasure in the U.S. context has been transformed by *Port Charles*'s shift to a six-months-on, six-months-off production schedule. While mimicking the production schedule of primetime programming, the shift also mimics one of the main limitations of prime time to engender the intense audience loyalty characteristic of daytime: viewers' inability to give ongoing feedback to the unfolding narrative. As we argued in *Soap Fans* (Harrington and Bielby 1995), the daytime industry in the United States deliberately cooperates with the secondary press to foster and maintain a sense of participation on viewers' parts: "we are all in this together." While obviously illusory to some extent, this sense of participation in the storytelling process is a key element of fan pleasure and loyalty and will be transformed through telenovela-ization.

15. For a full discussion of the issue see, Harrington and Bielby (2002).

REFERENCES

Allen, Robert C. 1985. *Speaking of Soap Operas*. Chapel Hill: University of North Carolina Press.

———, ed. 1996. "*As the World Turns*: Television Soap Operas and Global Media Culture." In *Mass Media and Free Trade: NAFTA and the Cultural Industries*, edited by E. G. McAnany and K. T. Wilkinson, 110-27. Austin: University of Texas Press.

———. 1997. "As the World Tunes In: An International Perspective." In *Worlds Without End: The Art and History of the Soap Opera*, edited by The Museum of Radio and Television, 111-19. New York: Abrams.

Antola, L., and E. M. Rogers. 1984. "Television Flows in Latin America." *Communication Research* 11:183-202.

Baldwin, K. 1999. "Soapie's Choice." *Entertainment Weekly*, January 22.
Barker, Chris. 1997. *Global Television*. Oxford, UK: Blackwell.
Barrera, Vivian, and Denise D. Bielby. 2002. "Places, Faces, and Other Familiar Things: The Cultural Experience of Telenovela Viewing among Latinos in the United States." *Journal of Popular Culture* 34:1-18.
Bellafante, G. 1995. "Soap Operas: The Old and the Desperate." *Time Magazine*, May 29, pp. 73–74.
Bielby, D. D., and W. T. Bielby. 2004. "Audience Aesthetics and Popular Culture." In *Matters of Culture: Cultural Sociology in Practice*, edited by R. Friedland and J. Mohr, 295–317. Cambridge: Cambridge University Press.
Bielby, W. T., and D. D. Bielby. 2003. "Controlling Prime-Time: Organizational Concentration and Network Television Programming Strategies." *Journal of Broadcasting & Electronic Media* 47:573–596.
Bielby, D. D., and C. L. Harrington. 2002. "Markets and Meanings: The Global Syndication of Television Programming." In *Global Culture: Media, Arts, Policy, and Globalization*, edited by D. Crane, N. Kawashima, and K. Kawasaki, 215–32. New York: Routledge.
Calvo, D. 2001. "Soap Opera Seeks to Speak to Latinos." *Los Angeles Times*, April 19, p. 52.
Cassata, M. 1985. "The Soap Opera." In *TV Genres: A Handbook and Reference Guide*, edited by B. Rose, 131–49. Westport, CT: Greenwood.
Cassata, M., and T. Skill. 1983. *Life on Daytime Television: Tuning-In American Serial Drama*. Norwood, NJ: Ablex.
Cunningham, S., and E. Jacka. 1994. "Neighborly Relations? Cross-Cultural Reception Analysis and Australian Soaps in Britain." *Cultural Studies* 8:509–26.
Cunningham, S., T. Miller, and D. Rowe. 1994. *Contemporary Australian Television*. Sydney, Australia: University of New South Wales Press.
Dawn, R. 2002. "The Future of Soaps: 2002." *Soap Opera Digest* 27:48–51.
De Lacroix, M. 2001. "PC: Fast-Food Soap Opera." *Soap Opera Weekly* 12 (6): 12.
Diliberto, J. 2002. "Soaps' Ratings Bubble Stays Afloat." *Soap Opera Weekly* 13 (14): 30–31.
Fiske, J. 1987a. *Television Culture*. London: Methuen.
———. 1987b. "Genre Study and Television." In *Channels of Discourse*, edited by R. C. Allen, 113–33. Chapel Hill: University of North Carolina Press.
Flint, J., and E. Nelson. 2002. "'All My Children' Gets Revlon Twist." *Wall Street Journal*, March 15, p. B-1.
Foulk, L. 2000. "A Reader's View." *Soap Opera Weekly*, August 22, p. 27.
Freeman, M. 2002. "ABC Soap Takes a Page from Telenovela Playbook." *Electronic Media*, February 11, p. 2.
Gledhill, C. 1997. "Genre and Gender: The Case of Soap Opera." In *Representation: Cultural Representations and Signifying Practices*, edited by S. Hall, 337–86. London: Open University Press.
Griswold, W. 1987. "A Methodological Framework for the Sociology of Culture." In *Sociological Methodology*, edited by C. Clogg, 1-35. Washington, DC: American Sociological Association.
Harrington, C. L. 1998. "Is Anyone Else Out There Sick of the News?!: TV Viewers' Responses to Non-routine News Coverage." *Media, Culture & Society* 20 (3): 471–94.
Harrington, C. L., and D. Bielby. 1995. *Soap Fans: Pursuing Pleasure and Making Meaning in Everyday Life*. Philadelphia: Temple University Press.
———. 2002. "A New Era? The (Global) Rise and (Domestic) Fall of U.S. Soap Operas." Unpublished manuscript.
Hassell, G. 2001. "Surge in Hispanics Means mas Dinero." *Houston Chronicle*, August 22, p. B-1.

Hoskins, C., and R. Mirus. 1988. "Reasons for the U.S. Dominance of the International Trade in Television Programmes." *Media, Culture & Society* 10:499–515.
Intintoli, M. 1984. *Taking Soaps Seriously: The World of* Guiding Light. New York: Praeger.
Jenrette, J., S. McIntosh, and S. Winterberger. 1999. "*Carlotta*! Changing Images of Hispanic-American Women in Daytime Soap Operas." *Journal of Popular Culture* 33 (2): 37–48.
LaGuardia, R. 1974. *The Wonderful World of TV Soaps*. New York: Ballantine.
Leahy, L. 2002. Editor's Note. *Soap Opera Digest*, January 15, p. 22.
Lembo, R., and K. H. Tucker. 1990. "Culture, Television, and Opposition: Rethinking Cultural Studies." *Critical Studies in Mass Communication* 7:97–116.
Liebes, T., and S. Livingstone. 1998. "European Soap Operas: The Diversification of a Genre." *European Journal of Communication* 13:147–80.
Logan, M. 2002. "Michael Logan on Soaps." *TV Guide* 49:36.
Lopez, A. M. 1995. "Our Welcomed Guests: Telenovelas in Latin America." In *To Be Continued: Soap Operas Around the World*, edited by R. C. Allen, 256–75. London: Routledge.
Lowry, B. 1998. "Change Is on the Air." *Los Angeles Times*, August 30, p. 8.
Matelski, M. J. 1999. *Soap Operas Worldwide: Cultural and Serial Realities*. Jefferson, NC: McFarland.
McAvoy, K. 1999. "The Crying Game." *Broadcasting & Cable*, May 31, pp. 22–24.
Nordenstreng, K., and T. Varis. 1974. "Television Traffic—A One Way Street?" Reports and Papers on Mass Communication. No. 70. Paris: United Nations Educational, Scientific and Cultural Organization.
O'Donnell, H. 1999. *Good Times, Bad Times: Soap Operas and Society in Western Europe*. London: Leicester University Press.
Patterson, R. 1995. "Drama and Entertainment." In *Television: An International History*, edited by A. Smith, 95–117. Oxford, UK: Oxford University Press.
Pool, Ithiel de Sola. 1977. "The Changing Flow of Television." *Journal of Communication* 27 (1): 139–49.
Pursell, C. 2001. "Port Charles in a Storm." *Electronic Media*, November 19, pp. 1–23.
Schmuckler, E. 1997. "Search for Tomorrow." *Working Woman* 22 (7): 30–35.
Sinclair, J., E. Jacka, and S. Cunningham. 1996. *New Patterns in Global Television: Peripheral Vision*. Oxford, UK: Oxford University Press.
Soap Opera Digest. 2001 a. "In Other News." June 26, p. 14.
Soap Opera Digest. 2001b. "Late-Breaking News." December 11, p. 6.
Soap Opera Digest. 2001c. "Late-Breaking News: B&B Says 'Hola.'" May 1, p. 6.
Soap Opera Digest. 2001d. "Love It/Hate It." October 23, pp. 58–59.
Soap Opera Digest. 2001e. "More Cancellation Rumors at PC." December 18, p. 5.
Soap Opera Digest. 2002. "Herring and Fans Weigh In on PC Changes." January 1, p. 10.
Soap Opera Weekly. 2002. "Industry Insider." April 9, p. 5.
Stanley, T. L. 2000. "Soap Operas Look for Ways to Rekindle the Romance." *Los Angeles Times*, November 24, p. F25.
Taylor, E. 1989. *Prime Time Families: Television Culture in Postwar America*. Berkeley: University of California Press.
Varis, T. 1986. "Trends in International Television Flows." In *Global Television*, edited by C. Schneider and B. Wallis, 95-107. New York: Wedge.
Winnicott, D. W. 1971. *Playing and Reality*. London: Tavistock.

Engaging the Audience:
The Social Imagery of the Novela

Reginald Clifford

This article reports on a study that was conducted for the TV Azteca chain in Mexico City and was used both to add to ratings data and also as a feedback mechanism for the development of new programs and modification of programs as they were being run. It is derived both from commercial necessities and theoretical perspectives. In this article, the focus is the *telenovela*, the soap opera format that dominates Mexican and Latin American drama programming.

Television is primarily a domestic medium that brings together the private domestic space with the public sphere of leisure (Silverstone 1994, 176). To grapple with the concept of *audience*, it is necessary to access everyday life and construct the concept of audience from there. The study on which this analytical model rests is rooted in grounded theory and on a research methodology that combines some elements of Repertory Grid (Murdock and Phelps 1973) and construct analysis together with an ethnomethodological element. The knowledge generated from the field is developed by an analysis of the social imaginary of telenovelas that involves metaphorical and semantic analysis that is then, in turn, analyzed against genre theory, in this case, melodrama. This enables both the establishment of the principles of the telenovela as a subgenre and the parameters for their production according to theme and time slot of melodrama-telenovela. These parameters are then rechecked with the domestic ecology and demographic information available to develop, maintain, or transform the themes and tones of the telenovelas considered appropriate for the schedule.

By focusing on the triad of the social imaginary, a genre-based analytic model, and ratings analysis, it is possible to create, maintain, and transform (after Carey 1989) the telenovelas that we air. This, of course, is possible only if this is approached as a team effort between production and channel. This model is built on the assumption that both the TV channel and audience are engaged in an emotional dimension that other genres do not reach. For

---

Reginald Clifford: "Engaging the Audience: The Social Imaginary of the Novela," first published in *Television and New Media*, Vol. 6, Issue 4, 360–69.

example, the relationship of audience and channel in the process of being informed and watching news programs is more rational in the way it relates to and involves citizenship and social competence.

To engage an audience is a different approach than that suggested in other metaphorical approximations of audience as a category, such as that of reading, textual analysis, media consumption, uses and gratifications or reception, although there is affinity for the latter. The concept of mass is reconceptualized, so that it is possible to distinguish the difference between convergence for similar motives and needs and convergence for dissimilar motives. The notion of mass as synonymous with heavy, dense, and perhaps rather sheeplike mass behavior is replaced by the metaphor of mass being gaseous. The image is of an audience in the thousands circulating and converging for a variety of reasons on a particular program or, in an increasing trend, to watch several at the same time. The metaphor of the audience behaving as a gaseous mass is useful because it describes audience behavior as the audience navigates its way through the time people give television viewing and moving between channels and genres according to whim, mood, or need, within the limitations of what is on offer. There are occasions when what is offered successfully engages a large segment of the audience and channel hopping slows, and there are occasions when surfing reaches high levels of search, particularly during commercials and between programs. The interviews showed that people have a clearer idea of what they do not want than what they do.

Telenovelas usually engage people in the intimacy of their home, the site where Silverstone (1994) suggests that one community forms to view another; it is the site of conflicts, rituals, and sharing in dimensions that are gendered, generational, and class-oriented. It is, as Veronica Vazquez (1997) states, "life itself." It is a site where the emotions of everyday life are internalized and externalized. Respondents frequently assert that a telenovela, particularly one with tones of realism, provides a means for broaching a subject that families enjoy discussing but may find difficult to raise. A son or daughter may want to probe the parental limits placed on certain subjects such as sex, parental control, drugs, or sexuality but does not wish to be perceived as being active in transgressing them. Conversely, a parent may want to probe the world of their children without appearing inquisitorial or nosey. This, for Mexico, is where telenovelas take the central stage.

The launching day of a new telenovela is always a time for bated breath. The jury is out, and the producer and broadcaster can only fidget until the ratings return the verdict. The creation of the program is done with as much care as possible. Innovation, if any, is calculated, and it is hoped that there may be a plan B lined up to follow should things go awry. Producers propose and the audience disposes; producers feel that they have as much say in how their programs will be received as viewers have in what is produced. Yet there seems to be a bandwidth within which a common ground can be "negotiated." The producer may make changes and the viewers may increase their attention. This bandwidth is the common ground where audience and program engage in a dance that explores dimensions of character and narrative, where the stuff of commonplace and the sustaining of community occur, where the emotions can be seen, and where the consequences of actions and decisions about love and life may be explored vicariously.

Since the arrival of TV Azteca on the scene, the telling of stories in this genre has acquired a new perspective, often called "realism." All telenovelas are now classified into two general kinds of melodrama: Cinderella style or realist. The first is considered to be classic and inextricably tied up with Televisa, while the second is viewed as the domain of TV Azteca.

The production of telenovelas is primarily focused on the Mexican market, and then they are marketed elsewhere. In this sense, there are certain "ground rules" involved in the order of things. For example, the Mexican audience, particularly for primetime telenovelas, is intolerant of foreign accents and only slightly more tolerant of foreign actors. Tolerance is increased as the accent becomes more mainstream Mexican Spanish. Another aspect is the nature of the "contract" that the production puts on the table. In the usual way, the overall premise of the story is established as soon as possible. What follows, then, is the analysis of the social imaginary of telenovelas. As mentioned earlier, telenovelas engage their audience as few genres do. The producer, the plot, and the viewers are involved in a complex cycle in which each agonizes over the other.

THE NOTION OF THE SOCIAL IMAGINARY AND
THE MEXICAN CONTEXT

In an effort to get closer to the audience and produce programs that would be an attractive combination of trusted and tried melodrama with new elements that would give it a value-added advantage, a different approach in research was undertaken. What follows is based on this research, in combination with genre analysis and day-to-day expert panel research. The approach aims to define the "social imaginary."

The model was based on an analysis of techniques known as ASBI (*análisis semántico basado en imagines*; see Clifford 1998a; Clifford, Gomez, and Arango 1998), a qualitative technique derived from work done in the early seventies by Graham Murdock and Guy Phelps (1973), which explored the role of mass media in the lives of secondary school students. The study itself involved a variety of methods, including a technique developed to explore people's constructs that was a version of the original Repertory Grid developed by George Kelly, an American psychologist (Murdock and Phelps 1973). He suggested that people classify and make sense of parts of their everyday world by developing a repertoire of constructs. ASBI develops this technique further by using photographs and one or two questions to start the interview. All subsequent questions were based on comments made by the respondent. The final product is a map or pattern of what I here call the "social imaginary."[1]

The researcher would approach an individual, and on occasion a couple, and request permission for an interview. It was common to start with one and find others, usually friends, joining in. This happened in parks in provincial towns. Roughly, one in three or four requests resulted in an interview. The researcher then asked questions about whether informants recognized particular telenovela stars and, if so, whether they watched the telenovela and what they thought about the characters.

The process itself gave rise to fascinating insights into the attitudes people held toward the telenovelas. In formulating the interview protocol, the word used for acknowledging an image or recognizing a character was *conocer* (know). Thus, the question, "¿A quien conoces?" (Whom do you know?) was used. This turned out to have a class bias. The upper- and middle-class respondents had little problem fielding these questions in general. To know someone (*conocer*) implied having read about, heard about (from radio), or seen on television. They would offer opinions on programs that they had heard about. They were also more willing to extrapolate situations from a telenovela to their own lives or to those of others whom they had never met. For the working class, and particularly those whose orality (Ong 1982) was very marked, to know (*conocer*) was something that could occur only through personal experience. Thus, they would talk only about the telenovelas they had personally seen.

Within the working class, there was the added hurdle of self-esteem. The respondents would often state that they knew nothing and had nothing to say. It was as if they could not fathom why a middle-class interviewer would want to know anything from them at all, for what could they say that was not already known to the researcher? If the suspicion that the point of the interview was to discover that their ignorance could be overcome, the respondents from this class would move away from the question-and-answer mode of interaction into recounting personal anecdotes. In this way, this class made it harder to be judged and was found wanting, and the richness of the interview increased accordingly.

The total run for exploring this project was 1,490 interviews carried out in seven cities in Mexico during February and March 1998 (Clifford, Gómez, and Arango 1998). It was divided into three parts: news, telenovelas, and a category of broad entertainment. Because each section was centered on television, the actual interview tended to be accumulative. Regardless of which topic the respondent was commenting on, he or she tended to lace his or her conversation with comments that corresponded to other genres. A person commenting on a telenovela might refer to news or entertainment at the same time.

Perhaps the first theoretical aspect that was produced by the fieldwork is the consistency with which the respondents spoke about the world beyond their own everyday experience. How the respondent has the world "figured out" became a central aspect of the fieldwork. "Se me figura que así es" (That's the way I have it figured) was a common refrain. The social imaginary impinges on the respondents' everyday life in ways that are constant. When one respondent said, for example, "Es que nosotros los Mexicanos somos así . . . bien canijos" (That's the way we Mexicans are . . . really astute and clever), she not only projected a sense of self but also a sense of others. The social imaginary articulates this broader sense of community and of civil society. It is where the assumptions about others are located. At the same time, the individual monitors parts of this social imaginary and leaves much of the monitoring of different portions of it to others.[2]

Consider an example. Someone joins the stream of people going to and from work, and before long, that person will develop a sophisticated collection of ideas and conjectures about the nature of traffic, its peak hours, the best routes, and so on. This person has an imaginary map of the city, more or less corresponding to how things are, derived from their own and others' experiences, their projections, and their beliefs. What and how a person imagines things to be are key elements in the construction of social imaginary. The social imaginary thus refers to the domain that is abstracted to generate a general set of expectations about the social life that lies just beyond everyday experience. Daily experience will either corroborate or often modify these general expectations about the social world. In a sense, it is virtual knowledge of the world that forms a background to the foreground of our everyday lives.

The fundamental methodological assumption is that by attending to how people talk about social life, their perceptions can be mapped as they evolve. For example, talk about adultery ranged from absolutes for the young adults—those just starting out their own married life—to older adults whose understanding of ambiguous conditions of "understandable" adultery was a matter of shades of grey rather than black and white, because they themselves were well within the age range of midlife crises (Sheehy 1984). For them, adultery provoked by an impossible partner or the feelings of despair brought on by aging is understandable but lamentable. Understandable adultery was, however, not confused with justified adultery. In general, the female protagonist must retain her virtue. She can give it only to the man she will eventually end up with, the love of her life; otherwise she is tarnished and risks losing her aspirational value. The moral constraints within melodrama of the telenovela form the value core that audiences enjoy repeatedly.

This appraisal is derived from careful attention to the way people speak about their relationships; it implies that change would manifest itself first in naming and talking. If these assumptions of linkage between macro and micro are correct, then the phenomena ascribed to them can be mapped and the relationships explored. At the same time, the inherent social conservatism is constantly underlined by what is acceptable and what is not and for whom.

VIEWING HABITS

During the actual period of the research, TV Azteca aired *Demasiado Corazón*, *Mirada de Mujer*, and *La Chacala*, and Televisa aired *Desencuentro*, *Huracán*, *Mi Pequeña Traviesa*, and *Esmeralda*. Of these, *Mirada de Mujer* was exceptionally successful and drew a group of viewers who claimed that they had never before watched telenovelas. The Televisa product was more traditional and "Cinderella" in type.

Viewing habits differed throughout Mexico. In general, the interviewees in the capital were most knowledgeable about television, including telenovelas, even if they had not watched much. There is a monitoring of the domain that permits the focusing of attention on some things while maintaining others in view, even if not directly. Monterrey and Guadalajara are less given to wide monitoring. And the rest of the cities varied in the range, fragmentation, and specificity of their comments. In some places, such as Tuxtla Gutiérrez, the state capital of Chiapas, television viewing habits are somewhat less marked, as they vie with other activities, notably, socializing outdoors in the evening when the heat of the day has passed.

There are ranges of issues determining how people engage the telenovela as a genre. Age, gender, and social class create general dimensions from which people engage the telenovela. In principle, it is seen as woman's genre. Men seldom feel free to admit that they watch a telenovela, much less enjoy one. They will often state that they relinquish the remote control so that their partner can enjoy her telenovela, ostensibly showing love and caring by doing so. This issue is less marked as one moves toward the upper class.

Viewing habits also vary along age and class lines. Middle- and upper-class middle-aged interviewees classified channel 2 of Televisa as being for servants, but only with respect to telenovelas—not news or entertainment. The young shared this view but also expressed differentiation between the Cinderella/realist divide. It would be appropriate to point out at this stage that the Cinderella/realist issue is not totally polarized. Realism in telenovelas has its limits, and it is really more of an issue of how credible the audience finds the story, because the element of aspirational illusion cannot go missing in Mexican melodrama.

Audiences watch telenovelas for different reasons. Men claim to be more attracted by a mix of love underscored by action and even violence. For middle-aged middle- and upper-class women, *Mirada de Mujer* was good because it was more real and *La Chacala* was different. Younger women of the same classes were more swayed by physical attraction and themes that evolved around the issues facing young adults. In general, middle-aged women and older still found the traditional telenovela of interest.

Another interesting class-related issue is that the young of the middle and upper class pay less attention to the qualities of acting and more to the elements of music, fashion, and style. They seek out elements that are crucial to their sense of glamour and excitement. Fanciful or realistic story-lines, the audience is grateful when it can derive some element it can talk about and value. *Mirada de Mujer* was greatly appreciated because of the excellent acting and exquisite dialogues. Respondents would say, "When something like that happens to me (referring to some particular event) or to someone I know, I just hope I remember that line."

The audiences of telenovelas are thus diverse. However, across the demographic groups, the telenovela creates communities that, in turn, engage vicariously in the vagaries of the television community. It is a site where anxiety, security, emotional empathy, morality (as different from rational empathy), and social competence are brought for exercise. The method used brings out the classification system in people, so that together with the similarities in why people congregate "virtually" around a telenovela, it is accompanied by the differences as well. Similarities tend to congregate around elements of gender, while differences tend to be expressed in class terms. But it is not so simple. For example, the lower classes find it more difficult to express what they wish to say, but then they will often encapsulate something in a meaningfully laden way. In other words, they will often say less but mean more, much in line with Basil Bernstein's (1971) conceptualization of restricted codes versus elaborate codes. The middle and upper classes engage in more critique and evaluation of the dimensions of emotion being explored, while the lower classes bring moral issues to bear on the issue in question sooner.

A further element that was developed from the research was the clarity of the sense-making process. This sense making is also a part of the larger narrative that individuals develop to create their own narrative. Giddens (1991) argues that the creation of romantic love is a recent phenomenon in which the individual can engage in the ongoing story about the self: "The more post traditional the settings in which an individual moves, the more lifestyle concerns the very core of identity, its sense making and re-making" (p. 81). Telenovelas participate in this process by working to create a set of expectations concerning everyday life clustered around operational, normative, and aspirational expectations.[3]

The telenovela provides a larger "window" (as media do in general) to life than is usually available in everyday life. The success is in the management of expectations, especially the ones that the audience finds aspirational. This explains, in part, why recurring themes and outright remakes of telenovelas have a particular fascination for audiences. Respondents claimed that they derived a sense of security and certainty from the telenovelas they watched. Melodrama-telenovela as a form of story telling is among the most predictable. In fact, every effort is made so that this aspect is clear from the start. The leading couple falls in love in the beginning so that the audience knows who ends up together; it then becomes a matter of how they finally overcome all the obstacles in themselves and those placed in their way by the antagonists and villains. The telenovela becomes a cleansing process in which the heroes suffer and grow as a result. This is the stuff of anguish in which uncertainty is wrung from every situation to produce high tension and catharsis as subplots are resolved only to resurface in further plots until the central plot ends in a grand finale.

NOTES

1. The process of interviewing people with this methodology is a combination of simplicity and complexity. The simple part is to ask three or four basic questions. The complex process consists in building the terrain as the respondent talks.

The simple part: The questions used in this technique are deliberately few, allowing the respondent to talk freely about the topic of the research.

    1. "Please separate those photographs that you can identify from those you cannot."
    2. "Of those that are left, identify the two most different photographs." (The researcher voices the name of each selection.) "Why are they different?"
    3. "Of the remaining photographs, which are most similar to one photograph and which to the other photograph? Or if neither, then what other category can be used to classify them? Please comment."

The complex process:

    1. Responses generated varied by respondent, as each could elaborate on the different categories that he or she established.
    2. Building the interview from within. This is achieved by going over the different comments made, and questions are then asked that extend or amplify what has been

said by the respondent. The researcher typically asks for examples rather than explanations or definitions that will tend to promote a more rational response.

2. The map of constructs that this technique generates can be split in two:

1. The personal experience of everyday life and a mapping of the dimensions and flux of change in the social imaginary enable an understanding of the social mind-set and the pragmatic exigencies at a given moment.

2. It allows mapping across time of how people change the way they talk about things and the way social changes begin to unfold. As certain combinations of things become thinkable and gain currency in a society, the stock of possible social options grows. This provides a means of linking the macroworld to the microworld in social terms while allowing us to explore the complexities of layering and sedimentation.

3. Operational expectations are the actual frontlines set that people use to navigate their everyday lives (e.g., how they drive in traffic, how they behave at work, and how they interact with family and in other social environments). They are very pragmatic expectations that concern how an individual expects others to behave in very concrete circumstances and prepares responses accordingly.

Normative expectations are those that involve behavioral norms—what is expected from individuals, their roles, and their social locations. This is derived from Meads's roles theory and Garfinkel's general ethnomethodological work (Collins 1994). They function as giving guidelines about what ought to be. Aspirational expectations are those that relate to the longings and dreams that individuals have about what and how they wish things to be. These expectations are not commonly found in everyday life, but they are not entirely foreign either. They tend to be particular occasions such as weddings where everyone can enjoy, if only vicariously, the glamour of the couple and the occasion. This is most visible when the outlay is a material one, such as those that revolve around wealth, stardom, and the winning of prizes. These involve the use of cars, clothes, and activities. There are also symbolic aspirational expectations such as rites of passage.

REFERENCES

Bernstein, B. 1971. *Theoretical Studies towards a Sociology of Language*. Vol. 1. London: Routledge.

Carey, J. 1989. *Communication as Culture*. London: Unwin Hyman.

Clifford, R. 1998a. "ASBI, Análisis Semántico Basado en la Imagen." In *Técnicas de Investigación en Sociedad, Cultura y Comunicación*, edited by Jesús Galindo. Reading, MA: Addison-Wesley.

Clifford, R., R. Gómez, and O. Arango. 1998. *Imaginario Social de las Telenovelas: Parte dos, Ciclo uno*. Coordinación de Asesores de Presidencia, TV Azteca. México City, México: TV Azteca.

Collins, Randell. 1994. *Four Sociological Traditions*. Oxford, UK: Oxford University Press.

Giddens A. 1991. *Modernity and Self-Identity*. Cambridge, UK: Polity.

Murdock, G., and G. Phelps. 1973. *Mass Media and the Secondary School*. London: Macmillan Educational.

Ong, W. 1982. *Orality and Literacy: The Technologizing of the Word*. London: Methuen.

Sheehy, G. 1984. *Passages*. New York: Bantam Books.

Silverstone, R. 1994. *Television and Everyday Life*. London: Routledge.

Vazquez, V. 1997. *La Vida Misma*. Coordinación de Asesores de Presidencia, TV Azteca. México City, México: TV Azteca.

PART II
CASE STUDIES

Cultural Identity:
Between Reality and Fiction
A Transformation of Genre and Roles in Mexican Telenovelas

María de la Luz Casas Pérez

In examining the way people use media, we surmise that media help in shaping the world we live in. They give us ideas, offer interpretation or preferred meanings, and help us make sense of reality. This is especially true of soap operas or *telenovelas*: they help viewers relate to social situations. As some researchers have stated, audiences are active and derive a variety of meanings from telenovelas (McAnany and LaPastina 1994). Hereby, we state that telenovelas also help construct cultural identity.

Examples will be given to demonstrate ways in which individuals focus, give meaning, and relate to other members of their group or class, developing a sense of cultural differentiation. These parameters are fundamental to understanding changing roles and social patterns on which, as discussed later, telenovelas are believed to have certain influence (Kottak 1990).

In defining *cultural identity*, several notions arise, namely, those of cultural expression, nationality, and national sentiment. These vary according to the position and particular philosophy of culture. Culture, and cultural expression, will hereby be referred to as the basic ingredient of the notion of cultural identity. As Paul Audley noted, "our culture is expressed not just in works of art or entertainment, but in all forms of expression that reflect attitudes, opinions, values and ideas, and in information and analysis concerning the present as well as the past. Just as an awareness of our collective past is an essential component of cultural identity, so too is an awareness of what is happening now" (1983, xxi).

Culture is a complex and dynamic ecology of people, things, world-views, activities, and settings, an ecology that fundamentally endures but also changes

---

María de la Luz Casas Pérez: "Cultural Identity: Between Reality and Fiction: A Transformation of Genres and Roles in Mexican Telenovelas," first published in *Television and New Media*, Vol. 6, Issue 4, 407–14.

in routine communication and social interaction: "today familiar resources ranging from food, language and religious rituals to TV programmes and popular music are combined by individuals and groups into distinctive cultural repertoires or tool kits" (Lull 1995, 66). Television has become an important part of daily routine. In some instances, and particularly for some people, life takes place according to television programming (Lull 1998).

TELENOVELAS AND LIFE DYNAMICS

Statistics related to telenovela viewing in Latin America indicate that viewers are mainly women, although male audiences are increasing. Research shows that audiences vary from Brazil to Venezuela, Colombia, Chile, Peru, and Mexico and that the purposes of telenovela production are also varied. In Brazil, telenovelas helped the government spread a changing image of the nation from rural-regional to urban-national (Kottak 1990); they also helped women deal with birth-control issues (Population Communications International 1997);[1] in Venezuela, telenovelas are a way of expressing female domination within the family (Barrios, as quoted in McAnany and LaPastina 1994). In most of Latin America, telenovelas are the preferred show for women, used as a way of communicating and as linkage among women of different generations (Covarrubias Cuellar, Bautista, and Uribe 1994).

Patterns of behavior are present in the way audiences deal with television. Rituals—regular, constant family activities—are repeated to negotiate encounters with television. Men are attracted to action movies; women prefer slow programs in which they can pay attention to details (Muñoz 1992). Telenovelas are changing, as are the people who watch them and the way they deal with whatever beliefs and values telenovelas reproduce. We may therefore assume that individual, cultural, and national identities are being transformed by new patterns of consumption and production of media content.

In Mexico, telenovelas are a guaranteed media product. Ninety percent of homes have at least one television set, and more than 80 percent of viewers indicate they watch television daily (Huerta Wong 2001). Changes have occurred in themes, plots, and in the way characters deal with everyday problems in telenovelas. Studies report men watching soaps more frequently than before. Recent evidence in Mexico seems to contradict the masculine hegemony of the television room (González 1994; Lozano and Martínez 2000; Huerta Wong 2001), suggesting there is no clear evidence of male dominance in the decision-making process.

MEXICAN CULTURAL IDENTITIES AND THEIR PORTRAYAL IN MEDIA

Several observations can be made about cultural representations of *lo mexicano* throughout the years. Those representations can be related to the emergence of particular media as well. For instance, the representation of male dominance in music and film in the forties exported a view of machos dressed in mariachi clothes, happily singing while facing danger. Females would be represented as companions of, or background to, the main characters, serving much the same purpose as nice scenery or a fine horse.

For years, Mexican telenovelas consisted mainly of a love triangle in which a young, beautiful, honest, and poor girl falls in love with a man, usually rich and usually of a higher social class, and has to overcome all sorts of trouble caused by an evil third party.[2] Some sacrifice would usually be required. Lovers would have to endure pain and sorrow to achieve true love, which would be the dominant force for cultural cohesion, with marriage as the ultimate social mechanism for its legitimization. No sordid or deviant behaviors would be presented, other than those of evil characters. Love and marriage would be considered the basic components of social integration and stability.

During the eighties and nineties, Mexico gained presence through telenovelas around the world but also began to receive cultural influences through media imports. Venezuelan and Brazilian telenovelas invaded Mexican TV screens, giving viewers new choices, themes, and representations of love and relationships.

With the North American influence for more explicit sex on the screen, a decline in commitment among couples, less focus on marriage as the only socially accepted institution for the legitimization of relationships, and more acceptance of premarital sex, Latin Americans looked for alternatives. A chaotic world was not explainable through the stability of family as institution; political and economic turmoil was not resolved through hard work; values were in crisis. Telenovelas started to include all these elements, offering sex appeal and visual cadence.

"As society changes, as fashions vary, as personal liberty fluctuates, as freedom of expression increases, as democracy develops, as alternatives are born, as justice is sought—then inevitably what we see on television is bound to change too, to keep up with modern life and trends" (Pearson 1999). Therefore, as the Mexican social context evolved, female telenovela characters began to work outside the home and male macho patterns started to fade. Women began to address issues related to domestic violence, male domination, and other issues usually avoided within the genre.

A SMALL TOKEN OF CHANGE IN MEXICAN TELENOVELAS

Along with the factors described above, much of the impetus for change came from shifts in the Mexican media conglomerates. In 1993, the Mexican government sold part of its media enterprises in a package that included newspapers, television frequencies, film theatres, and film production companies. Among these was TV Azteca's channel 13, a television station with national broadcasting range. Its license was granted to Ricardo Salinas Pliego, president of Televisión Azteca, today Televisa's main competitor.

Salinas Pliego quickly understood that to compete, he must produce telenovelas, the highest rating programs on Mexican television, with new ways to address the genre. He hired Epigmenio Ibarra, head of Argos Productions, to produce a series of telenovelas that soon provoked comments from academia and critics alike.

Ibarra was trained in film narrative:[3] he took the plot outside the studio, onto the streets. He made extreme changes in camera movements, dialogues, and themes. Characters were less fairy-tale-like and more like real, flawed people. He brought previously ignored subjects such as revenge, battered women, and betrayal onto the scene. He even portrayed government bureaucrats and police officers as telenovela characters, addressing issues of political corruption that were not censored by the government as evidence of openness and proof of the newly acquired freedom of expression in media.[4]

Televisa kept its channel 2 (also with national broadcasting range) primarily for the broadcasting of telenovelas, but it worked to diversify its audiences. The genre evolved and became multitargeted: Televisa's early afternoon telenovelas would be directed at children and young adults, late afternoon ones at housewives, and late evening telenovelas would be directed at adults, both male and female. The genre is still evolving, affecting the way Mexicans view themselves.

The process described above can be illustrated by viewer responses to two successful telenovelas in Mexico: one from Televisa and one from Azteca, emerging from data compiled in 2001 at the Tecnológico de Monterrey in Campus Cuernavaca, Mexico.[5] Episodes of Televisa's *Sin Pecado Concebido* (*Conceived Without Sin*) were examined alongside episodes of Azteca's *Lo Que es el Amor* (*What Love Is*). The treatment of new themes and subject matters was examined by content analyses of episodes of both telenovelas,[6] whereas issues of preferred meanings and interpretation were drawn from focus group sessions with regular *relenovela* viewers.[7]

The content analyses showed issues never accounted for in Mexican telenovelas, such as male impotence, baldness, homosexuality, AIDS, polygamy, menopause, battering of women and children, home violence, and fear of solitude, thus contrasting with strong male figures of earlier soaps and driving dramatizations more into reality and away from fiction. As to audience interpretation, focus groups conducted with regard to both telenovelas indicated that viewers saw a need for fantasy to remain true to the genre but also that they prefer stories closer to reality. Audiences look for stereotypes, which help to identify good from bad, but appreciate characters that are multifaceted, making plots more interesting.

The focus groups' findings suggested that Azteca's telenovelas appeal to young, more educated viewers, whereas Televisa's are popular with older, less educated audiences. More educated people reported watching telenovelas for entertainment and said that they do not believe the situations depicted, whereas less educated people insisted that they themselves had had problems similar to those presented and found the information given them helpful. Others reported that the treatment of subject matter leads to controversy within the household but that they watch anyway.

Some viewers who appreciated that telenovelas are now closer to reality and less predictable also claimed that youngest family members were not allowed to watch. Young viewers in the focus groups said that telenovelas gave them a sense of fashion and trends. Some indicated that they offer culture, showing new situations and providing interpretations of reality. A majority insisted that telenovelas depict reality by presenting Mexican society as it is. One woman mentioned that telenovelas "teach language and culture" and that some behavior is imitated by younger viewers.

THE FINAL EPISODE: MEXICAN CULTURAL IDENTITY IS CHANGING

Media texts are important components of evolving cultural texts written by complex societies. This is particularly true nowadays because of the globalization of culture and the dynamics of worldwide television production exchanges. In Mexico, the genre evolved in concert with political and economic change. A large, developing country having to deal for the first time with freedom of expression and democracy had to come to terms with the fact that reality was more sordid and crude than television had hitherto depicted.

Television producers working with the assumption that after several political and economic crises, Mexico's audiences doubted what they saw on television came to the conclusion that viewers were mature enough to accept reality with all its flaws. Political, economic, and cultural contexts were finally represented through telenovelas and articulated and interpreted through language and other highly elaborate modes and codes. New role models pertaining to international and cosmopolitan societies were introduced to Mexican audiences, ones now consisting of people from all genders and socioeconomic backgrounds instead of just housewives.

New ways of establishing relationships, dealing with personal and social crises, while still looking for love and affection, entered Mexican telenovela plots. While still supporting family values, a wider range of social roles for women have been established. Male characters are slowly moving away from *machista* attitudes, confronting more active, outgoing women.

Finally, Mexican telenovelas still carry a dose of fantasy and fiction, but they slowly resemble more real-drama situations. The hybridization of the genre is bringing about a new kind of media product, one that is probably unique in nature when compared to other soap operas in the world.

CONCLUSIONS

Cultural identity traits are interwoven with reality and fiction in Mexican telenovelas. Mexicans seem to prefer greater doses of reality instead of fairy-tale-type stories in new telenovelas; however, they remain faithful to the genre conventions when trying to evade problems. For example, new role models and patterns of behavior are being established for viewers—especially women, shown as professionals working outside the home and dealing with situations that were traditionally the province of the male. Nonetheless, stereotypes are still used to generate preferred meanings (for example, handsome men and women models promote desired patterns of beauty), and a basic element of telenovelas in relation to Mexican cultural identity remains: poor, honest characters suffer injustice at the hands of the elite, and love will prevail.

Mexican telenovelas now avoid cultural references and colloquial terms and language to enhance their usefulness for export as international products. Home consumption means that viewers are adopting a more cosmopolitan, internationalized jargon. The traditional characteristics of Mexican cultural identity—religion, language, national character, and history—are slowly being mixed with new elements, thus appealing to a wider, more globalized audience.

Mexican telenovelas today are deeply engaged in the overall issue of reflecting a complex, dynamic, yet conservative cultural community while transforming identity into that of a more cosmopolitan, mature, liberal, and modern society. Further research has to be conducted to generate more evidence that will support these conclusions. However, the evidence so far available suggests that themes and subject matters, treatments of content, and styles of production in the newest Mexican telenovela productions are beginning to influence patterns of cultural identity.

NOTES

1. Carolina and Scarlet, the characters of the main Brazilian telenovela *A Indominada* (*The Indomitable*) openly discuss their views on sex and reproduction. This intertwining of educational information and drama is part of the success of this production of Population Communications International/Brasil that has been designed to communicate sexual orientation and reproductive health information within the plot. A study conducted by the University of São Paulo on this telenovela alone indicates that telenovelas have contributed significantly to the reduction of birth rates in Brazil (Population Communications International 1997).

2. As pointed out by Katz and Liebes (as quoted in McAnany and LaPastina 1994), audiences recognize the fictional nature of the genre and the functioning of its rules, thus conceding that this formula is far closer to fiction than to reality; nonetheless, viewers accept the deal and play along (see McAnany and LaPastina 1994, 837).

3. Ibarra was mostly trained as a journalist doing film documentaries. This explains in part why his treatment of telenovelas related more to reality than to fiction.

4. The first Argos productions set the path for a radical transformation in social acceptance of certain subject matters, but the telenovela that truly transformed the institution of marriage and opened sexual taboos for discussion was *Mirada de Mujer*.

5. A group of students and professors of the Tecnológico de Monterrey in Campus Cuernavaca, Mexico, carried out the study between the months of August and December 2001. Special thanks for this data must be given to Dr. Juan Ricardo Cojuc, Dr. Ilya Adler, Silvia Soria, and their students.

6. The viewing sample for both telenovelas consisted of taped episodes from a typical viewing week (Monday to Friday), August 20-24. This particular viewing week was selected considering that both competing telenovelas shared the same time slot (which is considered primetime programming for each network), were at their peak viewing, and reported high ratings at the time. Quantitative and qualitative content analyses were applied to five episodes of each telenovela: five to Televisa's *Sin Pecado Concebido* and five to TV Azteca's *Lo Que es el Amor*. Ten key scenes were selected from each telenovela and carefully analyzed by three groups of students, leading first to the individual identification of visual, verbal, and nonverbal units of content and meaning, and then to discussion among groups at length. At the same time, four focus groups were conducted to gather elements of interpretation directly from audiences. Participants of a variety of sociodemographic characteristics were randomly selected

to participate, the only prerequisite being that they would be regular telenovela viewers. The bridge of comparison was thus created by the audience between the quantitative part of the analysis and the qualitative ways of interpreting preferred meanings.

7. For a complete review on theory and critique of the genre, see Pearson (1999).

REFERENCES

Audley, P. 1983. *Canada's Cultural Industries: Broadcasting, Publishing, Records and Film.* Toronto, Canada: James Lorimer and the Canadian Institute for Economic Policy.

Covarrubias Cuellar, K., A. Bautista, and B. A. Uribe. 1994. *Cuéntame en Qué se Quedó: La telenovela como Fenómeno Social.* Mexico City, Mexico: Trillas.

González, J. A. 1994. *Más (+) Cultura(s): Ensayos sobre Realidades Plurales.* Mexico City, Mexico: Consejo Nacional par la Cultura y las Artes.

Huerta Wong, J. E. 2001. "No le Cambies a mi Novela: Dominación y Negociación entre Géneros en el Acto de Ver Televisión." Paper presented at the annual conference at the Universidad de las Americas, Bienal Iberoamericana de Comunicación: Globalización, tecnologia y culturas, Puebla, México.

Kottak, C. P. 1990. *Prime Time Society: An Anthropological Analysis of Television and Culture.* Belmont, CA: Wadsworth.

Lozano, J. C., and F. C. Martínez. 2000. "Consumo y Lecturas Negociadas de Noticieros Televisivos en Monterrey, Guadalajara y México." Paper presented at the Congreso Anual 2000 de la International Communication Association, Acapulco, México.

Lull, J. 1995. *Media, Communications, Culture: A Global Approach.* New York: Columbia University Press.

———. 1998. "Constructing Rituals of Extension through Family Television Viewing." In *World Families Watch Television*, edited by J. Lull. Newbury Park, CA: Sage.

McAnany, E., and Antonio LaPastina. 1994. "Telenovela Audiences: A Review and Methodological Critique of Latin America Research." *Communication Research* 21 (6): 828–49.

Muñoz, S. 1992. "Mundos de Vida y Modos de Ver." In *Televisión y Melodrama*, edited by J. B. Martín and S. Muñoz. Bogota, Colombia: Tercer Mundo Editores.

Pearson, R. 1999. "Genre, Convention and Evolution: The Changing Face of the Mexican Telenovela." Master's thesis, University of Leicester, United Kingdom.

Population Communications International. 1997. *A Indomindada.* Available at http://www.comminit.com/la/descripciones/lapdsbrasil/descripciones318.html.

Fact or Fiction?
Narrative and Reality in the Mexican Telenovela

Rosalind C. Pearson

Telenovelas are to Mexico what soap operas are to England—an essential ingredient in the tradition, culture, and history of a country. The advent of television, the tradition of *radionovelas*, and the taste for melodrama awakened by the films of the Epoca de Oro period in the 1940s in Mexico gave the first telenovelas a highly successful style and format. Audiences were immediately captivated, and today, Mexicans young and old carry on with this sixty-year-old tradition, demanding an ever-increasing investment on the part of the television companies to provide for the steadily growing consumption of telenovelas.

Changes have inevitably occurred in the style and format of the typical Mexican telenovela, but the basic ingredients of a love interest, complicated family relationships, unreal dialogue, and the poor striving to be rich still form the basis of the average telenovela. Its length varies from as little as three months to occasionally, if successful, perhaps eighteen to twenty months. During this time, a huge amount of activity takes place, including the development of exaggerated and fantastic situations based on lies, gossip, and apparently, unattainable desires. The changes in recent telenovelas lie most obviously in the use of film techniques, development of narrative styles, and moves toward more socially realistic treatment of subject matter.

As closed narrative texts, telenovelas differ from their Australian, English, or American soap opera cousins. There are a very definite beginning, middle, and end to every Mexican telenovela; what happens on the way through these states in terms of narrative involves a style and treatment of subject matter

---

Author's Note: The research at Tecnológico de Monterrey was carried out by three groups of students under the guidance of Dr. Ricardo Cojuc, Dr. Ilya Adler, and Silvia Soria during the August-to-December 2001 semester.

Rosalind C. Pearson: "Fact or Fiction? Narrative and Reality in the Mexican Telenovela," first published in *Television and New Media*, Vol. 6, Issue 4, 400–406.

designed to make sure audiences are "hooked" enough to want to tune in every day to watch the heroes and heroines go through disaster after disaster, before somehow arriving at a happy ending. How close this treatment is to reality is at issue here; how much telenovelas are based on fact or fiction, or a mixture of both, is the question, and this article will attempt a discussion of the narrative style and structure of the Mexican telenovela in relation to the changes currently being experienced by the genre and in relation to how "reality" is negotiated.

FACT VS. FICTION

The issue of "reality" is particularly pertinent at the moment, especially with the advent of what is known as "reality TV." Reality TV shows have been seen in the United States, England, and other countries during the past couple of years, and some of these shows have been imported and shown in Mexico on cable television, with limited success. Now the home-made version, a Mexican version of *Big Brother* (produced by Televisa, starting in March 2002), is going out on a national network, and it will be interesting to see how this will impact telenovela audiences. In the meantime, the five or six hours a day of telenovelas shown on two national television channels (Televisa's channel 2 and TV Azteca's channel 13) are the staple diet for many millions of Mexicans who will perhaps find it hard to abandon their handsome heroes and beautiful heroines living out a semirealistic fantasy.

Telenovela scriptwriters can hardly be compared to Dickens or Balzac, but what they do have in common is an attempt to get "under the surface of ideology to reveal the 'true' relations between people and their source in class struggles" (O'Sullivan et al. 1994, 258). If we take this literally, the "true relations" refer to the inevitable struggle between men and women, be it married couples, boyfriends and girlfriends, brothers and sisters, mothers and sons, whatever the combination, that in the Mexican telenovela is always the crux of the action. Much of the resultant angst is due to "class struggles": the poor trying to be rich, a working-class fatherless son or daughter suddenly discovering a rich father, the typical Cinderella-type story. The dominant ingredient in any telenovela is the love story, but the smooth passage of this love interest is always thwarted, traditionally by melodramatic tensions of infidelity, betrayal, and lies, and more recently with the added tensions of politics and social issues. The melodrama is still very definitely there, but it is a level of melodrama that reflects perhaps somewhat more realistically the average Mexican's daily life.

Telenovela scripts, or texts, are narratives that "can be seen as the devices and strategies, the conventions and sequencing of events with characterization, which constitute a story, be it fictional or factual" (Newbold 1995, 444). A telenovela is a story, and every story has a narrative structure that is a very important part of understanding texts, as well as being essential to the recognition of genres. "Narratives are sequences of events, settings and characters arranged in a logical order through time, the sequence being driven by cause and effect" (Abercrombie 1996, 19). These events, settings, and characters are immediately recognizable and identifiable as being of today, thus "the use of representational devices (signs, conventions, narrative strategies, and so on) to depict or portray a physical, social or moral universe" (O'Sullivan et al. 1994, 257) is the basis of all telenovela narrative structures. We can therefore talk about telenovelas offering a *constructed reality* or a *reflection* of real life.

Even for documentary filmmakers, it is difficult to depict reality without imposing some form of subjectivity into the structure, but the telenovela as a story is what is deemed fiction, and fiction gives us stories about a world, as opposed to *the* world (Nichols 1991, 113), an imaginary world that allows the characters to do things that we would not necessarily call realistic. Fiction allows us to be tricked and entertained, intrigued and excited, tempted and concerned. We recognize a world and its people, places, and things, but "the resemblance is fundamentally metaphorical.... It is a likeness rather than a replica" (Nichols 1991, 109). Fiction offers a version of events, settings, and characters, but only insofar as they are useful to the narrative form and relevant to the plot and subplots forming the story. The narrative is essential to the unfolding of a story; as Ellis says, "the narrative is a tight organization of actions and themes in a pattern of crisis, innovation and repetition that is orchestrated to a particular resolution" (1999, 67). Nichols likens narrative to a "black hole" where everything is drawn "within its ambit inward, organizing everything from décor and clothing to dialogue and action to serve a story" (1991, 142). If this is true, then reality has to take a back seat; the only thing "real" about a telenovela is its loose connection to *the* world we recognize.

The language or dialogue used in telenovela narratives "can be interpreted to refer to or *reference* the world" (Hall 1997, 22). The language used is the clue to how audiences make sense of what they are seeing. Meanings are constructed through "representation" that provides the "link between concepts and language which enables us to *refer* to either the 'real' world of objects, people or events, or indeed to imaginary worlds of fictional objects, people and events" (Hall 1997, 17). Language is therefore used to convey meaning, but language, in all its richness, is not able to accurately convey, reflect, or represent the real world. Thus, language too helps in the construction of *a* world.

New telenovelas are often remakes of old stories, *refritos*, as they are called in Spanish. The public often know what is going to happen in a story, but what they do not know is *how* the story is to be narrated. The *how* includes what Fiske refers to as "the cultural specificity or ideology of a narrative (that) lies in the way this deep structure is transformed into apparently different stories, that is, in which actions and individuals are chosen to perform the functions and character roles" (1987, 138). This relates also to Solomon's belief that "the search for underlying patterns ... can relate a particular cultural or artistic experience to some universal truth about human nature or the society we live in" (1995, 457). Television programs—and telenovelas are no exception—present a view of the world that is acceptable and in line with the audience's expectations and beliefs, a view that is not questioned but assumed to be the norm. Our common sense guides us, and that is why we accept what telenovela characters do in a given situation; as Abercrombie says, "the world of television texts is therefore a commonsense world in which much is taken for granted" (1996, 32).

The narrative structure of a text that involves the telling of a story is commonly acknowledged to represent the dominant ideology and rarely attempts to upset the status quo of a particular culture. Good always triumphs over evil, order over disorder, and in the language of telenovela, love wins out despite crimes, murders, lies, treachery, and the like. The Virgin of Guadalupe (the Mexican Virgin) has a strong role to play in this sequence of events, being called on repeatedly to help the "good" characters win out over the "bad" characters. Since in popular culture, "the narrative structure is likely to be used in favour of the status quo" (Fiske 1987, 140), there is a feeling of comfort and security engendered by these texts, particularly the Mexican telenovela. The Bulgarian structuralist Todorov believed that "narratives are to do with very fundamental ways in which societies see themselves" (Abercrombie 1996, 23), and the telenovela, with its closed-text format and its beginning, middle, and happy ending, represents Todorov's theory of narrative in which a harmonious situation (the beginning) is disrupted (the middle) before the reestablishment of harmony (the ending).

The narrative conveys a meaning that is part of the way a society sees itself, or as Fiske (1987, 142) says, there is an "interweaving of voices which are shared by reader and writer and which cross the boundaries of the text itself to link it to other texts and to culture in general." We know that telenovelas are fiction and that fiction takes us into an invented world, but we also know that telenovelas are an accepted part of everyday life. The world created on the screen is a recognizable one, even more so today now that telenovelas have progressed to including more socially realistic themes. "The telenovela is a text of our time, a product of our culture, a total example and expression of our society. The telenovela portrays us, reinvents us, imitates us, reflects us" (Galindo 1998, 152, my translation).

Telenovelas, as fiction, entertain; they are dramatic, funny, tedious, emotional, occasionally horrific, exaggerated, and informative. Telenovelas, as representative of reality, reflect everyday life in Mexico; they highlight social issues such as drug abuse, domestic violence, rape, sex before marriage, insecurity in the streets; they inform and educate at the same time as entertain; they enter our imagination and charge our emotions. They are a microcosm of Mexican life and culture, with the drama of daily life translating into the melodrama of telenovela life. Melodrama synthesizes the real with the unreal, it pushes common occurrences into the realm of fantasy, and it provides a level of emotional involvement for audiences that guarantees their participation in the development of the telenovela. But as Gledhill points out, deciding "which meanings, which definitions of reality, will win the consent of the audience" (1997, 353) is all-important; that is the difference between success and failure.

The relation between the fictional and real worlds is necessarily complicated, as complicated as defining realism. Fiske goes so far as to say that "television [is] an essentially realistic medium because of its ability to carry a socially convincing sense of the real. Realism is not a matter of any fidelity to an empirical reality, but of the discursive conventions by which and for which a sense of reality is constructed" (Fiske 1987, 21). He says that realism "makes sense of the real" (p. 25), that it is "a reactionary mode of representation that promotes and naturalizes the dominant ideology" (p. 36). The dominant ideology, or preferred meaning, is always present in Mexican telenovelas, but so too are alternative meanings, meanings that the audience—depending on educational and social levels—actively interpret. "People can . . . enjoy soap operas or telenovelas even though they may be ideologically consistent with dominant values. But, at the same time, they may take up these pleasures and use them to critique these same values" (Brown 1994, 5). Scriptwriters and producers have the double-edged duty of keeping existing audiences captive while trying to attract new ones. It is all-important for the script—the narrative—to be creative, which means that "topicality, being up-to-date, [and] controversy . . . [are] all vital factors in the form's continuance" (Gledhill 1997, 361). This need for cultural verisimilitude is something that roots telenovela narratives in *the* world, a world separate from fiction but identifiable immediately with what is real.

This is particularly the case in what we term the "new-style" telenovelas seen on TV Azteca during the past seven or eight years. *Lo Que es el Amor* (*What Love Is*) seen in 2001-02 might not have turned out as it did if TV Azteca had not experimented with Argos TV and its ideas for reinvigorating the genre (see Pearson 1999). This telenovela features a group of "yuppies," working in the stock exchange, who never seem to actually do any work and to whom the most extraordinary things happen. Themes include topics such as male sexual impotence, baldness, obsessive behavior, gang fights, divorce, murder, blackmail, infidelity, lies, homosexuality, and cancer (to mention a few!), and their behavior, lifestyle, and clothing represent a completely upper-middle-class standard of living.

In research carried out at the Tecnológico de Monterrey, Campus Cuernavaca, in autumn of 2001, these "new-style" telenovelas were viewed by focus group members as "more realistic" and as entertaining enough to "make you forget reality for a moment." Themes were considered to be "realistic," but the handling of situations was not. What is presented and identified as a lifelike situation to begin with then moves into exaggeration and extreme circumstances, moving it away from reality. Themes hitherto considered unsuitable for telenovelas—or indeed television in Mexico—are now being treated, but at the same time, the stereotypical good and bad characters are still present.

Lo Que es el Amor came on at 9 p.m., in direct competition with *Sin Pecado Concebido* (*Conceived without Sin*) on Televisa's channel 2. This latter production was much more representative of the "classic" telenovela and had consistently higher ratings. Televisa is also moving with the times, but its move to a more socially realistic treatment has been much slower and more gradual. They are not losing audiences; they are slowly convincing audiences of the new trends. TV Azteca, as the new rival only in existence since 1993, needs to be innovative and trend-setting to win audiences, but what they are discovering is that audiences are not necessarily being taken away from Televisa; rather, the audience base is growing.

CONCLUSION

There is room for more telenovelas; there is room for more audience. New ideas and treatment of the typical telenovela are rejuvenating the genre and providing a much-needed injection to the format. We can conclude, therefore, that telenovelas today are indeed a mixture of fact and fiction, with the equation moving up and down as needed. Telenovelas are fiction and they entertain—this is a fact. Their relationship to reality is at the same time stronger and more pronounced, but their treatment of this issue is very much bound into the more traditional desires of audiences to be entertained and transported away from their own particular reality. "Television is pushed by the demand that it should entertain. It is pulled by the competition for audiences into any amount of trivia and sensationalism" (Ellis 1999, 69); television viewing is so much a part of life in Mexico that for some, television almost is reality. "Life is like a telenovela" is often the refrain uttered by Mexicans, old and young, male and female. Telenovelas are a way of life in Mexico, as are *chisme* (gossip), *mentiras* (lies), and *infidelidad* (infidelity). It is all indefatigably intertwined, so much so that the line between *the* world and *a* world is often difficult to distinguish.

REFERENCES

Abercrombie, N. 1996. *Television and Society*. Cambridge, UK: Polity.
Brown, M. E. 1994. *Soap Opera and Women's Talk*. Thousand Oaks, CA: Sage.
Ellis, J. 1999. "Television as Working-Through." In *Television and Common Knowledge*, edited by J. Gripsrud. London: Routledge.
Fiske, J. 1987. *Television Culture*. London: Routledge.
Galindo, J. 1998. "Lo Cotidiano y lo Social: La Telenovela como Texto y Pretexto." In *La Cofradía de las Emociones (Interminables): Miradas sobre Telenovelas en México*, edited by J. Galindo. Guadalajara, México: Universidad de Guadalajara.
Gledhill, C. 1997. "Genre and Gender: The Case of Soap Opera." In *Representation: Cultural Representations and Signifying Practices*, edited by S. Hall. London: Sage.
Hall, S. 1997. "The Work of Representation." In *Representation: Cultural Representations and Signifying Practices*, edited by S. Hall. London: Sage.
Newbold, C. 1995. "Analysing the Moving Image." In *Approaches to Media*, edited by O. Boyd-Barratt and C. Newbold. London: Edward Arnold.
Nichols, B. 1991. *Representing Reality*. Bloomington: Indiana University Press.
O'Sullivan, T., J. Hartley, D. Saunders, M. Montgomery, and J. Fiske. 1994. *Key Concepts in Communication and Cultural Studies*. London: Routledge.
Pearson, R. 1999. "Genre, Convention and Evolution: The Changing Face of the Mexican Telenovela." Master's thesis, University of Leicester, United Kingdom.
Solomon, S. J. 1995. "Defining Genre/Genre and Popular Culture." In *Approaches to Media*, edited by O. Boyd-Barratt and C. Newbold. London: Edward Arnold.

Whose Life in the Mirror?
Examining Three Mexican Telenovelas as Cultural and Commercial Products

Laura J. Beard

In "The Cofraternity of (Un)Finishable Emotions: Constructing Mexican Telenovelas," Jorge A. González asserts that telenovelas are, "together with the Boom writers, the most current and vital cultural product that Latin American countries export to the world and share among themselves" (60). Brazil's leading television network, Rede Globo, for example, which was the fourth-largest commercial television network in the world in the 1980s after ABC, CBS and NBC, had by 1988 exported television programs, particularly telenovelas, to 130 countries throughout the world (Tufte 2, 20). These popular serial television programs, broadcast during the afternoon and evening hours, are usually shown Monday through Friday and last for several months. In Mexico, the most popular telenovelas often have a one-hour episode on a weekend evening that shows the week's highlights so that viewers who missed episodes may catch up on the important parts. Thus, the production and the consumption of the telenovela differ both from U.S. soap operas, which are shown during the day and may last years, but also from U.S. situation comedies or dramas, which appear only once a week during the evening hours. As vital cultural products viewed by millions of people on a daily basis, telenovelas contribute to the social construction of gender in Latin America.

Judith Butler, in *Gender Trouble: Feminism and the Subversion of Identity*, stresses that it is "impossible to separate out 'gender' from the political and cultural intersections in which it is invariably produced and maintained" (3). Gender is a performative act, socially constructed and perpetually re-enacted and reinforced. As Butler sets out the terms of sex, gender and desire, gender is not merely the juridical conception of the cultural inscription of meaning on a pregiven sex, but also the designation of "the very apparatus of production whereby the sexes themselves are established" (7). Butler's discussion of gender thus explores how the possibilities of imaginable and realizable gen-

---

Laura J. Beard: "Whose Life in the Mirror?: Examining Three Mexican Telenovelas as Cultural and Commercial Products," first published in *Studies in Latin American Popular Culture* vol. 22 (2003): 73–88.

der configurations within culture are presupposed and preempted in part by the limits of what, within a given culture, that language sees as "the imaginable domain of gender" (9).

An important factor to be examined in the social construction of gender in Mexico is the role of telenovelas in the production and maintenance of cultural meaning. As popular commercial television programs successfully marketed to a large audience, telenovelas take part in forming what can be seen as "the imaginable domain of gender." Telenovelas can serve to maintain ideological hegemony or, very occasionally, to question certain aspects of a system. In *Alice Doesn't: Feminism, Semiotics, Cinema*, Teresa de Lauretis comments on how the discourse of dominant cinema performs "a political function in the service of cultural domination including, but not limited to, the sexual exploitation of women and the repression or containment of female sexuality" (26). Such an assertion can be made of telenovelas as well. As de Lauretis notes, often the only way to position oneself outside of a dominant discourse is "to displace oneself within it" (7).

In this article, I analyze gender roles as well as racial and class politics in three Mexican telenovelas that were airing on Mexican television during the 1999–2000 academic year I spent as a Fulbright Senior Scholar doing research on the social construction of gender in Mexico. In the telenovelas discussed, I look both for the places where the telenovelas assert their own ideologies "with a vengeance," as de Lauretis would put it (157), and for the ruptures and contradictions in the otherwise smooth fabric of those ideologies, places where resistance can be located and celebrated. Of the many telenovelas airing during that year I was in Mexico, the three discussed in this article were chosen as representative of the ways in which telenovelas both reinforce ideological hegemony and, on certain rare occasions and to a limited extent, question it. "Laberintos de Pasión" (Televisa) represents the genre of the telenovelas set on haciendas (large plantation dwellings), and demonstrates particularly rigid patriarchal gender and class roles. "El Candidato" (TV Azteca), while following in many aspects the norms of the stereotypical urban telenovela set in Mexico City amongst the rich and powerful, advertises itself as a *"telenovela interactiva"* and is of particular interest for the ways in which it includes aspects of the year's political presidential campaigns, as a comment on electoral politics in Mexico. "La Vida en el Espejo" (TV Azteca), one of the most popular telenovelas of the year, is innovative in its efforts to reflect life more realistically, to show, as its title indicates, "life in the mirror."[1]

"Laberintos de Pasión" is a product of Televisa, the largest producer of telenovelas in the world. Televisa produces 70 percent of the Hispanic language segment of the U.S. market and co-produces 50 percent of the series shot in Latin America ("Telenovelas: Love, TV, and Power"). The centrality of telenovelas in the Televisa company seems implicitly acknowledged by Televisa's webpage, which shows a sexy young woman and the greeting *"Bienvenido a la fábrica de los sueños"* before going on to note that it is *"el conglomerado de medios más importante en español"* (http://www.esmas.com/televisa). Indeed, Televisa San Angel, owned by Emilio Azcárraga (cited by *Fortune* magazine as one of the richest men in the world), is its own city, employing 6,500 people who work at 11 studios, a self-sufficient world where everything from the sets to the costumes is produced by Televisa, and where the actors even receive acting classes on site ("Telenovelas: Love, TV, and Power"). Seven or eight episodes are shot a day, six days a week, as continuing to produce the profitable cultural product maintains the fortune for the company and its owner. While the impact of the telenovela phenomenon on the international market can be seen in the example of Televisa, Televisa's fortune is based on its four national channels and 200 regional channels, with an indisputable hegemony that is built on strong relations with the political powers in Mexico. Televisa has its own set of ethical principles regarding what is appropriate for telenovelas, so that no matter what the topic, the story must conclude on a note of hope and love, allowing viewers to be able to go to bed free from stress. Televisa does not conceive of telenovelas as being educational but rather as reflecting some aspect of reality, with family and true love as the most important elements. Good acts should be rewarded and bad acts punished, affirm the Televisa executives interviewed in the video "Telenovelas: Love, TV, and Power." A traditional, hegemonic ideology is thus being strictly maintained by the telenovelas produced by Televisa.

In addition to the ethical principles that are a part of Televisa's own conservative ideology are those imposed by the Mexican government. Televisa has a Department of Literary Supervision, with employees who know the ethical and moral rules stipulated by the secretariat to the Mexican government which supervises and controls censorship. The department makes sure that Televisa employees all know these rules, together with the rules of the company. Readers can refuse a scenario that appears in a script and explain why it cannot be broadcast. An author who has many years of experience writing with Televisa knows the rules and abides by them, noted a Televisa executive interviewed in "Telenovelas: Love, TV, and Power."

Televisa's "Laberintos de Pasión" is set in the fictional town of San Vincente, mostly taking place on a ranch called "El Castillo." In the world of "Laberintos de Pasión," the man's home is truly his castle, for this telenovela showcases traditional gender roles where the father is the patriarch who rules absolutely in the house and on the ranch. Both male and female children are expected to obey the father, and the wife is not allowed to contradict her husband's dictums. The wife is passive, the husband controlling. The father on the ranch is Genaro Valencia, a violent man who had apparently murdered his first wife, appears to be responsible for the death of the beloved grandfather of the telenovela's heroine, Julieta Valderrama, and will, by the end of the telenovela, attempt to kill both his second wife and his foreman. Genaro has two sons, Pedro and Cristóbal, the first whom he favors and the second whom he considers weak. The main love story, complicated by both main and secondary love triangles, is between Pedro and Julieta. In this stereotypical, melodramatic telenovela, the evil Genaro wears a black hat and the good Pedro dons a white hat.

A representative scene exemplifying the traditional patriarchal gender roles and the absolute control males expect to exert over the women in their families is one aired on November 15, 1999. The daughter of a prominent family in town, Alejandra Sandoval, disobeys her father and leaves the house, in this case only going to talk to the village priest—hardly a grave transgression, but one that puts her on the street alone in the evening. Her father happens to see her on the street, becomes furious, yells at her, grabs her, and pushes her around. When another person in the town protests the father's treatment of the daughter, he responds, "Esta niña es mi hija y la trato como me de la gana." Throughout the telenovela, the women are seen as property of the men to be treated as such.

"Laberintos de Pasión" is a stereotypical melodrama, with love triangles, cases of forbidden love, and climactic announcements coming at the end of each episode to keep audiences interested enough to return for the next night's episode. One of the conventions of telenovelas (and soap operas) is for each *capitulo* to be interrupted a number of times by commercials, so that the scene preceding each commercial break ends with a tag line enticing enough that viewers will stay tuned to watch the rest of the show. When writers work on a script, they must order the segments of the scenes to work up to the tag lines before commercials, putting the second-best tag line before the longest commercial break and the best tag line before the end of the show to leave viewers hanging, wanting to come back the next day. In "Laberintos," not only are the tag lines carefully scripted, but the most climactic scenes take place during dramatic thunderstorms. In the episode of November 18, 1999, Genaro tells Cristóbal that he is useless, that their being related is only an accident as Cristóbal obviously shares none of his characteristics. Cristóbal, angry and hurt, goes crashing out of the house, rushing to Julieta to share his despair with her. She tries to comfort him, telling him that he matters to her, that he will always have her, Pedro hears her words, misinterprets them as declarations of love, Pedro and Cristóbal have a huge fight, Cristóbal goes off in his pickup truck, already drunk, and crashes, ending up partially paralyzed. The entire scene happens during a spectacular nighttime thunderstorm. Similarly, in the November 25, 1999, episode, when Gabriel, the man who raised Julieta, finally tells her that his love for her is not that of a father for a daughter but that of a man for a woman, Julieta goes running off into a thunderstorm.

A main case of forbidden love is that of Diego and Alejandra. Diego is the son of Magdalena, a servant at El Castillo. He falls in love with Alejandra Sandoval, the daughter of a prominent attorney in town. Not only would this love affair be deemed inappropriate according to the very strict class lines in San Vincente, but Diego does not realize that Alejandra is his half-sister. In the episode of December 3, 1999, Diego's mother goes to see Arturo Sandoval to tell him that she thinks it is time that Diego knows who his father is. While Arturo forbids her to tell anyone, she tells him that Diego and Alejandra are falling in love and that the only way to prevent it is for her to tell Diego the truth. At this point, Arturo's wife Sara enters and gets angry at seeing "that woman" in her husband's office. Sara has no idea of their previous relationship but thinks that the woman is of low class, *una cualquiera*. The lawyer tells Magdalena not to worry, to let him take care of the issue. He seeks to impose his will without letting his wife see what his connection to Magdalena truly is. He then announces to his wife that this time he really is going to send Alejandra away, to lock her up in a convent. Although his wife had disagreed when he tried to send Alejandra to a convent before, she agrees now because she does not want her daughter associating herself with a low-class young man. That the threat of their daughter having relations with a man of a lower class is enough to justify such a drastic measure shows how important the maintenance of class distinctions is to the characters of this telenovela. This episode also provides the attorney with another opportunity to announce, "Ella es mi hija y ella tiene que hacer lo que yo diga." A daughter is seen as the father's property to be disposed of at his will.

Not wanting to enter a convent, Alejandra runs away to her brother Benjamin to seek his help. Meanwhile, Rosendo has been sent by his boss Genaro to take care of Benjamin, since Benjamin is thwarting Genaro's nefarious plans to obtain Julieta's property. When Alejandra enters her brother's hotel room, she is attacked from behind and strangled to death. The episode ends with her body on the ground, and Julieta announcing to her father, with Benjamin also looking on, "Lo siento mucho, pero su hija está muerta." Alejandra is an object always already possessed by a male. She never controls her own fate.

"Laberintos de Pasión" has an unusual heroine, Julieta Valderrama, in that, unlike most unmarried young women in Mexican telenovelas, she has short hair. She is also blond and studied to be a medical doctor. Although a stronger character than Alejandra and in spite of her professional training, she is also expected to know her place as a female in this very patriarchal society. In the episode of November 24, 1999, when Rosendo (the evil foreman of El Castillo) encounters Julieta at night, he tells her she is too pretty to be alone in a house. When she claims she knows how to protect herself, he reminds her, "Aunque tengas muchos pantalones, eres mujer y eso te pone en peligro." The very fact that she is female puts her in danger in this society any time she is without the protection of a male.

In the episode of December 9, 1999, another of the evil characters, Javier Merino, shows up at night when Julieta is alone in Gabriel's house and assaults her. Julieta is resisting his attack, calling out for help, when Gabriel arrives and pulls Javier off her. The night's episode ends in that dramatic moment. The next night's episode opens in the same moment, with Gabriel's masculine fury aroused, ready to kill Javier, but Julieta asks him to stop, tells him it is enough, that he should just get rid of Javier. The scenes reinforce the sense that Julieta, or any woman, is not safe alone in a house, but always needs a man to protect her from the predatory impulses of other men. Other scenes in which Magdalena is attacked by Rosendo, or in which Alejandra is killed by Rosendo, also underscore this message.

Pedro talks to his uncle Mateo, the village priest, who tells him, apropos of Alejandra's death, that you never know when your day will come and so you need to work out your life to be happy. Pedro rides off on his horse to see Julieta, whom he finds sitting by the banks of the river, in the stereotypical romantic setting. When he tries to kiss her, she pushes him away, forgetting about his injury from a gunshot wound that has not been healing properly. When she then gets concerned, fussing over him, he looks at her tenderly, "Júrame que no me quieres, júrame que no estás moriendo de ganas de que te bese, júrame." Since she cannot swear to him, they kiss. But Julieta is promptly reminded of her proper place by one of her paternal proxies, Llauro, who tells her, "Acuérdate de que este muchacho está casado y por lo tanto tú no tienes el derecho ni de mirarlo." Rules are strict in San Vincente and Pedro and Julieta, for all their grand love and passion, should not be kissing by romantic rivers. Meanwhile, Pedro is reminded by his grandmother, in the episode of December 8, 1999, that "Si Dios quiere que sea para ti, asi va a ser, pasa lo que pase." In a Catholic culture, one can always put one's faith in God to work out the details of one's labyrinthine love life. While the telenovela enforces strict rules regarding proper behavior in a conservative Mexican society, it also must fulfill its generic role as a love story that makes people dream, following Televisa's ethical principles to leave viewers always with hope and love, free from stress.

Each episode of "Laberintos de Pasión" opens with the characters chasing each other through an outdoor maze of bushes, appearing and disappearing. Viewers usually get just enough of a glimpse to see who they are. The telenovela closes and cuts to commercial breaks with a mariachi theme song. Most telenovelas have their theme song at the beginning and the end of each episode, but not at commercial breaks. Having the theme song interrupt the chapters of the telenovela underlines the artificial aspect of this cultural product. For "Laberintos de Pasión" is quite contrived, playing off every cliché of the genre while it serves to maintain ideological hegemony in terms of gender roles and class and racial politics.

Both "El Candidato" and "La Vida en el Espejo" are productions of TV Azteca, which has, on its website, the slogan "Historias que te inspiran a pensar, sentir y sonar como nunca antes." TV Azteca has its own publicly stated belief regarding the purpose of television:

> La televisión es relater historias, tanto las historias verdaderas del periodismo en televisión que nos mantienen informadas acerca de lo que está ocurriendo en nuestro mundo, como los dramas y comedias que nos ayudan a comprender quiénes somos y hacia dónde vamos como una cultura, como un pais y un mundo. En TV Azteca, comprendemos el poder de la televisión, especialmente en México y el resto de Latinoamérica donde la gran mayoría de la gente recibe sus noticias y entretenimiento de la televisión. Los programas de TV Azteca llegan a los hogares de más de 100 millones de personas cada dia en México, Chile, El Salvador y Costa Rica.
>
> TV Azteca siente la obligación de promover un México y un mundo mejor, a través de la producción y transmission de programas que reflejan nuestros valores: familia, esfuerzo, aprendizaje constante y permanente, pasión, generosidad, honestidad, confianza, libertad, respeto, tolerancia y amor por México.[2]
>
> Ricardo B. Salinas Pliego

While family comes first on the list of TV Azteca values, as it did for Televisa, TV Azteca does seem to expand its values beyond family and true love. TV Azteca also puts thinking before feeling and dreaming in its list of inspirational effects of its stories, while Televisa is, quite simply, a factory of dreams.

TV Azteca describes its telenovela "El Candidato" as "un melodrama romántico situado en un contexto actual: el camino que sigue un país que intenta llegar en la democracia a la elección de su próximo presidente."[3] Advertising itself as a "telenovela interactiva" and showing an e-mail address on the screen each night, the producers of "El Candidato" wanted a response from the viewing public and promised from the beginning to incorporate their comments into the production of the telenovela. The description of the telenovela on the web site explains that

> La historia tendrá un fuerte arraigo con la opinión pública, para ello contará con un correo electrónico que servirá de puente para hacer llegar a la historia la problemática que vivimos hoy en dia los mexicanos.

Also on the web site is a questionnaire for viewer comments. After asking for certain biographical details about the viewer (name, year of birth, sex, city and country, educational level, civil status, occupation, e-mail, and where one usually has access to the Internet), the questionnaire offers the viewers the opportunity to express opinions about the telenovela (the story, the actors, the production, the plot, the episodes, the love story, the treatment of political themes, the acting). The questionnaire also asks viewers if they agree that TV Azteca produces formulaic telenovelas and why (my favorite question), what grade would they give "El Candidato," and what would they ask of the next president of the republic. Viewers get to participate not only with comments on the telenovela but also with their political opinions on what they think their next president should be like, an unusual aspect of "El Candidato." But the desire to know what the viewers want is common to all producers of telenovelas, for producers of this cultural product must give the public what that public wants. Telenovelas are a hugely popular, and profitable, product that generates general public loyalty to stations, and the multiple commercial breaks per episode generate a large percentage of the total revenue a station brings in. In Mexico, the North American Free Trade Agreement multiplied by five the price of advertising space, a significant boost for companies producing telenovelas in which eighteen percent of the broadcast time can be used for ads ("Telenovelas: Love, TV and Power"). Soliciting audience comments on the telenovela allows producers to incorporate material directly from their viewers' suggestions, if they so choose, thus solidifying viewer loyalty.

"El Candidato" tells the story of Ignacio Santoscoy, a politician from the Alianza Popular party, married to Marycarmen Manrique, the daughter of Don Juventino Manrique, a powerful political *cacique* whose wealth and connections have helped Ignacio rise to the top of the ranks of Alianza Popular. But in marrying Marycarmen, the elder daughter, to make Don Juventino happy, Ignacio ignored his love for Beatriz, the younger daughter and half-sister of Marycarmen, who was then sent off to Harvard to earn a degree. In the telenovela, she has returned, the love of Ignacio and Beatriz is reignited and the main love triangle of the telenovela is set.

In spite of her Harvard degree and exalted position in the party, Beatriz, portrayed by Lorena Rojas, remains the representation of woman as image, a vision of beauty, an object to be looked at, the site of visual pleasure. While seen occasionally in her office, she is more frequently portrayed in the domestic sphere (her apartment, her father's house or, less frequently, Ignacio's home) or in a sexualized space like the beach, where she and Ignacio share erotic encounters that are then replayed in other capitulos as flashbacks, emphasizing the female body as the locus of sexuality and desire.

As a signifying practice, the telenovela is a work producing effects of meaning and perception. Advertisements for "El Candidato" announce that "El poder tiene dos caras" and then, showing the face of Don Juventino, proclaim "ambición, intolerancia, corrupción" and, showing the face of Ignacio, "el lado sensato, honesto, auténtico." Considering that throughout the telenovela, Alianza Popular is clearly the symbol for the Partido Revolucionario Institucional (PRI), Mexico's ruling party for more than seventy years and the party still in power at the time the telenovela was being aired, this symbolism has to read not only as an acknowledgment that the PRI is corrupt, its politicians intolerant and ambitious, but also as an attempt to encourage viewers to believe that the new PRI candidates are honest, authentic, and level-headed, reformed characters indeed. If telenovela viewers could fall in love with Ignacio Santoscoy, as it was clearly hoped they would, they could vote PRI in the upcoming elections.

Another advertisement promises that the telenovela offers viewers "Cuatro maneras diferentes de vivir la vida en El Candidato: la pasión de Ignacio, el amor de Beatriz, el odio de Marycarmen, la envidia de Adrian." Not only are good and evil characters clearly distinguished here, but gender roles are appropriately maintained in the emotions portrayed by Ignacio and Beatriz. Ignacio, the virile telenovela hero, is allotted the passion, but Beatriz is allowed only love. Passion would be inappropriate for a woman in this society.

In "El Candidato," for Ignacio, the hero, to be able to leave his wife, the mother of his children, for Beatriz, Marycarmen must be seen as a bad wife and mother and Beatriz must be set up as her binary opposite. Marycarmen is continuously portrayed as conniving, cold, harsh, cruel to her children; she drinks to excess; she has a secret affair with Adrian, her husband's best friend, gets pregnant by him and then pretends the baby is Ignacio's in order to win Ignacio back. She later throws herself down the stairs when she and Beatriz are alone in the house in order to claim that Beatriz tried to kill her, and loses the baby. In the episode of November 15, 1999, Ignacio tells Marycarmen, "Jamás me hubiera imaginado que tú fueras capaz de jugar con algo tan sagrado como la maternidad." Not only is Ignacio setting Marycarmen up as the bad mother and showing his shock and disdain, but his words reinforce the hegemonic discourse of the sacredness of maternity. A woman's desire can never come before the sanctity of maternity in this society. In the episode of November 25, 1999, Ignacio, Beatriz and the children (of Ignacio and Marycarmen) pray to "diosito" to care for Marycarmen. They form a vision of the perfect Catholic Mexican family, with Beatriz in the place of the mother. This scene serves to show that she will be a better mother than Marycarmen, as viewers have had no scenes of such domestic tranquility or religious devotion with Ignacio, Marycarmen and the children. Scenes abound of Beatriz playing with the children, her niece and nephew, helping them with homework or answering their questions, encouraging them to continue to love and support their mother during this difficult time.

In "El Candidato," Don Juventino represents the same traditional patriarchal gender roles and power plays represented by Genaro in "Laberintos de Pasión" and he spouts some of the same types of lines as those of the attorney in "Laberintos." When his wife Griselda threatens to leave him if he does not tell her the truth about his daughter Beatriz, about what had happened twenty-eight years earlier when he showed up with the young girl, a gun in his hand and his shirt covered in blood, he tells her, "No cabe duda que mujer que no jode es hombre" (December 7, 1999). Like Genaro, in "Laberintos," he sends a strong man to do his dirty work, but because "El Candidato" operates in a higher level of society, among the rich and famous of Mexico City, Don Juventino's strong man usually hires hit men to take care of the dirty business.

An interesting aspect of the telenovela is the homosocial bonding between the male characters in the Alianza Popular. In *Between Men*, Eve Kosofsky Sedgwick argues that in many nineteenth-century literary texts, a homosocial bonding between men underlies the more obvious heterosexual narrative, explaining that a homosocial attachment is one of deep affection that, while erotic, is never actually consummated. Often the homosocial bond is maintained through the body of a woman, a woman who serves as a commodity of interchange between the men. In "El Candidato," we see Ignacio as the object of desire not only of the women but also of the men, with multivalent homosocial bonds created with both Adrian and Don Juventino. Don Juventino and Ignacio's bond is maintained through the bodies of two women, Marycarmen and Beatriz, as Ignacio is the husband of one daughter and the lover of the other daughter of Don Juventino. Don Juventino, in a telling episode on November 15, 1999, confesses to Ignacio, "Yo te quería." Adrian also negotiates his relationship with Ignacio through the body of a woman, having an affair with Ignacio's wife and impregnating her in an effort to possess Ignacio's phallus. Also in the episode of November 15, 1999, Adrian tells Ignacio, "Necesito estar cerca a ti." At some level, Ignacio is presented as the object of everyone's desire.

Another notable element of "El Candidato" is the way it incorporates current events into the drama of the telenovela. If Vicente Fox or Francisco Labastida says or does something noteworthy on the campaign trail on Tuesday, the corresponding candidate in the telenovela will make a similar comment or action in the Thursday or Friday night episode. Nor is it only political events that show up in the telenovela; popular cultural references are also contemporary. In the February 25, 2000 episode, Perla was excited about the nine Grammy awards won by Santana. Space is left in the main story line to add short scenes that make references to current events, scenes that can obviously be shot and edited in one or two days. In this way, "El Candidato" is indeed a telenovela interactiva.

"El Candidato" can be likened to the hugely popular Venezuelan telenovela "Por estas calles," aired in 1992, which broadcast that nation's problems into every part of the country as part of the telenovela's storyline. Storylines revolved around events in the life and administration of Carlos Andrés Pérez, even including news footage from coup attempts in the telenovela broadcast. "Por estas calles," however, went much further in its realism than "El Candidato," reaching the point that there were entire episodes without a single love scene, signaling that the telenovela had indeed changed. In "El Candidato," while the story of the presidential campaign events is an important and novel element, the telenovela still focuses on the love story between Ignacio and Beatriz with the attendant secondary and tertiary love triangles and complications.

The very popular "La Vida en el Espejo" attempts, as the title indicates, to represent life, to reflect life in a more realistic manner than most telenovelas. It is the only telenovela I have seen in which characters go to the bathroom, for instance. However, it still reflects the life of only one slice of the Mexican population—the wealthy in Mexico City—and thus, like other telenovelas, comes closer to providing for its viewing public a reality of desire rather than a reality of life.

The main characters are Santiago, his wife Isabel and their three children: Mauricio, the elder son, Eugenio, the middle child, and Diana, the younger daughter. Isabel has an affair with Eduardo, a younger man who had worked at the ad agency she and Santiago own. She leaves Santiago to be with Eduardo, but then repents, as she realizes that her family means more to her than the relationship with Eduardo. She wants to recuperate the love of her children and, if she can, get Santiago's love back, so she breaks it off with Eduardo. She ends up moving back into the family house and Santiago gets an apartment, because he feels that the children need their mother at home. Meanwhile, Santiago falls in love with a younger woman, Gabriela Muñoz. Gabriela works at a radio station, comes from a lower economic and social class, and is less educated.

The daughter, Diana, is still in high school. She goes through a period when she will not eat, will not go to school, is obnoxious to everyone, and is using drugs. After her mother is attacked by her ex-lover, Diana refuses to testify against him, shows no support for her mother, instead taunting her mother with the idea that she would rather have Gabriela Muñoz as her stepmother. In the episode of November 19, 1999, Diana's boyfriend wants to know what is the matter with her, why she is always so moody, why she never wants him to kiss her. When he does kiss her, at her invitation, she then screams at him to get off her. After these disturbing episodes, Gabriela encourages Diana to see a psychologist. Diana undergoes a miraculous conversion, starts being polite to people and changes the way she looks. She starts to dress in a more stereotypically feminine fashion, tames her hair, wears makeup, and makes up with her boyfriend. In the episode of November 24, 1999, they are kissing. That Diana starts displaying "appropriate femininity" once she starts seeing a psychologist underlines that only certain forms of female behavior and appearance, only certain gendered performances, are considered "normal" in this society.

The portrayal of Diana's transformation into a young woman who is performing her femininity appropriately after psychiatric counseling betrays how the patriarchal system only accepts certain performances of femininity and threatens to reject all women who fall outside those norms as mad. Other side stories of the telenovela also stress the traditional side of the patriarchal system. Julio is one of Santiago's best friends, a divorced, alcoholic womanizer, father of one son, owner of a jewelry store and a very fancy apartment. Julio, Santiago, Ernesto, another of Santiago's best friends, and Alvaro (Santiago's brother who has been living in the United States for many years) are the four members of the Club de Tony. The purpose of the Club de Tony appears to be to get together, to get drunk, and to say derogatory things about women in a form of male bonding.

In the episode of November 30, 1999, since it appears that Santiago and Alvaro's sister Cayetana is going to marry Gustavo Prieto, her childhood sweetheart from whom she was separated by the egotism of her brothers, Julio decides that Gustavo should become a member of the Club de Tony. Gustavo is invited to a reunion and has to swear the oath—on a copy of *Playboy*—"no reveler ninguna verdad revelada aquí a nínguna mujer." No one ever proposes making Mauricio a member of the club, but perhaps his gay identity precludes that invitation.

Indeed, much of the interest of the fall episodes comes from Mauricio coming out to his parents and their struggle to come to terms with this new reality. Having a gay character and the different issues it brings out is one of the unusual aspects of this telenovela. In one episode, for example, Isabel and Mauricio have a frank talk. She wants to ask him about his relationship with his partner Jimmy, but feels awkward doing so. He tells her not to, that if he were married to a woman, she would ask. So she asks him, what do they do? He says the normal things, we go to the movies, to a play, we go for drinks in a bar, we eat out a lot since neither one of us likes to cook. We have disagreements, make up, just like any other couple. But mostly we support each other, understand each other, love each other. He notes that the one difference is that they can't hold hands or demonstrate their affection in public. Then Mauricio asks Isabel about her relationship with Eduardo, what happened, why she broke it off. She goes on about the difficulty of being a woman in Mexico if one does not fit in with the expected norms of femininity and maternity. She then says that being a woman in Mexico is like being gay in Mexico. He tells her not to exaggerate. At least she doesn't have to worry about being attacked on the street for her sexuality.

Isabel and Mauricio's discussion of the difficulties of being female and of being gay in Mexico is one of the more striking moments in the telenovela. It offers a rare example where such issues are discussed, even if one might take issue with what the characters say about the topics. For while Mauricio tells his mother that she does not have to worry about being physically attacked for her sexuality, in episodes of "Laberintos de Pasión" noted above, women are repeatedly reminded that they are never safe alone, neither in the streets nor in their own homes. In fact, rape and sexual assault statistics suggest that women in Mexico *are* attacked simply because they are women. The 1992 *Boletín del Centro de Ayuda a Victimas de Violación* put out by the Puerto Rican Department of Health, citing rape statistics in various Latin American countries, asserts that a woman is raped in Mexico every nine minutes. But domestic and sexual violence against women, while widespread, is also vastly underreported. It is estimated that only one in ten rapes gets reported to legal authorities in

Mexico and perhaps one percent of rapes are punished (Jordan A1). In "La Vida en el Espejo," Isabel herself is assaulted by Eduardo after she ends their relationship, so she is aware of the ever-present threat of violence and rape for women even if Mauricio seems not to be cognizant of it.

"La Vida en el Espejo" also includes scenes in which Mauricio and his partner, Jimmy, a visiting professor from Stanford currently teaching in Mexico, discuss issues about being gay in Mexico. The November 25, 1999, episode opens with Jimmy in the shower—a nude man seen from afar, as the camera is on the opposite side of the bedroom. Jimmy and Mauricio are discussing whether they should move to San Francisco because in the United States individuality is more respected. The scene ends with the two of them in the bathroom, obviously about to have a sexual encounter, but they shut the bathroom door, so that whatever happens is off camera. Since they live alone in the apartment, there is no particular reason why they would shut the door, but their love scenes are always staged off camera and right after a cut. Much less intimacy between men is shown than would be the case were it a scene between a man and a woman.

In a later episode, two men break into Mauricio and Jimmy's apartment and beat up Jimmy. The assumption is that they were sent by Irene's father, who is furious that Mauricio and Irene did not marry, and even more furious that Mauricio is gay, and that the beating was intended for Mauricio. Gay-bashing is the subject of the November 23, 1999, episode, in which Jimmy and Mauricio are attacked by two men on the street.

Mauricio's sexual identity incites other violent reactions. The ad agency that Santiago and Isabel own has been working on a political campaign, but when the candidate for the Senate and his campaign manager find out about Mauricio's sexual orientation, via a scene in a restaurant in which the drunken father of Mauricio's ex-fiancee denounces Mauricio as a homosexual and Isabel as a prostitute, the agency loses the contract. The candidate says that he could never permit a homosexual to work on his campaign. Isabel is furious, pointing out to Santiago and Mauricio the candidate's hypocrisy as he had just been requesting that very week that the campaign slogans emphasize the equality of all Mexicans.

Mauricio feels terrible that the agency has lost the campaign. Both his parents say that it is not his fault, that it is the fault of the politician and his campaign manager or the fault of Irene's idiotic father. In one scene, Isabel tells him not to worry about it, that she has accepted his "condíción." Although the scene is supposed to be a positive one in which she is being supportive, her use of the term "condition" pathologizes Mauricio's gay identity.

Thus, although the telenovela attempts to portray gay characters in a positive light and, indeed, both Mauricio and Jimmy are attractive, intelligent, sympathetic characters, it is in the moments like these when Isabel pathologizes Mauricio's gay identity that "La Vida en el Espejo" falls short of the goals it obviously hoped to attain. But it certainly makes positive strides that put it well beyond the stereotypical telenovela.

A side storyline of the telenovela involves Santiago's brother, Alvaro, who is married to Sharon, a woman from the United States, and living in Denver with their two children. Although in his visits to Mexico he had always presented their marriage as a perfect one, it turns out Sharon was abusive. One intriguing aspect of this story is the ways in which Sharon, the only character who represents the United States, is presented as manipulative, abusive, and greedy. In her physical appearance, she contrasts with the Mexican women normally seen in the telenovela—she is large and unattractive. She serves as a synecdoche for the U.S., for Mexico's feelings towards its aggressive northern neighbor. It is also interesting to note that Alvaro, as the character who presents himself as someone who was taken in by/taken advantage of by Sharon, is portrayed by an actor with a less elegant appearance and less European features. Being that Santiago, Cayetana and Alvaro are siblings and share the same gene pool, the lack of physical resemblance with this character is striking. If Sharon is seen as representing the United States, then there certainly seem to be some racial politics involved in terms of who suffers most in Mexico at the hands of the United States.

The other more indigenous-looking characters in the telenovela are the domestic employees. The maid in Santiago and Isabel's house and the maid in Julio's house both have more indigenous features than their employers. The maid in Julio's house, Pancha, is portrayed by a great comic actress who plays her often stereotypical role to the hilt. Such casting, however, confirms traditional racial and class roles in Mexico.

Another interesting aspect of the sometimes transgressive nature of this telenovela is in the treatment of a character's bout with prostate cancer. Ernesto, one of Santiago's best friends, is treated with an operation and left impotent. He refuses to tell his wife, Paula, although she knows from the doctor, and is nasty to everyone. She makes an appointment with the doctor to learn about the injections, and one amazing scene shows the doctor explaining the condition and the treatment with diagrams and plastic models, showing how one applies the injection in order to effect an erection in the male. It is very explicit and obviously done with didactic intent. This telenovela seeks not just to entertain but to educate.

The dual intent to entertain and to educate is also seen in the treatment of teenage pregnancy. Eugenio, Santiago and Isabel's younger son, has barely finished high school and his girlfriend, Paulita, the daughter of his parents' best friends, is pregnant. The parents do not want their children to marry because they are too young, because they want them to go to university, etc. But Eugenio and Paulita are determined to marry. The relatives all have strong reactions to the pregnancy, which is considered a grave transgression. Eugenio's aunt Cayetana gives them a beautiful old house and helps them to get established. She is portrayed as a very conservative, Catholic Mexican woman, and her support of their marriage is in large part due to the fact that she believes that, having made this terribly grave error, they have to marry. Paulita's father refuses to speak to or of her and claims that he no longer has a daughter.

In the episode of December 7, 1999, Paulita has lost her baby. Again we see the didactic nature of the telenovela. Eugenio and Paulita explain to the others that the doctor said that 25 percent of women have a spontaneous abortion and that by the time Paulita was feeling the pains, the abortion had probably already taken place so that even if she had gone to the doctor immediately, it would have been too late. They are upset, but their parents tell them that they are young, they have each other, they will still have a family in the future.

While the executive from Televisa interviewed for the video "Telenovelas: Love, TV, and Power," denied that his company conceived of telenovelas as being educational, for many people involved in the production and consumption of telenovelas, they are an important vector for education and influence. In episodes regarding medical concerns, we can see how the popularity of the telenovela then constitutes the program as an important and relevant educational instrument, as the medium of mass communication is used to promote education and consciousness of public health issues. The emotional connection that the telenovela viewers feel with the characters in the storylines, their involvement with the lives of the characters, helps them to engage with the health issues and to see them as relevant in a way they might not in a health report in the evening news program.

But at the same time that "La Vida en el Espejo" seeks both to provide a more realistic view of life in Mexico and to ignite awareness of and provide information about important health issues, it is always first and foremost a telenovela in a developing country where television is an important commercial activity. The blurring of the lines between advertisement and entertainment is common in the world of telenovelas, and "La Vida en el Espejo" is no exception. The telenovela opens with the introduction of "El instituto Ponds trae para ti tu telenovela La Vida en el Espejo," and the logos for both the telenovela and the jars of Ponds cold cream are blue and white, further associating the telenovela and the commercial beauty product in viewers' minds. The product placement in the show is blatant. Isabel and her best friend Paula are both seen using Ponds cold cream in different scenes or are seen with jars of the cold cream on their dressing tables. But the most forced product placement is a poster of Ponds Institute on the inside of Diana's door. Since Diana is portrayed as a rebellious character who is not performing her femininity appropriately throughout most of the telenovela, it seems completely out of character for her to have a poster for cold cream adorning her bedroom. Nor is Ponds the only commercial product seen in the show. When characters drink beer, it is always Corona, and the bottles are positioned so that viewers can see the name. In an episode of December 8, 1999, a computer in a scene clearly shows the screen for Prodigy Internet. In the same episode, Eugenio wears a Pepe Jeans polo shirt. All these product placements bring in additional ad revenue for the studios and remind viewers that "La Vida en el Espejo" is a commercial product. Viewers who might get too caught up in the world of the telenovela, who—to borrow a term from narrative theory—are reading too much as members of the narrative audience, are reminded that these characters are not real when a commercial break runs an ad for Whiskas cat food with the actress who plays Paulita.[4]

In the end, "La Vida en el Espejo" does break with generic traditions in many ways, introducing a gay character in a main role and portraying him in a stable, positive relationship, addressing societal issues like prostate cancer, teenage pregnancy and alcohol abuse, portraying a strong female lead who insists on living her life the way she chooses and then dealing with the consequences of her choices. Characters have honest conversations about issues not often discussed so openly on Mexican television. While there are certainly many moments that are problematic and issues that are not addressed, this telenovela does provide a different view of Mexican life than that normally seen on the TV screen.

Telenovelas are an important part of the cultural phenomena of everyday life in Mexico and in Latin America. As Jesús Martín-Barbero affirms, "In the redefinition of culture, the clue lies in the understanding of the communicative nature of culture, understanding culture as a process that is productive of meaning, and not just as a 'circulator' of information" (Tufte 16). Culture produces meaning, and as vital cultural products telenovelas participate in the production of meaning about gender in Mexico. In a country where many more people watch the television or listen to a radio than read a newspaper, television programs, including the ever popular telenovelas, have a huge impact in the production of meaning about gender, race, class and sexuality.[5] Telenovelas have many faces, but holding a mirror up to them can reveal what images of gender, sexuality, race and class are being reflected back.

NOTES

1. I should note that I use the present tense even though the telenovelas are not running on Mexican television at the time of publication of this article.

2. The telenovela website I accessed while I was living in Mexico in 1999–2000 (www.tvazteca.com.mx/televidentes/telenovelas) is no longer accessible and this particular statement from the president of TV Azteca no longer appears on the site. However, the TV Azteca website still offers statements about its values. In the segment on "cultura corporativa," TV Azteca proclaims itself a "Señal con valor," with a short paragraph explaining that "Es quien te ofrece incondicionalmente amor, valores, educación y la gran habilidad de enseñarte a descubrir tus errores; formación, que durante toda la vida te ayudará a ser cada vez mejor" [www.tvazteca.com.mx/corporativo/cultura/index.shtml]. While unconditional love comes first, values and education are most highly stressed.

3. From the web site, "Información para televidentes" at http://www.tvazteca.com.mx/televidentes/telenovelas/candidato/index02.shtml. All further quotations from the website are from the same site.

4. In *Before Reading: Narrative Conventions and the Politics of Interpretation*, Peter J. Rabinowitz distinguishes between the actual audience (the flesh and blood people who read a book), the authorial audience (the hypothetical audience an author has in mind in creating a text) and the narrative audience (the audience who accepts the fictional characters as people). Telenovelas rely on an audience who "reads" in large part as members of the narrative audience.

5. In statistics published in 1996, 28 percent of Mexicans read a newspaper daily while 9 out of 10 people listen to radio and watch television (González and Chávez, 1996: 113, cited in A. González, "The Willingness to Weave," p. 36).

WORKS CITED

Butler, Judith. *Gender Trouble: Feminism and the Subversion of Identity.* New York: Routledge, 1990.

"Cultura Corporativa" at http://www.tvazteca.com.mx/corporativa/cultura, April 17, 2003.

De Lauretis, Teresa. *Alice Doesn't: Feminism, Semiotics, Cinema.* Bloomington: Indiana University Press, 1984.

González, Jorge A. "The Cofraternity of (Un)Finishable Emotions: Constructing Mexican Telenovelas." *Studies in Latin American Popular Culture* 11 (1992): 59–92.

———. "The Willingness to Weave: Cultural Analysis, Cultural Fronts and Networks of the Future." *Media Development* 1 (1997): 30–36.

González, Jorge A., & María Guadalupe Chávez. *La cultura en Mexico I: cifras claves.* Mexico: CNCA & Universidad de Colima, 1996.

"Información para televidentes" at http://tvazteca.com.mx/televidentes/telenovelas/candidato.index02.html, December 18, 1999.

Jordan, Mary. "In Mexico, an Unpunished Crime: Rape Victims Face Widespread Cultural Bias in Pursuit of Justice." *The Washington Post*, June 30, 2002.

Martín-Barbero, Jesús. *Communication, Culture and Hegemony.* London: Sage, 1993.

Sedgwick, Eve Kosofsky. *Between Men: English Literature and Male Homosocial Desire.* New York: Columbia University Press, 1985.

"Semillas para el cambio." *Boletin del Centro de Ayuda a Victimas de Violación,* Departamento de Salud, San Juan, Puerto Rico, 1992.

Telenovelas: Love, TV, and Power." Alexandre Valenti, dir. Videocassette. National Endowment for the Humanities, 2001.

Televisa website. http://www.esmas.com/televisa/, October 5, 2002.

Tufte, Thomas. *Living with the Rubbish Queen: Telenovelas, Culture and Modernity in Brazil.* Luton, UK: University of Luton Press, 2000.

Selected Bibliography

Allen, Robert C., ed. *To Be Continued*. New York: Rutledge, 1995.
Ang, I. *Living Room Wars: Rethinking Media Audiences in the Modern World*. London: Routledge, 1996.
Benavides, O. Hugo. *Drugs, Thugs, and Divas: Telenovelas and Narco-Dramas in Latin America*. Austin: University of Texas Press, 2008.
Cabrujas, José Ignacio. *Y Latinoamérica, ¿inventó la telenovela?* Caracas: Alfadil Ediciones, 2002.
Harrington, C. Lee, with Denise D. Bielby. *Soap Fans: Pursuing Pleasure and Making Meaning in Everyday Life*. Philadelphia: Temple University Press, 1995.
Marquez de Melo, J. *As telenovelas da globo: Produção e esportação*. Sao Paulo, Brazil: Summus, 1988.
Mazziotti, N. *La industria de la telenovela: La producción de ficción en América Latina*. Buenos Aires: Paidós, 1996.
Ross, Sharon Marie. *Beyond the Box: Television and the Internet*: Malden, Mass.: Blackwell, 2008.
Stempel Mumford, Laura. *Love and Ideology in the Afternoon: Soap Operas, Women, and Television Genre*. Bloomington and London: Indiana University Press, 1995.
Straubhaar, Joseph D. *World Television: From Global to Local*. Los Angeles: Sage, 2007.
Tufte, Thomas. *Living with the Rubbish Queen*. Luton: Luton Press, 2000.

Index

ABC, 25, 81, 116
Abercrombie, N., 112
ABS-CBN (Philippines), 66
Akyuz, G., 44
Albania, 39
Alice Doesn't: Feminism, Semiotics, Cinema (de Lauretis), 117
All My Children, 83, 85, 89n5
Allen, Robert, 3, 12–13, 15, 21, 23, 24, 82
Alonso, Ernesto, 54
An American Family, 16
The Andy Griffith Show, 15
Ang, Ien, 4, 27n5, 52
Angel Malo (Bad Angel), 64
Another Life, 6
Another World, 23, 88
Antola, L., 38
Aragón, Angélica, 55, 56
Argentina, 58, 62; economic crisis in (2001), 64
ARGOS, 55
Argos Productions/Argos TV, 105, 108n4, 114
Arias, Cuauhtémoc Blanco, 56
Arnold, Gillian, 56
As The World Turns, 89n3
ASBI (análisis semantic basado en imagine) analysis, 95–96, 99–100n1
Audience(s), 108n2; "bio-time" of, 70; concept of, 93–94; different types of (actual, authorial, narrative), 130n4; engagement of by telenovelas, 94; viewing habits of Mexican viewers, 97–99
Audley, Paul, 103
Aulette, Ken, 27n5
Australia, telenovelas of, 41, 47, 54, 56

Bandeirantes (Brazil), 39
Bardasano, Carlos, 67
Barrera, Vivian, 89n7
Bay Guardians, 69
Before Reading: Narrative Conventions and the Politics of Interpretation (Rabinowitz), 130n4
Behr, Felicia Minei, 85, 89–90n11
Belgium, 42, 51
Bell, Bradley, 83
Bernardi, Helena, 63
Bernstein, Basil, 98–99
Between Men (Kosofsky), 124
Beyond Cultural Imperialism (Golding and Harris), 33
Bhushan, Nyay, 67
Bielby, Denise D., 89n7
BNT (Bulgaria), 46
The Bold and the Beautiful, 13, 87, 89n9; introduction of Antonio to the cast of, 83
Bosnia, 66
"Boutique programming," 25
Brazil, 36, 52, 104; social realism of Brazilian telenovelas, 64; television/telenovela industry of, 37–38, 42, 54, 56
"Brazilianization," of television content and values, 37
Broadcasting system in Latin America, structural influences on, 35–36
Brown, Mary Ellen, 26n1
Brunsdon, Charlotte, 3, 11–12, 17, 25
Bulman, Gabriel Vazquez, 52
Butler, Judith, 116

"El Candiato," 117, 121–22; advertisements for, 123; homosocial

bonding in, 124; incorporation of current events into its storyline, 124; as an interactive telenovela, 122; plot of, 122; representation of patriarchal gender roles in, 124; representation of women in, 122–23
Cantor, Muriel G., 4, 26–27n4
Capitol, 13
Caracol (Colombia), 69
Carvajal, Alicia, 66
Castro, Fidel, 62
Caughie, John, 7, 8; on the "assumptions of genre" in television, 8; on the "novelistic" in television, 18, 29n39
CBS, 32n83, 81, 116; programming directed at women, 25
Cenicienta, 54
La Chacala, 97, 98
Cheers, 15
Chile, 64
"Chinovelas," 66
Christian Broadcasting Service, 6
The City, 82
Clarin, 53
Clase 406, 65–66
CNN, 19
CODITEL (Belgium), 51
"The Cofraternity of (Un)Finishable Emotions: Constructing Mexican Telenovelas" (González), 116
Colgate, successful sponsorship of telenovelas, 62–63
Colombia, 53
"Contra-flow," 33, 34, 38, 39; and Latin American fictional material, 41–42, 47
Coronation Street (book [British Film Institute]), 4
Coronation Street (television show), 5, 18, 52
Cristal, 38
Croatia, 42, 66
Croce, Jim, 84
Cuba, role of in the origins of telenovelas, 62
Culebrones (serpents), 62
"Cultural fronts," 68; multidimensional aspects of, 71
Cultural identity, 103, 107–8; portrayal of Mexican cultural identities in the media, 104–5
Cultural imperialism, 33–34, 47, 79; cultural flow, 47–48; internal and external, 37; refutation of, 38; "reverse" cultural imperialism, 34, 38, 42, 47, 62. *See also* "Contra-flow"
"Cultural proximity," 69
"Cultural syncretism," 79
Culture, 103–4, 130
Cunningham, S., 79

Dallas, 4, 5, 15, 27n5, 59; difference of from daytime soap operas, 4; as first true "prime time" soap, 7
Dark Shadows, 27n5, 82
Days of the Week, 4
Demasiado Corazón, 97
Denmark, 39
Desencuentro Huracán, 97
Desperate Housewives, 67
Discovery Channel, 59
Dobbin, Mickey Dwyer, 84–85
The Doctors, 82
Dodds, Peter, 56
Donahue, 5
Dynasty, 4, 5, 15, 16–17, 27n5

EastEnders, 5, 18
Ellis, John, 21, 112
Em Busca da Felicidade (In Search of Happiness), 62
Emergency, 15
Escobar, Ramón, 63
A Escrava Isaura (Isaura, the Slave), 38, 42, 65
Esmeralda, 65, 66, 97
Estonia, 46
Estrada, Erik, 89n9
ETB (Basque), 45

Family, 24
Fantasy Island, 15
Fernández, C., 54–55
Feuer, Jane, 7, 9, 13–14, 16, 17
Fili-Krushel, Patricia, 84
Film theory, 9
Fiske, J., 112, 113
Fox, E., 36, 39
Fox Broadcasting, 25, 53
FremantleMedia, 67
Friends, 69

Gabriela, 38, 39
Galavisión International, 40, 53
García-Márquez, Gabriel, 41
Gender, social construction of, 116–17
Gender Trouble: Feminism and the Subversion of Identity (Butler), 116

General Hospital, 4, 82, 84, 85, 89n3
Generations, 13
Genre theory, 9, 15
Geraghty, Christine, 4–5
Germany, 39
Giddens, A., 99
Gledhill, Christine, 11, 21, 29n33, 80, 113
Globalization, 48, 62; of Latin American audiovisual corporations, 39
Globo/Globo TV/TeveGlobo. *See* TV Globo
Going Home, 56
Golding, P., 33
González, Jorge A., 116
Grindon, Michael, 67
Grupo Alfa de Monterrey, 53
Guiding Light, 13, 63, 89n3

Haddrick, Greg, 56
Harris, P., 33
Hayman, Connie P., 85–86
HBO, 19
Heath, Stephen, 13, 18
Hill Street Blues, 4, 7, 15, 23
Home and Away, 52, 56
Homefront, 27n5
Hoskins, C., 88
Hotel, 15, 27n5
HRT (Croatia), 45
HTV (Croatia), 66
Hungary, 42

Ibarra, Epigmenio, 55, 105–6, 108n3
Iceland, 39
A Indominada (The Indomitable), 108n1
Ireland, 39
Italy, 40, 44

Jacka, E., 79
Japan, 41, 47
"Journées de la Télévision Brésilienne" ("Days of Brazilian Television"), 40
Joyrich, Lynne, 10
Jucaud, Patrick, 65

Kassandra, 61, 65
Kelly, George, 95
Knots Landing, 15, 27n5
Kosofsky, Eve, 124
Kreutzner, Gabriele, 4
Kuhn, Annette, 25

L.A. Law, 4, 15, 20, 22
La Pastina, A. C., 37

"Laberintos de Pasión, 117, 126; melodramatic nature of, 119; portrayal of forbidden love in, 119–20; "proper" gender roles of women in, 120–21; thunderstorm motif of, 119; traditional patriarchal gender roles in, 118–19; use of taglines in, 119
Lang, Jack, 40
Latin America, 63–64, 67, 69, 104; creolization of Latin America culture, 37
Lauretis, Teresa de, 117
Leahy, Lynn, 83
Lee, C. C., 35
La Ley Federal de Radio y Televisión, 53
La Ley de Silencio (The Law of Silence), 67
Liebes, T., 80, 82
Life, three realms of, 90n13
Little House on the Prairie, 24
Livingstone, S., 80, 82
LNK (Lithuania), 46
Lo Que es el Amor (What Love Is), 106, 108–9n6, 114
Localization, of global cultural products, 52
Logan, Michael, 81
Love Boat, 15, 22

Magyar TV (Hungary), 45
Marimar, 61
Marinho, Roberto, 53
"Marlena De Lacroix." *See* Hayman, Connie P.
Martín-Barbero, Jesús, 37, 57, 58, 130
Mary Hartman, Mary Hartman, 4, 16, 27n5
*M*A*S*H*, 15
Mato, Daniel, 53, 58
Mattelart, A., 52
Mattelart, Michele, 3, 52
McAnary, E., 37
MDA, 56
Mediaset (Italy), 44
Megachannel, 44–45
Megavisión, 53
Mellencamp, Patricia, 8
Melodrama: association of with soap operas, 11, 29n33; as a "contaminated" genre, 10–11; diffuseness of television melodrama, 10; film melodrama, 10; institutional forms used in the production of, 57; Latin American, 37; "melodrama aesthetic" and "melodrama style," 9; as a "meta-genre," 9; pervasiveness of, 10; as the

preferred form for television, 10; as a social experience, 68–71; television melodrama, 4, 5; and "women's fictions," 11
"Melodrama Inside and Outside the Home" (Mulvey), 9
Melrose Place, 22
Mercedes, María, 51
Mexico, 36, 52, 69, 104, 130n5; Epoca de Oro period of (1940s), 110; problem of rape in, 126–27; television industry of, 37–38, 42, 118; television viewing habits in different areas of, 97–99. *See also* Cultural identity, portrayal of Mexican cultural identities in the media; Social imaginary, the, and Mexican television contexts
Mi Pequeña Traviesa, 97
Milmo, Emilio Azcárraga, 53, 54; on the role of the telenovela, 54
Milmo, Emilio Azcárraga Jean, 53, 117
Mirada de Mujer (A Woman's View), 52, 55, 57, 61, 77n2, 97, 98, 108n4; María Inés character in, 55
Mirus, R., 88
Modleski, Tania, 17, 30n54
Monday Night Football, 25
MTV, 7, 19
Mulvey, Laura, 9–10
Muraro, H., 36
Murdoch, Rupert, 53
Murdock, Graham, 95
Murphy Brown, 15, 22; controversy concerning Murphy Brown's pregnancy, 5

Nada Personal, 55
Narrative theory, 113
National Geographic, 69
NBC, 81, 116
Neale, Steve, 15; on generic specificity, 16
Neighbours, 51, 52, 56
Netherlands, the, 39
News Ltd., 53
Nochimson, Martha, 30n60
Nordenstreng, K., 48
North American Free Trade Agreement, effect of on telenovela advertising, 122
Northern Exposure, 15
NYPD Blue, 22, 23

O Pogador de Promessas, 46
O'Donnell, H., 80

Oliveira, O. S., 37
One Life to Live, 82, 83, 85, 87
The Oprah Winfrey Show, 5
Ordaz, Díaz, 53
El Otro y Pecado Mortal, 54

Packard, Felicity, 56, 57
Paradise Beach, 25
Partido Revolucionario Institucional (PRI), 123
Passions, 82, 88
Paxman, A., 54–55
PBS, 19
Pearson, Rosalind, 52
Peyton Place, 7
Phelps, Guy, 95
Philippines, export of telenovelas from, 66
Pietri, Arturo Uslar, 64
Pimstein, Valentin, 54
Pingree, Suzanne, 4, 26–27n4
Plataforma Digital, 40
Pliego, Ricardo Salinas, 105
Poland, 38, 40
Poor Anastasia, 67
"Por estes calles," 124–25
Port Charles, 85, 87, 89n5, 89–90n11; "books" of, 84; criticism of its format change, 85–86; innovative serial programming of, 84; possible cancellation of, 85; use of specific musical themes in, 84
Portugal, 38, 42, 44, 45

Queer as Folk, 69

Radio, 69; "radio" novels (*radionovelas*), 62, 69, 110
RAI (Italy), 45
RCTV (Venezuela), 39
The Real World, 16
Red Bolivia, 53
Repertory Grid, 93, 95
RETE4 (Portugal), 44
Reyes, Alberto Nolla, 54
Los Ricos también Lloran (The Rich Also Cry), 52, 55, 61; popularity of in post-Soviet Russia, 65
Riggs, Marlon, 5
Roach, C., 38
Rogers, E. M., 38
Roseanne, 22, 32n83
Ross, Andrew, 30n58
RTP (Portugal), 44

RTV (Romania), 45
Ryan's Hope, 13, 82

S4C (Wales), 43
Sabbah, Françoise, 45
Sada, Garza, 53
Sahab, Claudia, 66
Sánchez, Jorge González, 57
Santa Barbara, 13, 65, 83
Sat 1 (Germany), 43–44
Schiller, H., 38
Seinfeld, 22
Seiter, Ellen, 4
Senda Prohibida (Forbidden Path), 54, 63
Serbia, 66
Shapiro, Angela, 85
SIC (Portugal), 40, 44, 45
Simplemente María (Simply Maria), 63
Simpson, O. J., 81
Sin Pecado Concebido (Conceived Without Sin), 106, 108–9n6, 114
Sinclair, J., 35, 38, 39, 48, 69, 79
Sinha Moça, 42
Skirrow, Gillian, 13, 18
Slovak Republic, 42
Soap, 4, 16
Soap Fans: Pursuing Pleasure and Making Meaning in Everyday Life (Harrington, Lee, and Beilby), 59
Soap operas, 30n48, 80–82, 88, 103, 110; audience considerations when changing the serial format of, 84–86, 88–89n1, 90n14; audience intimacy with, 17; Australian 51, 52; "camp decodings" of, 16; characteristic "look" of, 23–24; closed-captioning and simulcasts of for Spanish audiences, 83; "dailiness" of, 17–20, 30n60; decline in popularity of, 81; distinction between "prime-time soaps" and daytime soaps, 4, 17; duration of, 89n3; emphasis on interior sets in, 23, 24; ethnic/racial makeup of soap opera casts, 82–83; and feminist discourse, 31n72; and the "flow" of commercial television, 18, 22; gender issues involved in, 25–26; genres of, 80; "ideological problematic" of, 23; increase in popularity of, 89–90n11; interlocking storylines of, 21–22; issues concerning the reformatting of, 87–88; lack of closure in, 12, 21, 23; marketing of, 81, 89n5; as "meta-text," 13; narrative form of, 12–13, 17, 21–22; parodies of, 16, 30n50; the pleasure of viewing soap operas, 57–59; production of, 20, 23; profitability of, 89n4; "real time" in, 14, 29n42, repeats/reruns of, 89n2; similarities to melodrama, 11, 29n33, 57; social evolution of as a genre, 82–84; targeting of female audience by, 24–25, 32n78, 32n83; viewer consumption of entire broadcast runs of, 13. *See also* Soap operas, definitions of
Soap operas, definitions of, 3–4, 26n1, 80; as a continuing fictional television program, 16; defining soap opera "text" problems, 12; definition emphasizing the specific characteristics of the genre, 6, 15–16; differences from closely related programming, 4–5; differences from telenovelas, 57, 63; difficulty of defining soap operas as "text," 12–13, 14–15; as focusing on relationships within a specific community of characters, 22; functional definition of, 5–6; problematic nature of defining soap operas (forms, practices, and medium distinctions), 6–7; as programs presented in multiple weekly installments, 17; similarities to telenovelas, 63
SoapCentral.com, 86, 90n12
Social imaginary, the, and Mexican television contexts, 95–97, 100n2
Social interpretation, 70–71
Sony Corporation, 67
The Sopranos, 69
South Park, 69
Soviet Union, 39
Spain, 38, 40, 41
Spanish International Network (SIN), 53
Sreberny-Mohammadi, A., 38, 48
St. Elsewhere, 15
Straubhaar, Joseph D., 35, 37, 38, 62, 65, 69
STV (Slovak Republic)
Sunset Beach, 88
Swans Crossing, 25
Switzerland, 46

TCI (United States), 53
Tele3 (Lithuania), 46
Telemadrid, 45
Telemundo, 63, 67, 82

Telenovelas, 16, 89n7, 89–90n11, 103, 107–8, 110, 115, 130; appeal of to women, 104; audience reception of, 37; authenticity in, 37; changing content of, 64, 105–7; as closed narrative texts, 110–11; criticism of by Latin American elites, 64; cultural development of, 52; as cultural hybrids, 63; as cultural products, 116; depiction of reality and fiction in, 111–14; differences from soap operas, 52, 57, 63, 110–11, 116; different rates for the sale of to other countries, 46; emerging markets for in Eastern Europe, 45–46, 64–66; expectations concerning everyday life created by, 99, 100n3; exports of to the United States, 64, 69; failure of some telenovela themes in Eastern European countries, 65–66; future of telenovela exports, 39; as a genre inspired by American soap opera models, 37; global success of, 52, 61–62; importance of Europe as an export market for, 40–41, 41–42; lack of export success to Northern and Northwestern European countries, 42–43; lack of realism in Mexican telenovelas, 54; leading Latin American producers of, 62; and life dynamics, 104; "Maria" telenovelas, 54; narrative devices of, 111–12; narrative structure of, 113; "new style" telenovelas, 114; as the "opium of the poor," 64; the pleasure of viewing telenovelas, 57–59; popularity of in post-Soviet Russia, 65; problems of language in the export market, 43; realism in, 113–14; reasons for export growth of, 40; as remakes of old stories (*refritos*), 112; role of cultural proximity in exports to Southern Europe, 44–45; similarities to soap operas, 63; social and scientific myths concerning, 74–75; socio-cultural phenomenon of, 68; specific export markets for, 39, 64; sponsorship of by American corporations, 62–63; styles of ("realism" and "Cinderella"), 54, 63, 95, 97, 98, 111, 113–14; success of in Poland, Spain, and Portugal, 38, 64; Taiwanese telenovelas ("chinovelas"), 66; total number of viewers worldwide, 62; transition of from serialized novels to "radio novels" to telenovelas, 62; use of language in, 112; use of taglines in, 119; websites of, 130; worldwide export of, 37–38; writers' and directors' panels concerning production of, 55–56. *See also* Telenovelas, international debates concerning; Telenovelas, plotlines of; Telenovelas, as symbolic and complex forms

Telenovelas, international debates concerning, 34–39, 46–48; capital control over Latin American television industry, 36; ideological questions concerning local program formats, 37; inflow of foreign programs, 36; key problems of the debate, 34–35; North American structure of Latin American broadcasting, 35–36

Telenovelas, plotlines of, 106; poverty, 63–64; reversals of fortune, 63; sentimental fairy tales, 64; struggling single women, 63, 105

Telenovelas, as symbolic and complex forms, 70–71, 77; argumentation analysis of telenovelas, 73; development of a deep interpretation model of telenovelas, 75–77; and levels of analysis regarding telenovela production, 71; pragma-linguistic analysis of telenovelas, 73; semantic analysis of telenovelas, 73; stylistic analysis of telenovelas, 72–73; understanding the complex symbolic form (complex texts) of telenovelas, 72–73; understanding the social interpretations of telenovelas, 73–74

"Telenovelas: Love, TV, and Power," 118, 129

"Telenovelas and Soap Operas: Negotiating Reality from the Periphery," 52

Telesistema Mexicana, 53

Televisa (Mexico), 36, 47, 52, 62, 69, 97, 98, 106, 114; and censorship, 118; ethical standards maintained in its telenovelas, 118; globalization of, 55; history of the formation of, 53; interventionist actions of the government toward, 53; production of telenovelas by, 54–55, 111, 117–18; telenovela exports of, 38

Television, 29n39, 30n61, 69, 89n6; categories of television programs

using the serial format, 15; and the concept of interruption, 17; development of outside Latin America, 66–67; differences and similarities between American and British television, 19; distinctions between film and television, 9, 13–14; effects of cable television on major network programming, 81; as a genre-driven medium, 7–9; habitual daily viewing of, 17; interest groups in vying for power, 70; intertextuality of, 12; introduction of public concerns into private viewing spaces, 5; irretrievability of, 13; narrative function of, 18; nonfiction genres of, 18; "permeable borders" of, 11; as primary representative of postmodern sensibility, 7; problematic nature of defining specific television genres, 7–8; "reality TV," 111; relationship of to its audience, 11–12; resistance of television programming to categorization, 7; serial forms of ("serialness"), 21; theories concerning live television ("ideology of liveness"), 13–14, 17, 20; undermining of television's textuality, 11–12. *See also* Social imaginary, the, and Mexican television contexts
Texas, 13
Thalía (Ariadna Sodi Miranda), 51
Third World, the: as victims of Hollywood, 38; Western imperialistic influence on Third World culture, 37
thirtysomething, 4, 15, 20
Thorburn, David, 9, 10
Todorov, Tzvetan, 113
Tomlinson, J., 33
Tongues Untied (1990), 5
Torchin, Mimi, 27n5
Trinta, A. R., 37
TV3 (Estonia), 46
TV Azteca (Mexico), 55, 69, 93, 95, 97, 111, 114; and the changes in telenovela content, 105–7, 114; public statements of regarding the purpose of television, 121
TV Globo (Brazil), 36, 39, 40, 47, 48, 53, 62, 63, 67, 69; co-productions of, 66; as an exporter of telenovelas, 38, 65;
interest of in new export markets for telenovelas, 45–46
TVE (Spain), 44, 45
Tufte, Thomas, 52
Turkey, 46
Twin Peaks, 4, 8, 27n5
Tyszka, Barrera, 63

United Kingdom, 39
United States: Latino population of, 83; as the major exporter of television programs, 79–80
Univisión, 36, 67, 81–82

Varis, T., 48
Vazquez, Veronica, 94
Venevisión (Venezuela), 36, 39, 62, 69
Venezuela, 42, 53, 104
"La Vida en el Espejo," 117, 129–30; blurring of the lines between advertisement and entertainment in, 129; depiction of the difficulty of being a woman in, 126–27; depiction of gay life in, 126, 127; dual intent of (to both educate and entertain audiences), 128; plot of, 125; portrayal of American women in, 127–28; portrayal of the patriarchal system in, 125–26; portrayal of teenage pregnancy in, 128–29; product placement in, 129
Villa Maria, 66
Villeli, Fernanda, 54
Vink, N., 37, 38, 52
Virgin of Guadalupe, 113
Vujnovic, Marina, 63

The Waltons, 24
Wiegman, Robyn, 10, 11
Williams, Raymond, 31n70
Wills, Patricio, 63
Winnicott, D. W., 90n13
Wiseguy, 15
Women and Soap Opera (Geraghty), 4

Yearbook, 16
Yo soy Betty la Fea (I Am Ugly Betty), 52, 53, 66–67
Yugoslavia, 40

ZDF (Germany), 44

About the Editor and Contributors

EDITOR

Ilan Stavans is Lewis-Sebring Professor in Latin American and Latino Culture and Five College–Fortieth Anniversary Professor at Amherst College. A native from Mexico, he received his doctorate in Latin American Literature from Columbia University. Stavans' books include *The Hispanic Condition* (HarperCollins, 1995), *On Borrowed Words* (Viking, 2001), *Spanglish* (HarperCollins, 2003), *Dictionary Days* (Graywolf, 2005), *The Disappearance* (TriQuarterly, 2006), *Love and Language* (Yale, 2007), *Resurrecting Hebrew* (Nextbook, 2008), and *Mr. Spic Goes to Washington* (Soft Skull, 2008). He has edited *The Oxford Book of Jewish Stories* (Oxford, 1998), *The Poetry of Pablo Neruda* (Farrar, Straus and Giroux, 2004), *Isaac Bashevis Singer: Collected Stories* (3 vols., Library of America, 2004), *The Schocken Book of Sephardic Literature* (Schocken, 2005), *Cesar Chavez: An Organizer's Tale* (Penguin, 2008), and *Becoming Americans: Four Centuries of Immigrant Writing* (Library of America, 2009). His play *The Disappearance*, performed by the theater troupe Double Edge, premiered at the Skirball Cultural Center in Los Angeles and has been shown around the country. His story *"Morirse está en hebreo"* was made into the award-winning movie *My Mexican Shivah* (2007), produced by John Sayles. Stavans has received numerous awards, among them a Guggenheim Fellowship, the National Jewish Book Award, an Emmy nomination, the Latino Book Award, Chile's Presidential Medal, and the Rubén Darío Distinction. His work has been translated into a dozen languages.

CONTRIBUTORS

Laura J. Beard is Associate Professor in the Department of Classical and Modern Languages and Literatures at Texas Tech University.

Denise D. Bielby is Professor of Sociology and affiliated faculty in the Center for Film, Television, and New Media at the University of California, Santa Barbara. She is the author, with C. Lee Harrington, of *Soap Fans: Pursuing Pleasure and Making Meaning in Everyday Life* (1995), and co-edited, also with C. Lee Harrington, *Global TV: Exporting Television and Culture in the World Market* (2008).

Daniel Biltereyst teaches cultural media studies and international communication at the Department of Communication Studies at the University of Ghent, Belgium.

María de la Luz Casas Pérez teaches at Tecnológico de Monterrey, Campus Cuernavaca, Mexico.

Reginald Clifford received a doctorate from Loughborough University.

Jorge González teaches at the Universidad Iberoamericana, Mexico.

C. Lee Harrington is Professor of Sociology and affiliate in the Women's Studies program at Miami University, Oxford, Ohio. She is author, with Denise D. Biebly, of *Soap Fans: Pursuing Pleasure and Making Meaning in Everyday Life* (1995), and co-edited, also with Denise D. Bielby, *Global TV: Exporting Television and Culture in the World Market* (2008).

Ibsen Martínez is a Venezuelan columnist and playwright.

Philippe Meers served as research assistant at the Fund for Scientific Research in Flanders, Belgium.

Rosalind C. Pearson is director of communication and public relations at Tecnológico de Monterrey, Campus Cuernavaca, Mexico.

Christina Slade is Professor of Media Theory at the Institute of Media and Re/presentation of the Faculty of Arts, Utrecht University, Holland. She is the author of, among other books, *The Real Thing: Doing Philosophy with the Media* (2002).

Laura Stempel Mumford is the author of *Love and Ideology in the Afternoon Soap Opera, Women and Television Genre* (1995).